# 'BE NOT AFRAID!'

# 'BE NOT AFRAID!'

*André Frossard*
in conversation with

# Pope John Paul II

Translated from the French by
## J. R. Foster

THE BODLEY HEAD
LONDON SYDNEY
TORONTO

British Library Cataloguing
in Publication Data

Frossard, André
Be not afraid!
1. John Paul II, *Pope*
I. Title    II. John Paul II, *Pope*
III. N'ayez pas peur!  *English*
282'.092'4    BX1398.5

ISBN 0-370-30552-3
0-370-30816-6 paperback

Originally published in French as
'*N'ayez pas peur!*'
© Editions Robert Laffont S.A., Paris 1982
Translation © The Bodley Head Ltd and St. Martin's Press Inc 1984
Printed in Great Britain for
The Bodley Head Ltd
9 Bow Street, London WC2E 7AL
by Redwood Burn Ltd, Trowbridge, Wiltshire
Set in Linotron Plantin by
Rowland Phototypesetting Ltd
Bury St Edmunds, Suffolk
*First published in Great Britain in hard covers
and simultaneously in paperback 1984*

# Contents

# Publisher's Note

In order to give prominence to Pope John Paul's replies while leaving the page relatively uncluttered with quotation marks, a pair of bold double inverted commas is used to indicate the start and conclusion of each passage of the Pope's direct speech, thus: "   "

The translations of the Scripture quotations are normally taken from the Revised Standard Version of the Bible, Catholic Edition, copyright 1966 by the Division of Christian Education of the National Council of the Churches of Christ in the USA, and are reproduced with permission.

# 'BE NOT AFRAID!'

That October day when he appeared for the first time on the steps of St. Peter's, with a big crucifix planted in front of him like a two-handed sword, and his first words, *'Non abbiate paura!'* ('Be not afraid!') echoed over the square, everyone realized then and there that something had happened in heaven: after the man of good will who had opened the Council, after the deeply spiritual man who had closed it and after an interlude as gentle and fleeting as the flight of a dove, God was sending us a witness.

We had learnt that he came from Poland. My impression was rather that he had left his nets on the shore of a lake and that he came straight from Galilee, on the heels of the apostle Peter. I had never felt so close to the Gospel. For the words 'Be not afraid' were doubtless addressed to a world in which man fears man, fears life as much as, if not more than, death, fears the savage forces he holds prisoner, fears everything, nothing and sometimes even his own fear; but they were also, or might have been, the exhortation of a disciple in the dawn of Christianity to his brothers called to bear witness, and while the new Pope spoke, the memory of Nero's circus on which St. Peter's is built rose again from beneath the marble.

There was no room for doubt. The astonished crowd in the square, lifting their faces to a new light, my neighbours, who were weeping, and I myself all shared the same feeling: Christianity was going to start again . . . it was emerging once more from the tomb that everyone had thought finally sealed. This Pope would be the Pope of a Christian renewal, and with him the hope that had fled would return in strength among us. He would not be a traditionalist pope, as people later liked to insist, or even a traditional pope, but a pope from the days before tradition, in the line of the first apostles, rising up with his cross amid the same pagan empires as before, empires just as prone to self-deification.

Well, the heavens did not open after all. Nevertheless, as truly as the history of mankind is only the slow development at ground level of decisive choices made from age to age in the firmament of thought, time did hesitate that day and for a moment history let eternity speak.

But the Gospel does not belong to one epoch alone; it is renewed with each generation. One generation emulates Mary Magdalen, drawing its contemplative fervour from the Gospel, and builds Vézelay; another looks to the same source for its moral code and erects intellectual edifices in which the rigour of the lines is in harmony with that of the law. Ours is a time of all-prevailing doubt, of doubt regarded by some disillusioned people as one of the fine arts, of doubt about the future of science and of humanity itself; to us the Gospel offers simple faith, the sole remedy for the barbarity of the age. If this is not yet completely clear, it will be soon; and what is clear already is that we are going through a remarkably fluid period of history, one devoid of any solid moral or rational base, a time of collapsing values and ideologies in which he who wishes to go forward has only one choice left . . . to walk on the water. The man of faith who resides in Rome is one of those people who are not afraid to respond to the appeal from the bark of Christ. 'Be not afraid!' he says, and his voice carries.

It carries a long way. With it the words are suddenly rejuvenated and reacquire the substance of which our intemperate language had robbed them. When you look at apples painted by Cézanne or some other genius, you feel as though you had never seen apples before, or at any rate had never granted them the attention which they deserve. Similarly, the word 'land' sounds different according to whether it is uttered by a government surveyor or shouted from the masthead of a caravelle. Thus when John Paul II exclaims at a public appearance, 'Praised be Jesus Christ', the phrase ceases to be a sort of a ritual banality and immediately becomes the enunciation of a discovery. This ability to give fresh life to words is the gift of poets, of great mystics and, naturally, of the apostles of Christ, who are the appointed representatives of the Word. Whole peoples are not mistaken; in this domain they have a musical ear.

The Pope was thinking of them, of their anguish, of their uncertainties, of their questions so often left unanswered by 'the wise and understanding' when he said to me one day: 'Put some questions to me.'

I think I put seventy to him. He did not evade one of them.

Such was the genesis of the dialogue which follows.

# HIS
# PERSON

# I

However, if some of my questions did find John Paul just a little reticent, they were those dealing with his own person. John Paul II does not like talking about himself. His biographers are usually reduced to consulting the parish register of Wadowice,[1] where he was baptized on 20 June 1920. The register recounts his life in the bare style of official documents: became a priest on such-and-such a date, bishop, archbishop, cardinal on such-and-such a date. The entry ends with 'Elected Pope on 16 October 1978, took the name of John Paul II'. This last remark overflows the space for entries and continues below the last line on the page, without any comment except a slight hesitation of the pen and a crossing-out or a blot at the bottom edge of the page.

I have nothing against biographical summaries, but I should have liked the Pope to tell me a little more than the official register of Wadowice.

He asserted at first that my little question implied many others of a very personal nature, that he would not go into the details into which autobiographies so easily sink and that he would stick to essentials. After some philosophical reflections on 'inner time', which is not the time indicated by clocks, and on the disproportion familiar to us all between the psychological length of the early days of childhood and the fragmentary memories which they leave us, he came to the facts which are not to be found in the register of his native parish, or do not figure on the same page: the deaths which marked his childhood and adolescence.

"At twenty, I had already lost all the people I loved and even the ones that I might have loved, such as the big sister who had died, so I was told, six years before my birth. I was not old enough to make my first communion when I lost my mother, who did not have the happiness of seeing the day to which she looked forward as a great day. She wanted two sons, one a doctor and the other a priest; my brother was a doctor and, in spite of everything, I have become a priest."

1. A town some twenty miles south-west of Cracow. (Tr.)

John Paul never saw his mother in good health. It was no doubt she who taught him to pray. His memories of her are fairly vague. Nevertheless, he remembers feeling deprived when she made a journey to Cracow without him, probably to consult doctors. His brother, fourteen years his senior, was obviously 'nearer' to her. From adolescence onwards John Paul gradually came to feel the cruel loss of her absence. He was subsequently to notice, when preparing young people for marriage, that boys often looked for the image of their mother in their fiancées. There comes a moment, he told me, when boys brought up by their father (however well and tenderly) make the painful discovery that they have been deprived of a mother.

"My brother Edmond died from scarlet fever in a virulent epidemic at the hospital where he was starting as a doctor. Today antibiotics would have saved him. I was twelve. My mother's death made a deep impression on my memory and my brother's perhaps a still deeper one, because of the dramatic circumstances in which it occurred and because I was more mature.

Thus quite soon I became a motherless only child. My father was admirable and almost all the memories of my childhood and adolescence are connected with him. The violence of the blows which had struck him had opened up immense spiritual depths in him; his grief found its outlet in prayer. The mere fact of seeing him on his knees had a decisive influence on my early years. He was so hard on himself that he had no need to be hard on his son; his example alone was sufficient to inculcate discipline and a sense of duty. He was an exceptional person. He died almost suddenly during the war, under the Nazi occupation. I was not yet twenty-one."

Henceforward he was alone in an occupied country, one in fact doubly occupied from 1939 to 1941, by the Germans and the Russians.

"At that time I was a workman. I worked in a stone quarry which supplied the sodium factory in the district of Cracow called Borek Falecki. A few months after my father's death I was transferred from the quarry to the factory itself, to the section which purified the water for the boilers. How did I come to be engaged in manual work? In the autumn of 1938, after leaving the lycée in Wadowice, I had enrolled at the Jagellonian University of Cracow to study philosophy and Polish philology. A year later the university was closed by the occupying power, and its teachers, many of them elderly and eminent, were deported to the concentration camp at Sachsenhausen. Hence the stone quarry, where several of my fellow students came to work with me.

No doubt I owe much to one single year's study at Poland's most ancient university, but I am not afraid to say that the following four years, in a working-class environment, were for me a blessing sent by Providence. The experience that I acquired in that period of my life was priceless. I have often said that I considered it possibly more valuable than a doctorate, which does not mean that I have a poor opinion of university degrees!"

John Paul has himself obtained several degrees, and without difficulty, too. He has always found study easy and enjoyable.

But what about his vocation? It was not a late vocation, but it was slow in coming: "Towards the end of my years at the lycée the people around me thought that I would choose the priesthood. As for me, I did not give it a thought. I was quite sure that I would remain a layman. Committed, to be sure, determined without any doubt to participate in the life of the Church; but a priest, certainly not."

He quotes the epistle to the Hebrews: 'One does not take the honour upon himself!'[1] In this domain, one does not choose; one is chosen. The vocation from which he averted his thoughts came all the same. It awaited him as he emerged from the soirées at which he liked to recite poetry with other young men who shared his love of literature:

"After my father's death, which occurred in February 1941, I gradually became aware of my true path. I was working at the factory and devoting myself, as far as the terrors of the occupation allowed, to my taste for literature and drama. My priestly vocation took shape in the midst of all that, like an inner fact of unquestionable and absolute clarity. The following year, in the autumn, I knew that I was called. I could see clearly what I had to give up and the goal that I had to attain, 'without a backward glance'. I would be a priest."

'What did I have to give up?' We all remember seeing John Paul II choose some child in the crowd, raise it in the air and hug it, and

1. Hebrews 5:4

anyone who has seen that is bound to put to himself the question of human love. I put it to the Pope.

"I will answer you briefly. In this domain I have received more graces than battles to fight. A day came when I knew for certain that my life would not be fulfilled in the human love the beauty of which I have always felt deeply. As a pastor, I have had to prepare many young people for marriage. My status as priest has never separated me from them; on the contrary, it has brought me closer to them and has helped me to understand them better.

They met, chose each other and founded homes. I blessed their marriages, shared their joy as young parents and baptized the children who came into the world. They trusted me and we talked freely about all their problems.

The fact that my path differs from theirs did not make me a stranger; quite the contrary. I read once in the works of Max Scheler[1] that virginity and celibacy have a particular importance for a better understanding of the value of marriage, of family life, of motherhood and fatherhood. I think that this view is an extremely just and pertinent one. The human love of engaged couples, of spouses and of fathers and mothers recurred to me daily in what I thought and said; it was a subject bound up with all the experience of my life, on my own path or in the company of those who had taken another road. It has always been like that and it is the same today. It is a big subject which I never cease to examine, and I see more and more clearly how deeply it is inscribed in the words of Christian revelation. I think there is much to be done in this field. The situation in the Church and in the world is in this respect a challenge."

The word 'challenge' was often to recur in the conversation. It is usually to be taken in the sense of 'incitement' or 'instigation' to act or react for good, justice and truth.

"Christ asked of us purity of heart according to our station in life and our vocation. He demands it squarely. But what is more, he shows us the way to values which are only revealed to the pure vision and the pure heart. We cannot acquire this purity without renunciation, without inner struggles against our own weakness; but, once acquired, this maturity of heart and mind makes up a hundredfold for the efforts which it rewards. The result is a new

---

1. German phenomenologist philosopher (1874–1928); disciple of Husserl. (Tr.)

spontaneity of feeling, of gesture and of behaviour which facilitates relations with people, especially with children . . . I think I have answered your question."

He replied as a priest. But at that point in our conversation he was not yet a priest. Let us return to Poland, where the young man who did not think he was made for the priesthood had discovered his vocation. Normally his path would have led him to religious training. However, the Nazi occupiers did not close the universities just to open the seminaries, and the training of priests was carried out in the strictest secrecy. Theology had gone underground.

"In October 1942 I became one of the pupils at the clandestine seminary attached to the faculty of theology of the Jagellonian university. It functioned outside the purview of the occupying power. I prepared for the examinations during my free time and even, so far as it was possible, during the breaks in my work at the factory."

At this point John Paul experienced an intellectual discovery, a Copernican revolution of sorts. The new seminarist was given a manual to introduce him to metaphysics.

"Straightaway I found myself up against an obstacle. My literary training, centred round the humanities, had not prepared me at all for the scholastic theses and formulas with which the manual was filled. I had to cut a path through a thick undergrowth of concepts, analyses and axioms without even being able to identify the ground over which I was moving. After two months of hacking through this vegetation I came to a clearing, to the discovery of the deep reasons for what until then I had only lived and felt. When I passed the examination I told my examiner that in my view the new vision of the world which I had acquired in my struggle with that metaphysics manual was more valuable than the mark which I had obtained. I was not exaggerating. What intuition and sensibility had until then taught me about the world found solid confirmation."

This coincidence – it must really be described as miraculous – between life and a philosophy manual had a decisive effect:

"This discovery, which has remained the basis of my intellectual structure, is also at the root of my essentially pastoral vocation. Circumstances have never left me much time for study. By temperament I prefer thought to erudition. I came to realize this during my short career as a teacher at Cracow and Lublin. My conception of the person, 'unique' in his identity, and of man, as such at the centre of the universe, was born much more of experience and of sharing with others than of reading. Books, study, reflection and discussion – which I do not avoid, as you know – help me to formulate what experience teaches me. In these two aspects of my life and activity, the pastoral vocation prevailed over that of teacher and scholar; it gradually turned out to be deeper and stronger; but if the two vocations are a long way from each other, there was never any rupture between them."

Life, experience. What about friendship?

"I owe a profound debt of gratitude to several priests, especially to one of them, now very old, who in my early youth brought me closer to Christ by his goodness and simplicity. He was my confessor and it was he who knew at what precise moment it was right to say to me, 'Christ is calling you to the priesthood.' My gratitude is also due to the seminary teachers, to the professors of theology and to the curates who were my colleagues during my brief parochial interlude, particularly to one of them.

I cannot forget Cardinal Sapieha, who behaved like a real father of his country during the war and the terrible occupation.

I had many lay friends, at the university, at the factory and in the resistance. I ought to thank them all one by one: I strive to do so before God, thinking first of all of those who are no longer in this world. Among the latter I think of a very simple man who was one of those unknown saints, hidden amid the others like a marvellous light at the bottom of life, at a depth where night usually reigns. He disclosed to me the riches of his inner life, of his mystical life. He had cut short his studies to work as a tailor in his father's workshop: this work better suited his inner life. Under the occupation he was a real master of spiritual life for many young people united in a 'living rosary' round my parish. His name was John. In his words, in his spirituality and in the example of a life given entirely to God alone, he represented a new world that I did not yet know. I saw the beauty of the soul opened up by grace. I was not yet thinking of the priesthood when he gave me, among other books, the works of St. John of the Cross, of whom he was the first to speak to me. He belonged to this school.

Later, when I was a theology student, I learnt Spanish on my own in order to be able to comment on the thought of the Mystical

Doctor in my doctoral thesis, which was begun in Cracow and continued in Rome at the Angelicum. The final examination took place in two parts, in Rome and in Cracow. But that is not the important point. What counts is what I owe to the admirable person, unknown by the world, whose memory I have just evoked – the revelation of a universe. The shock was comparable to the one I felt, as I told you just now, in the depths of my metaphysical forest."

So the sodium factory worker, the clandestine seminarist at the secret university of Cracow – who has retained in his decisive bearing something of the Carpathian *maquisard* – became a priest, a bishop, an archbishop and a cardinal (see the register of Wadowice). This part of his life is known. But has his conception of the priesthood and of the priest's rôle changed since the day when he put on his vestments to say his first Mass?

"No, not in essentials. The Second Vatican Council gave us a new view of the participation of the whole people of God 'in Christ's sacerdotal gift'. The sacrament of Holy Orders, both hierarchical and ministerial, has been inserted into the universal context of the priesthood of the faithful. Nevertheless, the proper understanding of the ministry of priests (and *a fortiori* of bishops) cannot be anything but the ripe fruit of a special participation in the universal fullness of the priesthood of Jesus Christ himself, a participation born of the sacrament which gives the power to continue the sacrifice that contains all the power of the redemption; a sacrament which, on this or that day, puts an indelible imprint on the human soul by engraving on it the seal of the *Eternal Priest*.

The holy priests of past centuries always gave clearly communal, one might even say 'horizontal', dimensions, to their vocation and their service, by living first 'for others'. Yet it is clear, absolutely clear, that this 'horizontalism' was a function of an authentic vertical sense, not an abstract one but a really existential one, rooted in the mystery of Christ as a priest.

Thus, after Vatican II the living models who offered me such a powerful challenge when I was a seminarian and during my time as a young priest retained all their value in my eyes. On the contrary, I am sure that these models helped me in a decisive way to adopt the idea of the priesthood put to us by the Council in all its richness and authenticity.

Who were my models? They were many. I owe much to St.

Francis of Assisi, who did not think himself worthy of ordination and remained a deacon, and to his brother Albert Chmielowski, his most faithful disciple in my country. Brother Albert was one of those responsible for the spiritual renascence of Poland towards the end of the last century. His whole life as a student, as a painter torn by internal conflicts, then as a tertiary of St. Francis and servant of the poor – an ideal in which he found peace – can be summed up in these words of an excellent biographer: 'He gave his soul.' There you are! I ask you, what is a priestly vocation if not an appeal to give one's soul? We priests badly need models to teach us to be demanding towards ourselves, to show us how far the ministerial priesthood of Christ transcends us, and to lead us to 'look higher'."

The first two models cited by John Paul II were not priests. The third was, to perfection. It was the man known as the 'Curé d'Ars'.

"At the seminary I read with an excitement that owed nothing to literature Canon Trochu's book[1] on Jean-Marie-Baptiste Vianney, Curé d'Ars, whose whole life was a testimony to the power of Christ the priest. I do not think that we have the right to renounce such models on the pretext of adaptation or recycling. We cannot regard them as '*passé*' or 'out-of-date' and still less as stale illustrations of a 'one-dimensional theology' (you hear that said from time to time). We can, in fact we must, imitate them, by re-reading them in the light – or the glare – of modern times. If the Curé d'Ars were alive now, there is not the shadow of a doubt that he would devote all the heroism of his priestly life, all the evangelical love that radiates from his person to the apostolate and the pastoral service of to-day.

Can one imagine that he would be a worker-priest? I think so, if one takes account of the evangelical radicalism implied by this choice of path. However, it is probable that after some time his working companions would ask him to be less of a worker and rather more of a priest, to instruct them, visit the sick and teach their children the truths of faith."

Perhaps the worker-priest movement awaits its twentieth-century Vianney, a working-class Vianney. I did not raise the question, but I had the impression that it is a question which the Pope asks himself.

1. Mgr. Francis Trochu, *Le Curé d'Ars: Saint Jean-Marie-Baptiste Vianney (1786–1859) d'après toutes les pièces du Procès de Canonisation et de nombreux documents inédits*, Paris and Lyon, 1925. A good English biography is the one by Lancelot Sheppard, *Portrait of a Parish Priest*, London, Burns and Oates, 1958. (Tr.)

# II

The name 'Wojtyla', when pronounced correctly, has something African about it for Western ears, and many of those who heard it proclaimed in St. Peter's Square by Cardinal Felici thought that the electors had chosen a pope from the Third World. Moreover, the name must be difficult to pronounce correctly, for a friend of John Paul's, who was in the square out of curiosity, did not recognize the name of the Archbishop of Cracow and shared for a moment the general misunderstanding. When people realized that the new Pope was a cardinal from Poland the astonishment was even greater, as if the white smoke from the Sistine chapel had been the smoke of a gun shot.

Where, then, did the cardinals of Holy Church, who were to be seen a few days later climbing the steps of the throne with unequal sureness of foot to pay homage to their elected head, where did they find the courage to break with the tradition of five centuries and choose a pope from beyond the iron curtain, from the jealously-guarded precinct of a secular religion which believes that History always has the answer to the Eternal Word?

But when it broke a habit the Church was only linking up again with the Gospel.

"Were the apostles not Galileans, like Simon whom Christ calls Peter, a fisherman by trade, a man of impulsive temperament who in the hour of trial experienced the bitterness of failing? Moved by the Holy Spirit, this same Peter came to Rome and founded the Church which still endures, confident in the promises of Christ. When I said in Rome on the day of my election that 'I came from afar', I was thinking of Peter, a son of Israel, a Galilean: he, too, had come from afar."

People immediately spoke of the 'Polish Pope', sometimes with a fairly innocuous condescension, but it was nonetheless rather surprising, particularly as it came from intellectual circles which never tire of condemning the West's superiority complex. Are we really so abject that we have to make excuses for belonging to a heroic nation which has long been one of Europe's 'displaced persons'? Is it really necessary to crave the indulgence of certain

Christians for being the son of a nation which has never shrunk from testifying to its faith? Is there a case to defend? When I hear people speaking in a certain tone of the 'Polish Pope', I remember the pictures of the ruins of Warsaw pasted up after the war on the undamaged walls of Paris. I think of this people which has been periodically buried and only emerges into the light of day to have to fight again, and I am ashamed.

"After Peter's death the Church was led by men of every kind of origin. The *Pontifical Directory* gives a list of them. It is probable that in those far-off days people already spoke of the 'African Pope', the 'Syrian Pope' or the 'Spanish Pope' before acquiring the habit of referring more precisely to the origin of this or that Pope as *ex gente teutonica*, *gallica* or *anglica*. At the start there were popes, or rather bishops of Rome, who came from the empire, then some came from the new communities which had settled on its ruins or beyond its old frontiers.

During the last five centuries the college of cardinals has always elected Italians. When it suddenly interrupted this long tradition the college discovered another, older one that went back to Peter himself. The last few Popes, particularly Paul VI, did all they could to prepare the Church for this change, not only by looking back to the ancient tradition but also, above all, by taking account of the Church's situation in the contemporary world.

To be sure, the description 'Polish Pope' covers a variety of purposes. It would be better to say 'Pope from Poland'. It is very probable that in days gone by reactions to a 'foreign' pope varied in accordance with the different levels of historical consciousness and national feeling, which are certainly not the same everywhere or in every age. It has been asserted, not without reason, that as Bishop of Rome the Pope should belong to the nation of his diocesan bishops. I do not want to miss this opportunity of expressing my gratitude to my Roman diocesans, who have accepted this Pope from Poland as a son of their own country. The charisma of universality must be well anchored in the soul of this people whose Christian ancestors had already accepted Peter, the Galilean, and with him the message of Christ intended for all the peoples of the world."

The Pope reminded me that down the ages Poland has generally been described, even in the official gazette of the Apostolic See, as the *antemurale christianitatis*, the 'rampart of Christendom'[1]; and that the Pope recalled from the ramparts brings us the experience of this long Polish watch which still goes on. However, we are not all historians, and many elements in the 'Polish experience' have escaped our notice.

"The 'Pope from Poland' is the first Slav Pope. His origin and his language link him to all the Slav peoples who inhabit eastern Europe and a good part of central Europe. Consequently, he and his people inherit the common ground between two Christian traditions and of two cultures, those of the West, centred on Rome, and those of the East, linked to Constantinople. It is pertinent to recall that the apostles of the Slavs, SS. Cyril and Methodius, came from Thessalonica, that is, Constantinople's sphere of influence. Nevertheless, history tells us that for their mission to the Slavs they sought support and confirmation from Rome. Right at the beginning of its history Poland received baptism through the intervention of a Czech princess, the wife of the first sovereign of my country attested by history. The union with Rome shaped our thousand years of Christianity. At the same time, especially after the union with Lithuania at the end of the fourteenth century, Poland entered into close relations with the Ruthenian peoples – who lived on each side of the line Lwow-Kiev – and through them with the eastern tradition. Thus our heritage is a fruit of this meeting between East and West."

I dedicate the words which follow to those who have forgotten that in western Europe in the fifteenth and sixteenth centuries freedom of conscience did not even have a notional existence.

"Poland's remarkable attitude to freedom of conscience was displayed as early as the Council of Constance in 1414, at which Paul Wlodkowic, the rector of Cracow University, categorically opposed any forcible conversion to Christianity (he was referring to the activities of the Teutonic knights who had settled beyond Poland's northern frontier). At the time of the Reformation, which found followers even in Poland in the sixteenth century, King Sigismund Augustus declared: 'I am not king of your consciences.' He acted accordingly, with the result that, unlike in the West, no

1. A title to the Church's gratitude recalled by Paul VI in a letter of 17 December 1965 to Cardinal Wyszynski, the primate of Poland (*Acta Apostolicae Sedis*, AAS, 58).

one was ever burnt at the stake in Poland. Thus the assertion of the inner freedom of the human being is part of the spiritual heritage of the Pope from Poland."

Though one in faith and language, the Polish people has not always been united in life. The unpleasant memory of its partitions (by Tsarist Russia, by Frederick the Great's Prussia, and by the Austria of Maria-Teresa and Joseph II, among others) has been a stumbling block to law and morality for two centuries. In losing everything the Poles acquired a sense of freedom which owes nothing to rhetoric and everything to experience. 'Freedom', the Pope said, is not 'possessed', it is 'conquered'. When he speaks of it, and of the rôle which it must play in the development of the human being, he employs an extremely vigorous expression: 'One's life as a person and a social being must be "built out of it".'

All through my childhood I used to hear old soldiers of the First World War speak of the endless horrors of a battle in which the whole genius of the strategists seemed to consist in filling the shell holes with living soldiers until the enemy had run out of ammunition. They told how, thanks to a wound or a period of leave, they would go back for a few days or weeks 'to the rear', and how what they saw there – acts of cowardice, petty betrayals, a dubious sense of well-being – helped them to return, if not without fear, at any rate without regret, to the fire-scorched fraternity of the front line.

All other things being equal, and forgetting the artillery, I think that the Poland of to-day is in the front line, as usual, and that our fine Western democracies, with their surplus of goods and deficit of morals, represent 'the rear' pretty accurately. I said so to the Pope.

"It may indeed be said that Polish Christianity is on the firing line as regards the most recent stage in our history, this encounter of Christianity and of the Polish Church with the Marxist system, an encounter which has lasted for thirty years.

In 1966 my country celebrated a thousand years of Christianity. Since then Providence has marked out as Peter's successor a pope from Poland. He is ready to serve the Roman Church, but also to fulfil his mission and to exercise his responsibilities on a universal scale. He prays the Holy Spirit that the 'Polish experience' may serve his mission and prove fruitful."

The Pope spoke of 'Providence'. Did Providence surprise him on 16 October 1978?

"I think that the conclave's vote that day surprised many people besides me! But what God commands, which may seem humanly impossible, he gives us the means to carry out. That is the secret of every vocation. Every vocation changes our plans, disclosing a new one, and it is astonishing to see how much inner help God gives us, how he tunes us in to a new 'wave length', how he prepares us to enter into this new plan and to make it our own by simply seeing it as the Father's will and accepting it. And all this whatever our weakness and our attachment to our personal views.

When I speak to you like this, I am thinking of other situations which I have met in my pastoral experience, of those incurable invalids condemned to the wheel-chair or chained to their sick bed; people who are often young and conscious of the implacable advance of their illness, prisoners of their sufferings for weeks, months or years.

The comparison may surprise you perhaps, but it was forced on me on the day of my election, and since you wanted to know what my first thoughts were I am giving them to you just as they came into my mind. Of course, first of all I had to reply to Cardinal Villot who, in accordance with the regulation, had to ask the person elected if he accepted his election. So I conformed to this regulation (clause 86 of the apostolic constitution *Romano Pontifici eligendo*), which requires the person to accept his election if possible, seeing in it the will of God and the intervention of the Holy Spirit. In spite of my unworthiness, such a directive made it my duty to accept, in a spirit of obedience and of faith in Christ, my Lord and Redeemer, and of total surrender to his Mother. All this was contained in my reply to the cardinal Camerlengo, and I repeated it when I gave my first blessing *urbi et orbi*."

When the regulation calls on the person elected to accept his election 'if possible', it seems to allow for the disclosure of incapacity or inaptitude unknown to the assembly. However, since the election of a pope is not the result of an electoral campaign, the person elected, far from thinking himself the best candidate, tends to consider himself the least suitable. That is why the regulation, after this 'if possible' which spares his conscience, invokes 'the will of God' to assist his humility to obedience.

But the Pope returned to the subject of the permanent invalids who form an intimate part of his spiritual life and whom he scarcely ever dismisses from his mind. He spoke to me of the secret and powerful infusion of grace into the suffering of these bodies which become, so to speak, radiant.

"Bereft of all strength, dying a slow death, how could these incurables, in human terms, accept their lot? Yet gradually some of them begin to realize that suffering, too, is a privileged vocation in the mystery of Christ and the Church. They live the words of St. Paul: 'In this mortal frame of mine, I help to pay off the debt which the afflictions of Christ still leave to be paid.' More than once I have noted that this terrible irreversibility could be accepted not as a calamity, but as a sign of election and vocation, engendering that inner peace and even that joy which come to man when he discovers the meaning of his life and his identity, that is, the name by which God calls him. In my conversations with the most severely tested people, I have often been struck by a serenity, an unexpected happiness in which I could see only a tangible proof of the intervention of grace and of the presence of the Holy Spirit in the heart of man.

Well, when on 16 October 1978 I was invited to accept, in the course of a single afternoon, the new 'plan' that God disclosed to me through the voice of the cardinals, I benefited, I am sure, from the aid of all those who help to pay off in their flesh 'the debt which the afflictions of Christ still leave to be paid', of those souls who are totally devoted and deeply hidden in the mystical body, of all the many who supported the assembly of cardinals with their prayers and their sacrifices; and I benefited from the prayers and sacrifices of those near to me. I am confident that it will be granted to me to draw on these same sources to carry out God's plan by responding to the call which I accepted on the day of my election. *Virtus in infirmitate perficitur*, says St. Paul. 'My power,' says God, 'is made perfect in weakness.'"[1]

There is a well-known saying, 'He who enters the conclave a pope leaves it a cardinal.' However, it is possible to enter as a cardinal and to emerge as Pope. I wondered if you have the same idea of the Pope when you look at him and when you are Pope. I wanted to know if Karol Wojtyla's conception of the papacy was the same since he had become John Paul II.

1. II Corinthians 12:9

(26)

When I put my question I was thinking of the sovereign pontiffs of days gone by, raised by ceremony above the human condition. The reply was original. The Cardinal of Cracow emerged from the conclaves as Bishop of Rome.

"The pastoral ministry of the Bishop of Rome in the see of Peter finds its meaning and its plenitude in Tradition, especially in the magisterium of the last Council. I am thinking not only of the third chapter of *Lumen gentium*[1] on the hierarchical organization of the Church and in particular of the episcopate, which follows the chapter devoted to the people of God; I am thinking of the whole teaching of the Council. It is clear that at the present time Peter's successor can only carry out Peter's ministry in the spirit of this teaching.

Providence allowed me to participate in all the sessions of the Council. I am profoundly convinced that Vatican II endowed the Church of our epoch with the authentic language of the Holy Spirit, and that we must follow it by embodying it in both our communal and our individual lives, in accordance with each person's vocation and the 'size of gift' that he has received. This concerns every Christian, every religious, every priest, every bishop and consequently also the Bishop of Rome, Peter's successor. I was convinced of this on 16 October 1978. I trusted the Holy Spirit who addressed the Church and the present world by the voice of Vatican II. I believe the same thing to-day and I try, so far as my strength allows, to profess and put into effect what I believe.

The Council emphasized the collegiality of the bishops' responsibility and mission in the Church. The primatial ministry and the mission of the Bishop of Rome should be understood and carried out in this spirit. The synod of bishops of 1969 spoke forcefully in its extraordinary session of 'effective collegiality' and 'affective collegiality', not to separate them, but to remind people that they are complementary in the life of the Church. Christ said to the apostles, who as a college of Twelve formed the model for the episcopal college: 'You are all brothers.' I think that Peter's

1. 'Light of nations'. The 'constitutions' or teachings of the Councils are called (like encyclicals) after the first words of their texts. Of the constitutions produced by Vatican II, the ones most often to be quoted by John Paul II were *Lumen gentium* and *Gaudium et Spes* ('The joy and hope').

successor should never forget these words, that they should be engraved on his heart. And since fraternity is part of every Christian's vocation, it must *a fortiori* be part of the bishops' collegiality.

The hierarchical structure of the Church should serve to make a reality of Christ's words, 'You are all brothers.'

The Christian hierarchy is a perfect inversion. This is symbolized in a cruel but explicit way by the crucifixion of Peter upside down. It follows from the good divine order of things – in which humility produces grandeur – that the greater emerges quite naturally from the lesser.

The mission of Peter's successor and his universal ministry are deeply rooted in his responsibility as Bishop of Rome, who presides as such over the assembly of the whole Church and the fraternal college of bishops. One can even say that the universal dimension of the Church is rooted in the local dimension of his responsibility. This corresponds to the whole eucharistic and ecclesial order, in its institution and in its history. I have thought from the start that the primordial duty of Peter is to be Bishop of Rome. It seems to me that the imperative condition of any initiative or action of a universal character is to feel oneself bishop of this concrete community and to act if possible in person as bishop of this particular Church.

I say, 'as much as possible in person'. It is obviously unnecessary to explain these words. Everyone is aware that a pope has a great deal to do, and I can see your next question: 'Since the Pope cannot do everything, what should his first priority be?' I think that his first task is to gather the people of God in unity.

The experience which I acquired in Cracow has taught me that it is important to visit the communities personally, starting with the parishes. Of course, this is not an exclusive duty, but I consider it of the first importance. Twenty years' experience has made me realize that, thanks to the bishop's visits, a parish comes to be all the more closely integrated in the architecture of the Church and thus adheres more closely to Christ. My visits to the Roman parishes are necessarily shorter and I have had to give up the sort of programme which I used to follow at Cracow. This vaster and more detailed programme falls to the lot of the auxiliary bishops.

These encounters through the Word and the Eucharist serve

basically to 'gather together the people of God', as we ask in the third Eucharistic prayer.[1] This is the central fact.''

I made a mental note that when he was speaking of his function rather than of his person John Paul II sometimes said 'Peter's successor' and sometimes just 'Peter'. This very evangelical way of expressing himself reminded me first of all of Christ's founding prophecy. 'You are Peter, and on this rock I will build my Church,'[2] words cast into the wind for a few fishermen, themselves netted as though by chance, and confirmed by the centuries. It subsequently caused to me to reflect that the succession of popes has nothing of a monarchical line about it, that a pope does not succeed another pope but directly succeeds Peter, in short, that there is no intermediary between the first and the last of them, so that there is no sense in comparing them, as people have done, with one another, Pius V with Paul VI, since all of them have been in turn the same 'Peter'. It is only a step from this reflection to imagining that all the Popes were appointed on the shores of the Lake of Tiberias, and I took this step. The Holy Father corrected any eccentricity there may be in this view and kindly redefined what I was trying to say.

"Remember the last words of Christ to his disciples: 'I am with you always, to the close of the age.' They concern all the generations of disciples, of confessors and of successors. In this first community, starting from the Twelve whom the Lord sent 'into the whole world', all the generations were to some extent appointed and called. From this point of view, one can agree that in the apostle Simon Peter of Bethsaida, who was the first to preside over the Church of Rome, all his successors down the ages and 'to the close of the age' were appointed and called.

When Christ said, 'I am with you', it transcended all the limitations to which man as a historical being is subject, as are all human institutions and even the Church itself, in so far as it is made of men.

Christ, the Son of God, also accepted, as a man, the limits of history. His life here on earth was brief . . . When he said at the Last Supper, before leaving his apostles, 'I will not leave you

1. One of those which encompass in particular the consecration of the bread and wine.
2. Matthew 16:18

(29)

desolate; I will come to you,'[1] he was speaking of the Spirit which they were to receive as the price of his departure ('It is better for you I should go away . . . if only I make my way there, I will send him to you'). All through the centuries, when the Holy Spirit institutes bishops, Christ is present. *Lumen gentium* tells us that 'he is present in their assembly.'

When we think of the succession of bishops across the world, and especially in Rome, we situate them in history. Yet we do not possess the right to detach this historical succession from the fundamental dimension of the Church, the dimension of mystery."

# III

Whereas for many of us faith is the permanent subject of inner debates that are not always constructive, with John Paul II it seems 'natural'. I wondered if it had always reigned in him as though over a peaceful countryside.

"It seems to me that one can say of man that he is 'religious by nature', or of the human soul that it is 'naturally Christian', but the relationship between faith and natural religiosity remains to be determined. Faith as a personal response to the Word of the living God, finally and definitively expressed in Jesus Christ and by Jesus Christ, is a problem to be examined more closely."

We shall return to the big question of the influence of environment and education on the blossoming of faith. In the next chapter, which deals essentially with faith, the Holy Father goes even more deeply into his thoughts on this extremely important point.

"From my earliest years I found myself in an atmosphere of faith and in a social milieu deeply rooted in the presence and action of the Church. In spite of this – perhaps because of this – it seems to me all the more important to assert that faith 'as personal response to the Word of God expressed in Jesus Christ' is created and develops ceaselessly; my own experience allows me to make this assertion. At the same time I am convinced that never at any period of my life

1. John 14:18

was my faith a purely 'sociological' phenomenon resulting from the habits or customs of my environment, in a word, from the fact that others around me 'believed and acted like that'. I have never regarded my faith as 'traditional', although I have conceived a growing admiration for the tradition of the Church and that living share of it which has nourished the life, history and culture of my country.

Nevertheless, when I look objectively at my own faith I have always observed that it has had nothing to do with any kind of conformism, that it was born in the depths of my own 'self', and that it was also the fruit of my intellectual search for an answer to the mysteries of man and of the world. I have seen more and more clearly that faith is a gift. With inner maturity came the evidence that it contained my personal and *free* response to the Word of God expressed in Jesus Christ, the Word incarnate. Thus *my* faith [the Pope stresses the 'my'] was from the start a gift of God. I have lived it little by little, and more and more fully, as an inner reality that was purely and simply 'given'."

For 'cradle Catholics', as English and American Catholics describe those who have the luck – sometimes not appreciated – to be born into a Catholic family, faith presents itself in the final analysis as a proposition suggested by environment and education. This does not by any means exclude – far from it – the freedom of choice on the basis of which personal faith 'is *created* [the reader will have noted the term] and develops continuously.'

It is also possible to move unexpectedly from the most settled unbelief to the most obstinate faith. Converted at the age of twenty by a silent explosion of light which took me by complete surprise amid the shadow world of my scepticism, I wrote (thirty-five years later) two books on this moment of time – a moment I still cannot recall without a start. The Holy Father had read them.

"You have an unusual, one might even say an exceptional, experience of this transition from atheism to faith. However, you have not raised the subject with me, nor the question of personal faith or the faith of the Church confronting unbelief and militant atheism, so I shall not speak of it either."

Not for the moment, at any rate, though I was not going to let such a question drop! I was going to remind the Holy Father a little later on of the cry of that young man in the Parc des Princes in Paris, who was to pose him questions that I had not yet posed.

# IV

For a long time the only part of the papal apartments that I knew was the little window – or at any rate it looks little from St. Peter's Square – at which by long tradition the Popes appear at midday on Sunday to bless the crowd; they appear white and tiny against the yellow wall of the Vatican, like an almond on a Madeira cake and arousing the same kind of family joy. When I was first given access to this formerly inaccessible dwelling, where the sovereign pontiffs were said to live in frightening solitude, I was so excited that I scarcely noticed, in the chapel with the luminous crystal ceiling, a bronze Way of the Cross on one wall and an icon of Our Lady of Czestochowa on the altar. The Holy Father, kneeling in prayer, looked huge. The cape on his wide shoulders called to mind a snow-covered landscape and I wondered how it had been possible to get a mountain into such a small space. (Since the attempted assassination of 13 May 1981 the snow will have melted to reveal the bare rock). I had before me a block of prayer. After Mass, said quite meticulously and with the stately pace of an orbiting planet, twenty minutes were devoted to the thanksgiving, a practice almost obsolete elsewhere, during which John Paul II remained kneeling on his prie-Dieu, the arm-rest of which is the size of a lectern. He prays, I had almost said as he breathes, and yet his prayer is action.

What part does prayer play in his activity? Had he never thought of the contemplative life?

"My vocation has always been mainly active in character. It is true that there was a time in my youth when I considered another direction, but my contacts with the Carmelites came to nothing. It was my bishop, Cardinal Sapieha, the metropolitan of Cracow, who settled the question. He did not see sufficient grounds to justify a change of direction. Neither, come to that, did I.

So I was not called to a contemplative life but, ever since the distant days of my 'conversion', to the inner life – and hence to my priestly vocation. I have all along been conscious of the primary importance of prayer and, essentially, of contemplative prayer, for any activity deriving from my vocation. So it has been at every stage of my life, first when I was a country curate, then in the city, as a teacher, as a bishop and finally since 16 October 1978. [He did not say 'as Pope': this is not a 'stage'.] In this respect I do not see any appreciable change. Perhaps the curate was obliged to stay up later to find the time for prayer and especially for meditation. Subsequently it was easier for me to make room for both in my day's programme."

He added, "When I was in a position to arrange it." I do not know if it is the case to-day. I have the impression that the Vicar of Christ is no more in charge of his timetable than the country curate was.

"If my past and present life can be described as 'active', let us not forget that the 'act' *par excellence* of each day is the Holy Mass, which constitutes the most perfect synthesis of prayer and the heart of our meeting with God in Christ. Over thirty years' experience of priestly life has taught me that to reach this summit, to arrive at this synthesis and this fullness, one must approach it through prayer and emerge from it towards the prayer of the whole day, knowing perfectly well that this day will be filled to overflowing with activities and engagements of every sort. Everyone knows that the priest's day is liturgical, not only thanks to the Mass but also through the liturgy of the hours,[1] which confers on the day its special rhythm. On the whole, work takes most of the time, but all activities should be rooted in prayer as though in a spiritual soil. The depth of this soil must not be too thin: inner experience teaches us how to form it, day after day, so that it is sufficient."

At the beginning of this book I said that one of the qualities of John Paul II's discourse was to give back to the most hackneyed words the force that they had long since lost through ill treatment. I have often wondered about such poor anaemic, extenuated words, so thoroughly emptied of their substance that contemporary thought is reduced to stuffing them in order to preserve some semblance of life: by what miracle could they suddenly recover their freshness and muscularity? Here is the reply: before being uttered the words must be *prayed*.

"I come back to contemplation. Although I do not live according to a contemplative rule, I can see very well that this ground of

1. The breviary

prayer in which each day is rooted comprises many profoundly contemplative elements and moments of great importance for my ministry and above all for the proclamation of God's Word. The ancient principle, *Contemplata aliis tradere* (hand on to others the fruits of prayer), is still topical and life-enhancing. It concerns in the first place the one who 'hands on', the preacher or servant of the Word: he is entitled to communicate – uniquely and exclusively – only *contemplata*, thoughts passed through prayer."

There remains what we more commonly call 'prayer', which is not so close to contemplation as to petition or, I might even say, to petition for a reprieve.

"There was a time when I thought that one had to limit the 'prayer of petition'. That time has passed. The further I advance along the road mapped out for me by Providence, the more I feel the need to have recourse to this kind of prayer and the more scope I find for it. By the same token I become more and more aware of the prayer which encompasses me; and I feel more and more keenly how great is my debt."

To speak of prayer with John Paul II is also to speak of the Virgin Mary. In the West, and more particularly in France, devotion to Mary undergoes strange vicissitudes. It is not an exaggeration to say that all French people have been, or will go one day, to Lourdes; yet some twenty years ago when there was a question of promulgating the doctrine of 'Mary Mediatrix' the newspapers were full of protests. This astonished me, for women are natural mediators. It is they who intervene between father and children, between the children themselves, between husband and neighbour, between nothingness and life – if it is indeed they who bear children – between the family and misfortune – for men are glad to see them do what must be done in times of mourning – and even between ourselves and God, to the extent that it is they who are most often to be seen in church. If we carried the objectors' reasoning to its logical conclusion we should arrive at the surprising notion that all women are mediators except the Virgin Mary.

However, the Holy Father is to speak of devotion to Mary in the dialogue on 'Morals'. It is clear that this devotion is a vital key to understanding his personality, which cannot be understood either unless we take account of the factors he has just enumerated. In the first place there was his admiration for his father – no question of an

Oedipus complex in this attractive story of filial gratitude – who was exemplary in every respect and whose unobtrusive moral strictness he has never forgotten. Then came solitude at twenty, that is, the age when one needs one's parents more than ever, if only to define oneself in relation to – or in opposition to – them; which of the two is of little importance provided the love is there. Without mother, father, sister or brother, the sun of his existence rose on the devastation of his family and the crushing of his country. What remained to him in this desert, which he was to traverse with his misfortune, without complaint, without hesitation? His faith, which was never to be called into question and which, together with an already remarkable strength of character, protected him from the giddy enthusiasms and follies of youth. 'I have received,' he said, 'more graces than battles to fight': enough said to dispel certain rumours about sentimental attachments at the start of his career. Above all, or, better, at the heart of all that his life comprised in those days, there was the murmur, imperceptible at first but secretly insistent, of the voice that called him – his vocation. It was a priest who was to decipher the message, rather in the way that one reads a telegram to its addressee. The pre-paid reply was grace.

It is clear that great importance must also be attached to his years of manual work and to his experience of working-class life. We have had popes of every kind of ancestry, including peasants, but it is the first time since factory chimneys began to sprout from the surface of the earth that the chemical industry has contributed to the education of a pope. It is curious that such a man should have been given to the Church at the end of this industrial century and still more curious that the doctrinaire advocates of social action apparently find no particular cause for satisfaction in the fact.

We should not forget either the intellectual discovery of his early days in his first contact with philosophy when, after a dark struggle with a manual of metaphysics, the sun rose, as it did for Jacob after his night's wrestling with the angel, on a new world.

To these personal experiences should be added a so to speak national and permanent factor, the spirit of resistance to oppression, which had every occasion to develop in him thanks to the sinister incidence of a particularly brutal occupation.

All these elements have contributed to form a man of exceptional character, who knows what people are talking about when they speak to him of poverty, solitude and violence, the three key words of the end of this century. But the world does not consist solely of unhappiness, especially for a Christian, and since John Paul II rose up among us, dressed in white, armed with a tranquil courage and a sort of obstinate good will, a passage of the Gospel often comes to my mind. It is the final episode in St. John's Gospel, which reminds us that Christianity is primarily a story of love:

> When they had finished breakfast, Jesus said to Simon Peter, 'Simon, son of John, do you love me more than these?' He said to him, 'Yes, Lord; you know that I love you.' He said to him, 'Feed my lambs.' And a second time he said to him, 'Simon, son of John, do you love me?' 'Yes, Lord,' he said to him, 'you know that I love you.' He said to him, 'Tend my sheep.' He said to him the third time, 'Simon, son of John, do you love me?' Peter was grieved because he said to him for the third time, 'Do you love me?' And he said to him, 'Lord, you know everything; you know that I love you.' Jesus said to him, 'Feed my sheep.'

When the Popes ascend the Roman throne of Peter, do they hear this same question? It seems to me that down the ages the whole history of the Church is connected with it, that all the errors and deviations from which she has suffered were so many restrictive or presumptuous ways of replying, one replying 'yes' with reservations, another reposing excessive confidence in himself. The right reply is Peter's – the third.

"In the episode recounted by St. John (which takes place after the Resurrection), the questions and answers have their own eloquence and their specific weight. To Christ's question, 'Do you love me?', Peter does not reply directly, 'Yes, I love you,' but – and his reply is significant – 'Lord, you know everything, you know that I love you.' He does not protest his love. He does not behave as he had a few days earlier, when he declared, 'Though they all fall away because of you, I will never fall away.' He feels the need to base his reply, his confession, not on the evidence of his conscience, not on the certitudes of his own heart, but, in St. John's expression, on 'him who knows what there is in the heart of man'.

That is why his reply is so truthful, and for us so convincing. It must have convinced Christ himself, since he ratified it three times by saying, 'Feed my sheep'. These words express the highest degree of confidence, for these lambs, these sheep are all those who have been redeemed, as St. Paul says, 'at a very high price', at the price of the Cross and the Resurrection. The price of the redemption is infinite; so therefore is that of the souls redeemed. All this is comprised in the concise order, 'Feed my sheep.'

The Church often reminds us of this dialogue between Christ and Peter. He who has to do Peter's service, in the chair once occupied by the first apostle, is confronted from the start by this moving interrogation and he gives thanks to the fisherman of Bethsaida for replying as he did and not otherwise, 'Lord, you know everything, you know that I love you.'

The question, 'Do you love me?' is the most difficult question that one can ask. It is as well if he who puts questions on love knows the mystery of hearts, for that makes it possible to reply as Peter replied. That is how human love must reply. And the Church. And the world, including the world of to-day."

That is how he replied himself, obviously. But before asking him what he believed and how he believed, I wanted to know if, with so much to do, he still found time to read.

"I have always read a great deal, although I have never been a bookworm, except possibly in my youth, at the age when one begins to discover the beauty of literature. In scientific work proper, to which I have only been able to devote a few years of my life, I did not seek erudition but what seemed essential to the progress of my research. Time to assimilate and reflect counted for more. It has always been like that, though of course more regularly at some times than at others.

To-day, of course, I have less time for reading than before, yet I can say that in a sense I read more, especially what can help to keep me informed. That is possible thanks to the remarkable method employed by my assistants, which gives me a swift grasp of essential publications, while still enabling me to go into detail if it is necessary or opportune.

I read 'systematically' works of theology, spirituality and philosophy and books on the human sciences. At the moment, for example, I am reading much more theology than philosophy. Some books I read right through from cover to cover, others I leaf through, as I do periodicals. In the domain of the natural sciences some texts sometimes gain my whole attention. I read them with great profit, although I am not particularly well prepared for this kind of reading.

As for 'belles-lettres', they are a luxury for my holidays. But I do sometimes read something 'not in the programme'. Quite recently I read an extensive selection of the poems of Milosz and Rainer Maria Rilke, which had not been possible earlier. But that is exceptional."

For John Paul takes few, if any, liberties with his timetable. Apart from the few days of relaxation which he spends at Castel Gandolfo, where in any case he ends up by working as much as in Rome, he does not concede a moment to himself. So far a general anaesthetic has proved the only means to make him stop working.

Although he has rather less time to read, he finds time to write, and he writes a great deal. Confronted with the stream of doctrine and oratory that flows out from St. Peter's and spreads over the world in encyclicals, homilies, instructions and various allocutions, insidious journalists wondered in perplexity who could provide the Pope with so many ideas, and after making enquiries, came to the regretful conclusion that the Pope thought for himself. He sometimes writes powerfully eloquent things on a simple theme, like the inaugural allocution of his pontificate. He also sometimes writes difficult things such as, in days gone by, *The Person and the Act*, an extremely heavy-going book. In Poland they say that reading it for their sins is enjoined on great sinners, who on the whole prefer to remain impenitent.

When the subject is faith he sometimes writes kneeling in front of the Holy Sacrament, rather as Thomas Aquinas used to put his head in the tabernacle before speaking of the Eucharist. But I do not think that he still writes poems; if he does, he keeps them hidden, which is a pity. They were the bunch of flowers on the battlement of the keep. On second thoughts I am not sure that it is in fact a pity. Poetry is connected with prophecy and there are prophecies which are better left unheard. I am thinking of a poem which has acquired a disturbing echo since the attempted assassination of 13 May, the poem which St. Stanislaus murmurs to himself before a King of Poland who was unreceptive to Christian feelings:

> My words have not converted you
> My blood will convert you.

# FAITH

# I

I confess I find this next section of the dialogue a rather moving experience, for what I have to transcribe now is a kind of extremely elevated – and entirely humble – spiritual confession, in which a man who never speaks but for the good of his brothers and of the people entrusted to him submits his own faith to a frank and uncomplacent examination, so that people who question themselves in secret may hear from the Pope 'prayed words' which will put an end, if not to their questions, at any rate to their solitude.

As I have already said, with John Paul II one is never very far from the Gospel, and we shall broach the subject via a parable, that of the lost sheep.

In Paris, at the splendid, boisterous evening in the Parc des Princes, a young man was seen to go up on the platform with a paper in his hand and put a series of questions to the Holy Father; he spoke in a feverish tone, with that blend of arrogance and deference with which the young often address their elders. He was an atheist, he said, but he did not wish to miss the chance to believe which the Pope's presence offered. When he had read his paper he disappeared into the crowd amid the hymns and applause, other questions came and his own remained unanswered. Months later John Paul II was still reproaching himself for letting this sheep of his slip into the well of anonymity.

"I am glad you have brought up the Parc des Princes and my meeting with young people during my visit to Paris. How did it come about that I did not reply to that young man's question, or rather series of questions? Is it possible to forget such important questions? Yet that is what happened. Don't forget that at that point in the evening several young people, including a handicapped girl, were on the platform, and they too were firing questions at me which I was considering attentively."

That evening, it must be remembered, the enthusiasm and spontaneity of the young audience left the programme in ruins and the Pope abandoned his prepared address, improvising instead.

"As soon as this young man began to speak it was clear that his point of view differed completely from that of the others and that his questions did not appear on the list which I had been given. The problem he raised was a fundamental one. It was impossible to deal with its full scope and complexity in a few words, but at the very least I should have said that it deserved a more thorough reply than the circumstances permitted . . . Immediately afterwards I began my speech, which was devised as a global reply to all the questions. My allocution soon turned into a sort of dialogue with fifty thousand participants. The meeting grew more and more heated, as meetings always do with young people, with the result that I quite simply forgot to reply to the only interlocutor who, off the programme, had declared that he was an atheist."

The opportunity was not to recur. There was to be no other evening of the same kind. "And as you know," the Pope said, "the programme of my visit to Paris was a particularly heavy one. It began at seven o'clock in the morning and finished at midnight!"

Midnight at the earliest. I remember being held up at one of the gates of Paris about that time with some fifty other drivers. It turned out that the Pope was to pass this way. We all got out of our cars, and he finally appeared from a tunnel; the inside light of his car was on and we caught a glimpse of him in his great red cloak. He gave us a friendly wave, there were cheers and everyone quietly got back behind the steering wheel. It was the first time that I had seen Parisian motorists caught in a fifteen-minute traffic jam without losing their tempers. If there is any question of beatifying John Paul II in days to come, I hope that this miracle will be put on the file.

However, the Holy Father wants everyone to find here the reply that he did not give amid the enjoyable uproar of the Parc des Princes, a reply which will be considerably supplemented during the course of this book.

"It was only after my return to Rome that I remembered the question that had been left unanswered. I immediately wrote to Cardinal Marty, asking him to find the young man and to present my apologies to him. Shortly afterwards the cardinal replied that the necessary had been done and that 'all was well'.

At the time I was extremely sorry about this omission. To-day, after re-reading at leisure the questionnaire you have given me, I feel less regret at not replying at the time as I meant to. That might have closed the debate instead of opening it. *Felix culpa*! Happy fault! Thanks to this omission we are going to talk about FAITH."

My religious knowledge is by no means encyclopaedic and I must admit that I have not taken note of all the pontifical documents published since I entered the Church by the window rather than through the door. Nevertheless, I have been fairly attentive to encyclicals, from Pius XI's letter condemning Nazism to John Paul II's on work, but I do not recall reading a text on faith in the simplest, most ordinary and most 'worrying', not to say painful, sense of the concept, which is comprised for the non-believer – and often for the believer too – in the three words, 'Does God exist?'

"The young man in the Parc des Princes asked me: 'Holy Father, in whom do you believe? Why do you believe? What is it that is worth the gift of our life and what manner of being is this God that you adore?' You told me that this series of questions could involve a complete examination of the problems posed by faith. I take the same view. Thus the reply cannot be fragmentary; perhaps it should even be considered from several angles; for this young man did not simply ask 'what manner of being is this God' in whom the Pope believes and whom he adores; he also wanted to know 'why' he believes.

Yet it seems to me that these are not the essential points. What matters is this moment when faith was questioned by unbelief, the emergence of two inner attitudes corresponding to two ways of existing and of being a man. Of course, in every period of history, and even all through the Christian era, there have been unbelievers alongside the believers. Nevertheless, in our day, these contrary attitudes seem to me more conscious and more radical. To-day there is simply no longer any way of talking about faith without taking into account unbelief and atheism.

Moreover, these two words are not identical in meaning. Strictly speaking, atheism is the opposite of theism. On the other hand, faith is not identical with theism or with some conception or other of the world [the Pope used the word *Weltanschauung*] that admits the existence of God. Faith is much more than that: it is an inner response to the Word of God in the sphere of thought and of the will to be human; thus it implies a special intervention by God. 'In many and various ways', says St. Paul to the Hebrews, 'God spoke of old to our fathers by the prophets; but in these last days he has spoken to us by [his] Son.'

Thus theism is organically included in the notion of 'faith' but fundamentally transcended. Faith is obviously 'theist' (in that it believes in the existence of a God), but it is not solely theist. In its very essence it is 'theological', that is, it does not confine itself to citing God; it speaks of him and with him.

Let us go back to the young man in the Parc des Princes who asserted that he was an 'atheist'. His words are worth re-reading attentively. This is what he says: 'I am an atheist. I refuse to accept any belief and any dogmatism. I also mean that I do not combat anyone's faith; but I do not understand faith.' The admission is precise. When he says 'I am an atheist,' this young man wishes not so much to deny the existence of God as to assert primarily that he himself does not believe in him. What he rejects is what he calls 'belief' and 'dogmatism', as though he regarded both as indispensable if we are going to admit the existence of God, or at any rate if we are going to admit it in a certain way. Yet one can see that he refrains from attacking the faith of those who do believe. Not only does he refuse to combat it or to treat it in a negative way, but he displays a certain interest in it, in a fact, that is, which he claims not to understand, although he would like to. That is why he addresses the Pope. That, at any rate, is what emerges from the questionnaire."

I admired this patient decipherment of a message which had mainly struck me by its constant use of the word 'I', an attitude which in my view makes the search for Christian truth very difficult.

"You must take account of all I have just said, not only to repair an omission but also because the assertion made in the Parc is significant for a whole generation. When the young man refuses to admit ready-made beliefs that do violence to his intelligence he explains at bottom, indirectly, why he cannot understand faith.

For faith does not do violence to the intelligence, it does not subject it to a system of 'ready-made truths'. We have just established the distinction between the theist conception of the world and faith: in both cases an *authentic commitment* of our intelligence is involved. As a conception of the world, theism results from a process of reasoning or from a certain way of understanding the universe, while faith is a conscious, free response of the spirit to the Word of the living God. As such, it commits the whole person. The fact *that* I believe, and *why* I believe, is organically linked to *what* I believe."

# II

However, not all ears are equally attentive to this Word to which we are invited to make a 'conscious and free response', and one thinks of the words of the Gospel: 'When the Son of Man comes, will he find faith on earth?' Even the most convinced Christians seem to-day to take from the Gospel only what can contribute to social change or to the expression of their individual freedom. The idea is spreading among them that God being 'unknowable' it is useless to speak of him; and if one cannot speak 'of him' one cannot speak 'to him' either. This makes contemplation and prayer equally vain; it also makes our 'conscious and free response' vain.

Can we know God?

"As a matter of fact, we tackled this problem when we analysed the statement of the young man at the Parc des Princes. You seek further details. The question is a vast one and the bibliography enormous. You know what terms the Church employed in the pronouncements which she made during the First Vatican Council. All that is well known. But if we want our conversation to continue as a conversation and not turn into a treatise, I suggest another, more concrete method."

For the second time the Pope was going to talk to me about my books. I know what people will say. They will say that I am making use of the Pope's good will to publicize my works, that I am only too happy to take revenge in this way for certain misconceptions or criticisms, and that I must have led the conversation myself onto this ground. *Nego simpliciter*: I purely and simply deny it, as theologians say when they are angry. I have no revenge to take; the friendship of the Holy Father is my most precious possession and I have no intention of wasting it on advertising. At any rate, I am not at all happy at having to transcribe the part that concerns me in the passage which follows, and my first thought was to act as if I had not heard. This the Holy Father did not want. He bade me repeat his reply just as he had made it, for a very good reason: the question 'Can we know God?' presents such a multitude of facets that it is impossible to know which way to tackle it. It is comparable to another well-known question, 'What is God?', which Thomas

Aquinas put to himself as a child and which he continued to answer for forty years. It so happened that the account of the sudden enlightenment which converted me provided the Holy Father with a point of departure, and – as he had just said – a concrete one. Starting from this point, he was to be led first of all to tell us something which is important for history, namely that there has been no mystical experience in his life, and subsequently to deal with the problem of the knowledge of God in the form in which it arises for every Christian who lives his faith and on his faith.

Every Christian, I am sure, will be touched by the simplicity with which the Holy Father opens his heart; I imagine that a number of people will be surprised to learn at what level of limpid profundity the faith is anchored in him – and in them.

"I take account of the fact that I am talking with a writer who twelve years ago published a well-known book, *Dieu existe, je L'ai rencontré*.[1] I had occasion at the time to read this curious account of your personal experience. A few months ago you brought me a second book, with which I immediately made myself acquainted, entitled *Il y a un autre monde*.[2] This book, too, is a work of autobiography which aims at defining more closely the facts recounted in *Dieu existe, je L'ai rencontré*. What seems to me the most significant point in your second book is the comparison between two conversions, your own in 1935 and that of Alphonse Ratisbonne[3] a century ago. The two events coincide on one point: a total inner transformation which was completely unexpected and immediate – a transition from unbelief (or 'atheism') to faith without any preparation. One would think that in both cases an invisible force makes the conscious subject swing towards the opposite pole, situating him in a different world diametrically opposed to the previous one. Or rather, one life is abandoned for another. You yourself, like Ratisbonne earlier on, changed in the twinkling of an eye from the unbeliever that you were into a completely believing Catholic, apparently without traversing any previous ground or any prior process of instruction.

1. *God Exists*, Collins Publishers, 1970. (Tr.)
2. 'There is another world' (Tr.)
3. Alphonse Ratisbonne, a Jew who had a vision of the Virgin Mary in a Roman church in 1842, and subsequently founded the order of Our Lady of Sion for Jewish converts.

The title of your first book is both magnificent and provoking. In the French title, what is meant by the words 'I have *met* him'? In human relations it signifies 'perceive'; we cannot say that of the meeting with God. It would be contrary to the words of St. John the Evangelist, 'No one has ever seen God',[1] and to the witness of Moses, to whom God says in the Old Testament, 'You cannot see my face; for man shall not see me and live'.[2] Accordingly you do not claim in any way to have seen God at the moment of your conversion. The title of your book simply means that you have experienced his action in you, that you have, so to speak, felt the inner touch of his light and his power. That is the only explanation of this violent transformation and of the fact that in your new state of mind you saw where you were immediately, you were instantly aware of your identity. What is more, you feel at the same time that you are yourself, possibly even more yourself than before. Your conversion has not stripped you or deprived you of your personality; quite the contrary. This is a weighty empirical argument against the thesis of man's so called 'alienation' by religion."

There is another argument, and one in favour of the Church. As the Pope had just emphasized, I did not 'see God'; certainly not. But I did see his light. And it is not generally known, or it has been forgotten, that this light is not the physical light that strikes and rebounds indifferently, but a light of truth, a light that really instructs, that informs as it illuminates, that teaches you more in a moment about the Christian religion than ten volumes of doctrine. And the curious thing is that this wordless instruction is exactly the same as that of the Church. Whether Christian truth comes to you through spiritual sunstroke or via the faith handed down by tradition, it is the same; the two things coincide perfectly. The convert discovers America, and the Church's geographers, who have never been there, are at least as familar with it as he is. This is a strong argument, so it seems to me, for the truth of Christian teaching. I am sorry that it has been so infrequently employed.

But Pope John Paul II was going to return to the birth of his own faith, of which he had already spoken to me in the first part of this conversation.

"What I have just said does not answer your last question, but it

1. John 1:18
2. Exodus 33:20

prepares the ground. Let us stop for a moment at this point. Personally I have not had the experience which was your lot. From my childhood I lived in an atmosphere of faith from which, to tell the truth, I have never cut myself off, although the circumstances and context of my existence, especially in my youth, often changed or were superimposed on each other. We have already had occasion to speak of this. For me, the fundamental problem was not one of a conversion from unbelief to faith, but rather one of a transition from an inherited, received faith that was more emotional than intellectual to a conscious, fully mature faith given intellectual depth after a personal choice. This slow and gradual transition by different paths, this journey which I myself directed only up to a certain point on the map, seemed to be guided from outside, no doubt, by the succession of events; but it was also guided at a level of my inner life deeper than my reflections, choices, responses or reasoning. I am aware that in this long process, which is still going on, *I am not alone.*"

To what extent is the knowledge of God a matter of the intelligence and to what extent is it a question of faith accepting the word of the divine Revelation?

"In replying to you I should like to reply to myself. But first of all we must settle a question around which we have already circled. I have just mentioned the faith 'inherited and received' through my parents, the environment in which I lived and grew up, my parish, my teachers and spiritual directors, my colleagues and so on. But while admitting this conditioning I do not think that my faith can be called 'traditional', that it is simple conformism, the fruit of adaptation to others, one of those things that one makes one's own by mere assimilation. No, I cannot accept such an interpretation of my faith or, if you like, of my 'theism' – to employ this term once again. Certainly not. I cannot accept this point of view. For without forgetting in any way what I owe to others (including to my country's history), I must state in all conscience that the series of convictions and attitudes which gives me the right and the duty to consider myself a Christian is at the same time the fruit of my own thinking and of my personal choice through and through.

But you want to know what this series of convictions owes to a rational progress towards God and to an intellectual apprehension of the Word and the mystery enclosed in It: this is your problem of the knowledge of God by reason (what one could accurately call 'theism') and of its welcome by faith, which is born of Revelation and through Revelation. Well, in continuing to examine the depths of my religious awareness – which I naturally know to be that of a believer – I note that the faith which is mine does not begin in me independently of the intellectual conviction that God exists but conjointly with it and, so to speak, on the same terrain."

That is how intelligence and the gift of faith are distinguished and unite in the architecture of spiritual life, like human craftsmanship and light in a stained-glass window.

"This intellectual conviction of the existence of God, obviously linked to some idea of what he is, flows, so to speak, into every dimension of the revealed mystery. There was a period in my life when the intellectual aspect predominated. However, while growing deeper with time, it has asserted its own identity and more or less faded into the background to make ever more room for what is mystery, for what enters the soul in the words of Revelation; these words have been allowed to blossom out and grow clearer in my religious consciousness.

What I have just said can serve as a reply to your question, is God 'unknowable' or can one know him even without faith? My own reply, keeping to the terrain of my consciousness and following its evidence, is this: I know that 'I believe' in God, but I also know that this 'I believe' is in correlation with an intellectually perceived knowledge. This fact, and the fact that down the centuries so many men who were unaware of the Revelation recognized (and still recognize) that God exists and have a certain idea of him, authorizes me to conclude that one can reach him by reason alone, although generally such knowledge is inadequate and imprecise."

Pascal says that a philosophical proposition, false as it may appear, is always true 'from one aspect or another' and that one must discover this aspect before discussing the others. John Paul II was to give the 'theology of the death of God' the benefit of his own Pascalian attitude. As the reader will know, this phrase embraces a number of Christian thinkers who assert very different things, while sharing the common factor that these things are generally somewhat obscure. However, 'from one aspect or another' they are true.

"In our day and especially in our Western civilization, in Europe possibly even more than in America, one meets more and more often the phenomenon of an intellectual atheism which to my mind is more 'agnosticism' than 'atheism' as such. The agnostic says, 'I do not know if God exists, I have no proof of it,' while the atheist asserts, 'I know that he does not exist.' This widespread phenomenon has certainly contributed to the birth of the various 'death of God' systems and even, subsequently, to that of a 'theology of the death of God'. This formula, which appears to contain an internal contradiction, seems less absurd when we view it as an attempt at reflection, which may be theological, on the modern phenomenon of agnosticism and atheism, and when we try to examine its roots in the mentality of people to-day. I might add in passing that the catch-phrase 'theology of the death of God' seems to me a negative equivalent to the title of your book, *God exists, I have met him.*"

I did in fact write this book and choose this title (which expresses precisely what I had to say) as a reaction to the appearance of a whole funerary literature in which one writer announced that God had 'died in Jesus Christ' and another preached 'God without God'. They all spoke of death where I had found life and, what is more, eternal life. One of the characteristics of contemporary religious thought is that the wheat and the tares grow so tightly intertwined that one is almost sure to uproot a truth while pulling up an error. The delicate hand of John Paul II is needed to untwist the 'theologies of the death of God' from their tares.

As for religious agnosticism or quite simply atheism, the origin of their development is to be sought, according to the Pope, 'in the subordination of ontological problems to epistemological problems'. In the language of philosophy *ontology* deals with the being of things, while *epistemology* is concerned rather with the manner of knowing them. For the benefit of the reader less familiar than the Holy Father with this language, let us put it another way: the intellect may have tired of scrutinizing the mysterious transparency of being and has transferred its gaze to the *matter* in which being clothes itself to make itself manifest. It is as if Cinderella, after quarrelling with her godmother, gave up her golden coach to analyse pumpkins. Human thought will only depart from the observable and measurable in order to construct systems or fashion chimaeras.

"Agnosticism and atheism are products of positivist epistemology. Contemporary man puts this epistemology into practice every day, without worrying too much about its theoretical aspect or about the mode of knowledge which it limits to the visible world, which is sometimes perceived with the aid of extremely refined apparatus that makes it possible to reach the ultra-microscopic dimension of matter. But whatever the investigative power of our instruments, what we perceive is of a material order, and solely material. This form of knowledge, known as experimental knowledge, has taken hold of men's minds and cut them off from everything 'trans-material' or 'trans-phenomenal'. In the context of the various methodologies which, however useful and effective for a profounder examination of the visible world, nevertheless imply a positivist methodology, not only is there no place for what is 'invisible' but the 'invisible' actually loses its meaning. It is to this state of mind that the expression 'death of God' alludes.

And if God is not 'dead' in my intelligence, that is due in particular to my conscious refusal to accept the familiar methodological and epistemological mechanisms that have led to his 'death' in the mind of contemporary man. This does not mean that I do not admire the progress and conquests of science – far from it. I appreciate all that has been gained in the realm of research and experiment by the positive sciences. But I do not accept the positivist rule. I do not agree with it because it has a narrow and hence erroneous notion of experience, which deprives man of realities accessible to his capacity for knowledge. I am afraid that the next stage in this epistemology will be, after the 'death of God', *the death of man*, which one can see looming up over the horizon of our culture and civilization.''

The 'death of man'? This was by no means a sudden surge of pessimism in a man who never surrenders to this kind of feeling. Pessimism is engendered by doubt, and doubt is something crafted by the ego: if faith really is, as the Pope has just told us, a 'commitment of the whole person', there is no room for doubt. The Pope does not despair in any way of the human race. Just as the 'death of God' is nothing more than a transitory eclipse of the divine in minds obstinately concentrating on matter, so the 'death of man', the psychological counterpart of the 'death of God', is a provisional eclipse – or let us hope so at any rate – of the reflection of God in man's consciousness.

In any case, neither God nor man is dead in John Paul II's philosophy. He explains this partly by his categorical opposition to positivism, to the extent that this philosophy claims to reduce knowledge to what is perceived by the senses.

"But this is only a negative explanation. There is a positive explanation, which obliges me to return to a point mentioned in my autobiographical sketch. I mentioned to you then the great experience, almost an intellectual revolution, occasioned in me at the beginning of my studies by my first contact with an ordinary manual of metaphysics or 'philosophy of being'. It may be that in this inner commotion there was some analogy with, or foretaste of, the experience which forms the heart of your books. This intellectual discovery of days gone by, which could be defined according to Aristotle as a discovery of 'primary philosophy', or of the most elementary dimension of both our pre-scientific and our scientific knowledge proper, formed a durable basis in my mind for the intellectual knowledge of God. There we have a broad scope for intellectual encounters with him. The philosophy of being opens up in this respect wide vistas to the human spirit, and these vistas are more important from some points of view than the five 'ways', still known as proofs of the existence of God, enumerated by St. Thomas Aquinas. I will not repeat them or attempt to evaluate them here. To my mind, each of these 'ways' is a variation inscribed, to define it more exactly, in the context of *being* and *existence*. Thomas Aquinas was not only a continuer of Aristotle's work in the realm of 'primary philosophy'. He renewed and reformed this philosophy, as has been shown by French Thomists like Maritain and Gilson.

From another point of view, immensely important results have been obtained by the philosophy of religion in the domain of the intellectual knowledge of God. This philosophy employs a different method from that employed by the philosophy of being. It is based on the analysis of religious experience and thus takes account of human subjectivity. This kind of analysis is particularly close to my way of thinking. It is concerned directly with the knowledge of *God*, not just with the *Absolute*, as in the purely metaphysical point of view proper to the philosophy of being. This does not prevent me from being convinced that the approach towards 'being' and 'existence' (to be more precise, 'being' under the aspect of 'existence') remains an essential basis for the knowledge of God through reason."

# III

Thus the intellect can form an idea of God and, contrary to an opinion that has become a commonplace, reason can perfectly well demonstrate him even if it cannot display him. I even wonder if it has ever succeeded in demonstrating anything else. This is so true that for two or three centuries people have striven either to limit its jurisdiction to what can be seen or counted, or to forbid its raising certain questions such as those 'why's' of which the biologist Jean Rostand said that of course they are nonsense . . . of course they have no right to emerge from a human mouth . . . but we nevertheless have great difficulty in swallowing them down again once metaphysical nausea brings them up into our throat.[1]

However, reason gives us only a blind knowledge of God, and it is not from reason but from Scripture and Revelation that men's hopes have come since the conscious beginnings of the Judaeo-Christian religion. And if these are two other means of knowing God, how and in what state of mind should we read Scripture, and how is Revelation communicated to us, assuming that by this term we mean the personal teaching of God? I put this question to the Holy Father for two reasons. The first is that for some time the Bible has been subjected to such radical treatment that, if we are to believe some commentators, everything in this venerable book should be treated with caution except for the footnotes written by themselves. This would make the Bible less a means of knowing God than a means of knowing biblical scholars. The second reason is that it seems to me more important than ever to know whether Judaeo-Christianity really is the somewhat surprising result of a conversation with God and whether our common religion is in fact a *revealed* religion.

"In what 'state of mind' we should read Scripture and 'how Revelation is communicated to us' are questions which require a little preliminary organization. However, if I stick to the way in which you formulate them, they answer themselves. For if you admit, as you do, that 'Revelation is the personal teaching of God,'

1. Jean Rostand, *Ce que je crois* ('What I Believe'). Grasset.

it is clear that to read the Bible, in which this Revelation has been put in writing so as to last, the right attitude is that of the disciple. This attitude does not at all conflict with that of the scholar, if it is properly understood that the scholar is not so much a man who teaches others as a man who can show that he is a maturer disciple by going more deeply into the subject of his study.

The intellectual knowledge of God consists rather of reading his presence in the book of the Universe (for Einstein, this meant, for example, the discovery of the wisdom revealed by the structure and organization of the world). If the reading of Scripture is to shape faith – or rather, if it is to shape *our* faith – then it must not only thoroughly understand the biblical texts; it must penetrate beyond their content to him who in the text of Scripture communicates himself. It is a quite distinct mode of knowledge – not so much a question of *knowing* God as of *making his acquaintance*."

Yes, that is what the Pope said: through the words of Scripture God 'communicates himself'. This would mean that there is no distinction to be drawn between what he *is* and what he *says*; he is included in his message, so that the reading of the Bible is really a communion, a sort of first version of the Eucharist. I should have liked to learn more, but the Pope wanted us to stop there for the moment. Besides, another question came to my mind. For the Christian, Scripture is first of all the Gospel. Now Christians have gradually gained the idea that the texts of the four evangelists – Matthew, Mark, Luke and John – were written after the event in the language of fable, to make the new truth accessible to primitive minds. According to this view, what is known as the 'primary meaning of the Gospel', that is, what might be termed the journal-istic account of the divine event of the Incarnation, is only an imaginative, pastoral way of explaining an unprecedented doctrine too difficult to understand in its purely spiritual dimension.

This destructive conception of the Gospel would make Chris-tianity into a profoundly esoteric teaching concealed for the delec-tation of the knowledgeable under the multi-coloured finery of the story. Yet it was the 'primary meaning' of the Gospel that made it so successful. It was because it was received as a true piece of news, not one more mythology, that it conquered so many hearts in so many centuries. It was because they believed that a man, really born of a virgin, had really suffered for them, really been crucified under Pontius Pilate and really risen again on the third day that innumerable martyrs went to their death. These martyrs are called witnesses, not followers, because they gave their lives for a person, not for their own ideas, and that is why we in our turn, in days of old, began to believe. Jesus declared, 'I thank thee, Father, Lord of heaven and earth, that thou hast hidden these things from the wise and understanding and revealed them to babes.' If these words had never been uttered, or if they had only been uttered to mislead the humble, the message being really addressed to 'the wise and understanding', then the Gospel would be a lie and God would be mocking the simple minds to whom he promises his Kingdom. Hence my question: Does the Gospel describe *facts* that really happened at a definite time?

The Holy Father's reply began with a quotation from the constitution *Dei verbum* (Concerning the Divine Revelation) of the Second Vatican Council:

> Holy Mother Church has maintained and maintains with entire constancy and steadfastness that the four above-mentioned Gospels, whose historicity she affirms without hesitation, faithfully relate what Jesus the Son of God, while he passed his life among men, did and taught for their eternal salvation until the day when he was taken up into heaven. The apostles after our Lord's ascension handed on to their hearers the things that he had said and done, in the light of the fuller understanding that they themselves, having been taught by the events of Christ's glorification and illumined by the Spirit of truth, enjoyed. The sacred writers, when they composed the four Gospels, made a selection of some of the many things that had been transmitted orally or in writing. Some of these they related in an abbreviated form or explained with due regard for the situation of the Churches. They retained the character of the original preaching, in such a way as always to impart to us an honest and true account of Jesus. This was their intention when they wrote either from their own memory and recollection or from the testimony of others 'who from the beginning were eyewitnesses and ministers of the word': that we might know 'the truth' of those words in which we have been instructed.

This long excerpt from the conciliar text, said the Pope: "gives in my view a full answer to your question, with all the details necessary to define it. It is well known that the other texts in the

New Testament began to appear in parallel with the four Gospels. Here I shall turn once again to a passage from the constitution *Dei verbum* which touches our problem. We read in the constitution:

> The canon of the New Testament contains, besides the four Gospels, St. Paul's epistles and other apostolic writings set down under the Holy Spirit's impulse, by which, according to God's wise counsel, the facts regarding Christ our Lord are confirmed, his true doctrine is more and more fully expounded, the saving power of his divine work is preached, the Church's beginnings and her wonderful extension are related, and her glorious consummation is foretold.

As we can see from these two quotations, the critical spirit of the exegetes and of the commentators on the Scriptures has always concentrated on the historicity of the four Gospels themselves and on the historicity of their content. In this respect the conciliar constitution condenses in a few words a synthesis of the researches of numerous historians and biblical scholars."

I should like to recall in particular the first lines of the first text: the Gospels 'faithfully relate what Jesus did and taught.' Faith does not demand more, but it does not demand less. Otherwise the Gospel would not be 'news' but at the most a novelty. Christmas, Easter and the other big dates in the Christian calendar would not be feasts but subjects for religious dissertations which there would be no point in setting to music.

"However, the historicity of the events reported in the Gospels enables me to add a remark on the subject of the knowledge or 'knowability' of God which you raised just now. This God in whom as Christians we believe is not only the *invisible creator* that our intelligence can attain through the world and the creatures in it. He is a God who *comes* towards man and as a result *enters* history . . .

[Which is our natural abode.]

Man is a being involved in history and therefore subject to passing time, but he is conscious of the passage of time, which he must fill by fulfilling himself. He has to establish himself in time and employ it to make himself into a unique being who will never be repeated. Historicity differs essentially from limitation by time, for all the beings in the world around us pass away with time. Man alone has a history and he alone creates it. It is true that he creates it while enmeshed in impermanence, but at the same time he creates it through that element in him which resists and overcomes the fleeting character of his existence. When I speak of 'historicity' I am not thinking of the creation of history as culture or knowledge; I am thinking of the very mode of existence of man as man, of each man without exception.

So conceived, the historicity of man explains the appearance of God on the horizon and his entry into history. The Revelation reaches its zenith in the events forming the life of Christ which are recounted by the four Gospels and confirmed by the other writings of the New Testament, as the constitution *Dei verbum* says. The whole Revelation is historical in the sense that it refers to 'historicity' as man's mode of existence in this world. It proclaims the 'great works of God', namely the effects of his transcendent action – or rather of his gift to man. In history these works assume the concrete form of the history of salvation."

I suggest that the reader pays the greatest attention to the demonstration that follows. It is based on undeniable, rock-solid evidence: there is something in the human being – as the Holy Father had just said – which resists the entombing effect of time, which pushes him to produce a work, to write a name in marble or in the heavens, to build pyramids or, more prosaically, to have children. This confers on him a sort of biological perpetuity. This irreducible principle which makes him live through his own history, and which is a sort of memory, reflection and seed of eternity, is the very thing that reminds him that he is made 'in the image of God'. It is in this profound and primordial part of the personality that faith takes root.

"God gives himself to man created in his own image, and this 'image' and 'likeness'[1] alone can make this communication possible. This communication creates the innermost, transcendent, final thread in the history of each man and of humanity as a whole. It is also a 'trans-historical' thread, since, while taking account of the transitory character of man, inscribed in time together with the whole visible world, it also reveals in him the element that does not pass away, that resists time, destruction and death. As we have just said, this is the *historicity* of man – this arrest, this hold on what passes away to extract from it *what does not pass away*, what serves to immortalize the most essentially human element, the element

1. Genesis 1:26. 'God said, Let us make man in our image, after our likeness.'

through which man is the image and likeness of God and surpasses all the creatures subject to an ephemeral existence. *Historicity* is also the existence of *some one* who, while 'passing away', retains his identity.

Understood in this way, the historicity of man is the focal point of Revelation in which faith and its history, and consequently the history of salvation, are fashioned.

That said, the historicity of man so regarded is one of the sources of theist thought, of the intelligence going to meet God. It is precisely in his historicity and because of it that man is prompted to seek a Being who embodies everything in him that resists *transitoriness*, or in other words the ultimate Transcendent of his own transcendence, the eternal model of whom he is, as man, the image and likeness.

Thus it is not only the world (or the Universe) that is at the root of the rational knowledge of God, but also and perhaps above all man himself-in-the-world, man in his historicity, that is, at the same time in what transcends him."


# IV

John Paul II has a remarkable capacity for work, thanks to the combined effect of a strong constitution and good organization. Before the assassination attempt of 13 May an impression of extraordinary strength emanated from his person. When he said Mass in St. Peter's Square the folds of his ample white robe flapped round him like the pleats of the Victory of Samothrace, that gust of wind in stone. The first time I saw him at close quarters, he was walking through a gallery in the Vatican between two rows of visitors and a squadron of *monsignori* was panting after him. Since the assassination attempt he is returning to his old ways but, to risk a metaphor, he does not yet let his horse bolt as he used to do.

As for the organization of his time, it is both strict and flexible for the different parts of his normal days. He rises at a quarter to six – not very easily, he tells me. Mass at seven o'clock, after a long meditation. Quite often a short audience of some ten to fifteen minutes precedes breakfast, at which there is always one or more guests. From nine to eleven the Pope works in his office and does not receive visitors. In Cracow he used to lock himself in his chapel, where a small desk, placed near a window, was turned towards the altar. Cardinal Wojtyla would write for two hours in the rays of the Holy Sacrament, and in two hours this man whom prayer keeps constantly under arms, so to speak, can get through a considerable amount of work. At eleven o'clock the audiences begin; they go on until half-past one or a quarter to two. Lunch, like breakfast, brings guests whom the Pope wishes to honour or from whom he awaits a briefing. Then he has half an hour's rest before going on to his terrace to recite the Divine Office. From half-past three to half-past six he works in his office with his closest assistants. Then the ministers and senior civil servants of the Curia, the government of the Church, come with their files. Dinner, which is called 'supper' in the Vatican, is served towards eight o'clock. At nine o'clock the Pope returns to his study and the chapel to complete the daily office, the 'hours' of which have been recited in the intervals. The Holy Father often goes to bed after eleven o'clock, having devoted his whole day to the Church in prayer, thought, word and action, without deducting a minute from it for other purposes.

John Paul II brings the same conscientiousness to everything he does – the reader will have noticed this from the meticulous nature of his replies to my questions – so much so that a dialogue like ours, which he regards as private, although he has decided to make it public, never encroached on his working hours, all of which he feels he owes to the Church. However, he does allow himself a few minutes of freedom at Castel Gandolfo, or on Sunday mornings or again during mealtimes, which are not all reserved for important visitors. The big dining-room is decorated in grey like a picture gallery (there are some very fine old works on the walls), with a Polish statuette to be seen in one corner, representing St. Anne carrying the Virgin Mary, who in her turn holds to her heart the Infant Jesus. The ceremonial here is always the same. The Holy Father sits down on one side of the table, all by himself, his guest opposite him and his two secretaries at each end. As soon as grace has been said the Pope points a finger at the sheets of paper which you bring him. 'Well,' he says, 'where are we?' He eats very quickly, and less than people claim, without paying much attention to what is set before him. He pushes aside the empty plate much as if he were sweeping aside an objection, and listens to you in the attitude familiar from many pictures of him, elbow on table, cheek resting on hand, gazing out of the corner of his eye. He follows the steps in the argument and, reaching the conclusion before you, waits for you patiently. For patience is one of his most deeply seated characteristics. 'I am not in a hurry,' he likes to say. But his mind never deviates from its course and every decision, once taken, is immediately applicable, to the surprise of those concerned. What they took for hesitation was only the caution of the climber who makes sure of his footing. The Pope takes out only one kind of 'insurance' – prayer, a long session of which precedes all he says and does.

However, when a pope is willing to answer your questions, you are overcome by the double fear of asking too many or of asking too few. This is quickly followed by the feeling that you have not put the right question. I thought it was my duty, in my questionnaire, to make myself the representative of those who have never been given the floor and have only themselves to question, like Hamlet in his utterly simple soliloquy: 'To be, or not to be?' Does God exist, or doesn't he? Hence the questions which I had asked the Holy Father about the knowledge of God, Scripture, the historicity of the Gospels and the reality of the events which they report. But what about faith, of which people talk so much without ever telling us what it comprises? Is it possible to give a definition of this faith which is described by some people as a gift of God, by others as a commitment, and again as 'that which gives substance to our hopes'?

"Perhaps we should first come to an understanding about the very term 'definition', but let us leave that aside for the moment. Personally I would not discount the old catechism definition which I learnt at primary school: faith is 'to admit as truth what God has revealed and what the Church gives us to believe.' However, I will not send you back to the catechism, for this definition, as it stands, can incur the criticism that it does not attach sufficient importance to the person, the subject that experiences faith, even though the very phrase 'admit as truth' clearly implies the existence of the subject. It also indicates the cognitive character of faith in its reference to the truth that motivates it. The young man at the Parc des Princes also showed us this, by contrast with unbelief and atheism.

Yet your question goes further. There is a link and a sort of continuity between the three definitions which you put forward as equivalent: each of them expresses a different aspect of the splendid reality of faith.

First of all, the *gift*. Allow me to quote once again the Second Vatican Council:

> It has pleased God in his goodness and wisdom to reveal himself and to disclose the mystery of his will, whereby men through Jesus Christ, the Word made flesh, have access to the Father in the Holy Spirit, and become partakers of the divine nature. By this revelation the invisible God, out of the abundance of his love, speaks to men as to friends and is conversant with them, that he may invite them to share his company and admit them to it."

This text of the constitution *Dei verbum* (Section 2) is interspersed with references to the Old and New Testaments, most of them quotations from Exodus, the Book of Baruch, the Gospel of St. John and the epistles of St. Paul.[1] In it Christ is called, as in a number of religious writings, the 'Word incarnate', an expression which many people find mysterious and the explanation of which has alone produced more than one book. To be brief, let us say that in the history of mankind, before words deteriorated to the point of becoming inoperative, speech – the 'word' (in Greek, *logos*) – was the start of action and at the origin of things. For the Egyptians and the Hebrews, among others, the mere human word had power in a certain way over what it named; the divine Word was creative, a sort of intermediary between God and nothingness. Thus when we read in the Bible, 'God said, Let their be light,' the words to note for the point which concerns us here are 'God said'; it is because he spoke that *things exist*. Christ, through whom according to the Christian creed 'all things were', is the Word in person, creative and redemptive. 'In the beginning was the Word,' says St. John's Gospel. This makes the Universe a sentence of God's, the end of which we do not yet know.

---

1. Here they are, in the order in which they are quoted: Ephesians 1:9 ('The mystery of his will'); Ephesians 2:18 ('Access to the Father'); Exodus 23:11; Colossians 1:15; I Timothy 1:17 ('the invisible God'); Baruch 3:38 ('hold converse with mortal men'); Romans 16:26 and 1:5; II Corinthians 10:5–6 (for the whole text).

But the Pope returned to the quotation from the Council.

"These admirably compact and precise words do not yet speak of faith but of Revelation. Revelation is 'God communicating himself'. It thus possesses the character of a gift or a grace: a person-to-person gift, in the communion of persons. A perfectly gratuitous free gift which cannot be explained by anything but love.

All this concerns Revelation. What about faith?

We read further on in the same text: 'To God who reveals himself we must bring the *obedience of faith* by which man entrusts himself entirely, freely, to God, bringing to *him who reveals* the complete submission of his intelligence and heart and giving with all his will full assent to the Revelation which he has made.' Thus faith is man's reply to the Revelation by which God 'communicates himself'. The constitution *Dei verbum* expresses perfectly the essentially personal character of faith.

In the words 'man entrusts himself to God by the obedience of faith', one must see, if only indirectly, the thought that faith, as response to the revelation by which God 'gives himself to man', implies through its internal dynamism a reciprocal gift on the part of man, who in a way 'also gives himself to God'. This *gift of oneself* is the profoundest and most personal structure of faith.

In the act of faith, man does not respond to God with the gift of a bit of himself, but with the gift of his whole person. Of course, in this reciprocal relationship the disproportion remains."

So misapprehension is frequent. Those who say, 'faith is a gift,' implying that they have not received it, are at the same time both right and wrong. Right, because there really is a gift on the part of God. Wrong, because this gift is not one of those which require only a banal acknowledgement of receipt; it only takes effect when there is reciprocity.

"Man gives himself or 'entrusts himself' to God in faith, by the response of faith in the measure of his created – and therefore dependent – being. It is not a question of a relationship between equals; that is why *Dei verbum* uses with superb precision the words 'entrusts himself'. In the 'communion' with God, faith marks the first step.

According to the teaching of the apostles, faith finds its fullness of life in love. It is in love that the confident surrender to God acquires its proper character and this dimension of reciprocity starts with faith.

Thus while the old definition in my catechism spoke principally of the acceptance as truth 'of all that God has revealed', the conciliar text, in speaking of surrender to God, emphasizes rather the personal character of faith. This does not mean that the cognitive aspect is concealed or displaced, but it is, so to speak, organically integrated in the broad context of the subject responding to God by faith. We shall speak of this later.

Have I answered your question about faith regarded as a gift? No, not yet. If we stuck to what I have just said we should be on the slippery slope to Pelagianism, which the Church very quickly overcame long ago."

Pelagianism is the teaching of Pelagius, a fifth-century monk who had his own ideas about original sin. He confined its effects to Adam, and invested human effort with a certain privilege by teaching that grace was proportional to merit, a view that is radically contradicted by all we know about the love of God or about parents' love for their children, who do not have to take any trouble to be loved. Pelagius's teaching was condemned by the Council of Carthage in 418, but it has reappeared since under various disguises. I suspect that this monk, with his ledger-like mentality, is at the root of the maxim that countless worthy people are sure they have read in the Gospel, although it does not feature there: 'Heaven helps those who help themselves.'

"Faith, a response to God's Revelation, is nevertheless not a gift made to God by man by his own means alone but, essentially, an inner gift in which man's confident surrender to God grows and flourishes.

We read in the constitution *Dei verbum* that the obedience of faith (through which man freely puts himself completely in God's hands by showing the 'God of Revelation' total submission of the mind and will and by assenting with all his heart to Revelation) is at the same time the fruit of an inner action of the Holy Spirit, and that it depends entirely and essentially on this action. We read in fact: 'In order that this faith may be forthcoming, there is need for God's prevenient and assisting grace, together with the inward aid of the Holy Spirit to move the heart and turn it towards God, open the eyes of the mind, and bestow upon all, in the words of Vatican I, "sweetness in consenting to and believing the truth".' And further on: 'And that the understanding of revelation may become more profound, the same Holy Spirit continues to perfect faith by

(65)

his gifts.' In this sense, faith is an inner gift of God which enables us to respond to Revelation, that is, to the Word in which God reveals himself. It is a Word proclaimed 'in many and various ways' by the prophets and finally by the incarnation of the Word. In receiving this Word we receive God himself, who reveals himself through it. This acceptance of the Word incarnate is at the same time an act of surrender to God or, in some ways, a commitment. In reply to your question, such is the second aspect of faith."

Once again the Pope was going to employ two words current among philosophers but less current in ordinary language – which is my language – the word 'ontological' and the word 'transcendent'. 'Ontological' refers to the being of things. For us, 'transcendent' describes what rises above the common, exceeds ordinary merit or escapes the laws which govern other things. 'Transcendence' is much appreciated by philosophers, but it does not possess the same meaning in all schools. In geometry – which always has the last word – a 'transcendent' curve is one into the calculation of which the infinite enters. I think this definition is the one nearest to the thought of the Holy Father when he speaks of the transcendence of man.

"Before I tell you how I am inclined to conceive this commitment, allow me to examine once again the fundamental meaning of this word in the light of the confident surrender to God.

I have already drawn your attention to the difference between the catechism formula, 'accepting as true all that God reveals', and surrender to God. In the first definition faith is primarily intellectual, in so far as it is the welcoming and assimilation of revealed fact. On the other hand, when the constitution *Dei verbum* tells us that man entrusts himself to God 'by the obedience of faith', we are confronted with the whole ontological and existential dimension and, so to speak, the drama of existence proper to man.

In faith, man discovers the relativity of his being in comparison with an absolute *I* and the contingent character of his own existence. To believe is to entrust this *human I*, in all its transcendence and all its transcendent greatness, but also with its limits, its fragility and its mortal condition, to *Someone* who announces himself as the *beginning* and the *end*, transcending all that is created and contingent, but who also reveals himself at the same time as a Person who invites us to companionship, participation and communion. An absolute person – or better, a personal Absolute.

The surrender to God through faith (through the obedience of faith) penetrates to the very depths of human existence, to the very heart of personal existence. This is how we should understand this 'commitment' which you mentioned in your question and which presents itself as the solution to the very problem of existence or to the personal drama of human existence. It is much more than a purely intellectual theism and goes deeper and further than the act of 'accepting as true what God has revealed'.

When God reveals himself and faith accepts him, *it is man who sees himself revealed to himself and confirmed in his being as man and person.*

We know that God reveals himself in Jesus Christ and that at the same time, according to the constitution *Gaudium et Spes*, Jesus Christ reveals man to man: 'The mystery of man is truly illumined only in the mystery of the Word incarnate.'[1]

Thus these various aspects, these different elements or data of Revelation turn out to be profoundly coherent and acquire their definitive cohesion in man and *in his vocation*. The essence of faith resides not only in knowledge, but also in the vocation, in the *call*. For what in the last analysis is this obedience of faith by which man displays 'a total submission of his intelligence and will to the God who reveals himself'? It is not simply hearing the Word and listening to it (in the sense of obeying it): it also means responding to a call, to a sort of historical and eschatological 'Follow me!' uttered both on earth and in heaven.

To my mind, one must be very conscious of this relation between knowledge and vocation inherent in the very essence of faith if one is to decipher correctly the extremely rich message of Vatican II. After reflecting on the whole of its content, I have come to the conclusion that, according to Vatican II, to believe is to enter the mission of the Church by agreeing to participate in the triple ministry of Christ as prophet, priest and king. You can see by this how faith, as a commitment, reveals to our eyes ever new prospects, even with respect to its content. However, I am convinced that at the root of this aspect of faith lies the act of surrender to God, in which *gift* and *commitment* meet in an extremely close and profound way."

1. *Gaudium et Spes*, 22. This constitution of Vatican II was often to be quoted by the Holy Father, who played a large part in drawing it up.

John Paul II calmly reels off his demonstration from one theme to another as though winding off an electric cable, and you wonder how long he is going to take to set it up when he suddenly makes the decisive connection which illuminates the whole doctrinal edifice. This last exposition is a good example of his method. Starting from almost banal statements about Revelation and human nature, he arrived at powerful new conclusions, among which I myself had particularly noted the point that faith is what establishes in the very core of our being the coincidence of the divine with that essential part of ourselves which refuses to die.

It remained to elucidate that beautiful but mysterious definition attributed to St. Paul and included in my question: 'Faith is that which gives substance to our hopes.' Does it mean that faith gives us now, in darkness, what we shall later see in the light of a new world? Or does it mean, as I have long believed, that faith is in some way the raw material of our share of charity in the eternal exchange which will be our joy? In what sense are we to take the sentence from the Letter to the Hebrews?[1]

But the Holy Father understands Greek and the reader will remember that he studied philology at the university. I was to endure the consequences:

"Through the spectacles of biblical criticism the term 'substance' corresponds to the Greek *hypostasis* and has its own separate history in the theology of the councils. At Nicaea, it indicated rather 'Essence' and later 'Person', whence the definition of the doctrine of the Trinity, 'one nature in three hypostases',[2] and that of the christological dogma, the 'hypostatic union of two natures'.[3] In the Bible, *hypostasis* has a meaning closer to its root, 'what is underneath', and hence 'base' or foundation. Consequently while the *hypostasis* of the Letter to the Hebrews was rendered by the word 'substance' in the Vulgate,[4] more modern translators no longer employ the term. They translate it either in a more 'objec-

---

1. Hebrews 11:1
2. God in three persons.
3. The Divine nature and human nature in Christ.
4. The Vulgate is the Latin version of the Bible, partly produced in the fourth century by St. Jerome, under the supervision of a small college of rabbis for the Hebrew texts, and adopted by the Church. Being in Latin, the Vulgate was therefore at the time a publication in the 'vulgar' tongue.

tive' way by speaking of *foundation*, *guarantee* or *security*, or else in a more subjective way by saying *certainty* or *reason for hope*.

Moreover, the passage in question of the Letter to the Hebrews forms part of a long train of argument (forty paragraphs) about faith, and is only complete in the form, 'assurance of things hoped for' and 'conviction of things not seen'.

After these philological remarks, I shall not be afraid to say that, according to the author of the letter, faith gives us in an *invisible way* a *reality* which is at the same time the *object of our hope*.

Faith, implying the firm conviction that this *invisible reality* exists, is *ipso facto* the foundation of the hope that we possess of attaining it.

To sum up, we can assert that the old definition in our catechisms has been considerably developed and enriched thanks to biblical studies and the conciliar texts. To be sure, one could and even should say more about it. In the Letter to the Hebrews alone, which we have just cited, we read that faith enables us not only to *know God* but to *please him*, and that is the *strength* of the martyrs and confessors.[1] As for myself, there was a time when I studied the question of faith in the works of St. John of the Cross. You know that he speaks of the *nights* of faith to convey in a metaphorical fashion that this participation essential to the knowledge of himself which God grants us in faith transcends the human faculties on the plane of the senses as well as on the spiritual plane. It is precisely this supra-sensory and supra-intellectual character of faith, manifesting itself in an intense inner life, that guarantees that one is approaching the Reality given to man in faith and sought by him with all his strength.

This analysis of faith, the work of a great mystic, I find particularly convincing. That does not diminish in any way the scope of your questions," he added, ever charitable, and doubtless to console me for the loss of 'substance' which I had just experienced.

However, one difficulty remains. In the Letter to the Hebrews there is talk of the 'things hoped for' without any further details, as if it were pointless to say any more to Christians. And we may suppose in fact that the martyrs going to their deaths had no hesitations about what their faith led them to hope for. I am not at all sure that all the Christians of to-day, especially Christians of the

1. Hebrews 11:6 32–38

western world, who have long been spared the hard necessity of bearing witness, have the same clear and distinct vision of the promises of their religion. Faith and hope proceed along the same path, hope a step in advance of her companion; but where are they going to? What are these 'things hoped for'?

"Another question which would need a whole treatise! Let us try to avoid that by taking up the thread of our conversation. I have not forgotten for a moment that I am dealing with the author of the book *Dieu existe, je L'ai rencontré* and of its successor, based on the same experience, which speaks of the existence of the 'other world' and discusses precisely the *invisible world*, the *reality* we hope for. The text of the Letter to the Hebrews which we have just analysed is in perfect agreement with others in which the inspired author speaks of the 'hope that is in us' and of which every Christian 'must give account' to men."

It is in fact a forgotten truth that the Christian does not own Revelation and that he must account to others for the grace which he has received. I made a mental note to return to this point, while the Holy Father was starting on another train of thought.

"If to believe is to admit as truth what God has revealed, to have Christian hope is to await with supernatural certainty 'what God has promised man because of the merits of Jesus Christ'. Or, better, it is to tend towards that, to order one's life in the light of the future which man and the world possess in God.

I think that the thrilling moment described in your two books, the moment of a violent inner transformation, of conversion from unbelief to faith, was at the same time the start of hope: the discovery of the future of which I have just spoken. Previously you did not admit it and you did not order your life in this light; from that moment onward you began to live in this sector and to tend towards this future.

As for myself, I have never experienced such a violent trans-formation. As I told you, the years of my childhood and adolesc-ence passed in an atmosphere of faith, of faith handed down and freely continued. I was very conscious, sometimes agonizingly so, of the 'last days' and especially of the 'judgement of God'. In the catechism in use at my primary school, the 'last days' figured in the chapter on *Christian hope*, which discussed successively death, judgement – personal and final – heaven, hell and purgatory. At the centre of this catechetical eschatology lay – or at any rate that was my impression – the *judgement of God*. This vision of the last days possessed above all the character of a great examination of one's whole life, of one's good and bad actions. The moral aspect predominated, transferred to the plane of the after-life, of which God is the master and supreme guarantor.

Of course, this vision is in conformity with Revelation; various texts can be cited in its support, beginning with the grandiose fresco of Chapter 25 in St. Matthew's Gospel.[1] I am convinced that this picture forms an essential part of the faith and ethics of a huge majority of mankind, and not only of believing Christians. If we base ourselves on this vision of things we can 'give account of the hope that is in us' – but it does not correspond to all the riches of this hope. The future that we have in God according to the words of eternal life is infinitely richer, more closely linked to present time and to the whole past of man and the world since the beginning and all through revealed history. It is in virtue of the *future* that this history is known as the 'history of salvation' and in fact is just that."

Christians who sometimes have a great deal of difficulty in organizing their beliefs will no doubt find some comfort in the following words, in which the Holy Father confesses that the final 'synthesis' of his faith did not come about of its own accord or particularly early:

"I must admit on this point that it was the Second Vatican Council that helped me, so to speak, to synthesize my personal faith; in the first place Chapter 7 of the constitution *Lumen gentium*, the one entitled, 'The eschatological character of the pilgrim Church and its relation with the Church in heaven'. I was already a bishop when I took part in the Council. Before that, I had obviously studied the treatise on the end of time, and this at two universities. At the Angelicum in Rome I had devoted much time to the articles of the *Summa theologica*[2] dealing both with *beatitude* and the *beatific vision*. Nevertheless, I think it was the conciliar constitution on the Church that enabled me to discover the synthesis of this reality for which we hope. That is why I want to

1. After two parables about the Kingdom of Heaven, Chapter 25 of St. Matthew pictures the judgement of the nations ('Come, O blessed of my Father', etc.). We shall revert to this text a little further on.

2. By St. Thomas Aquinas, *'doctor communis* of the Church', whose teaching, even when it is contested, has for centuries been the basis of the training of the clergy. The 'beatific vision' is the vision of God.

answer you text in hand, so to speak. The discovery that I made at that time consists in this: whereas previously I envisaged principally the eschatology of man and my personal future in the after-life, which is in the hands of God, the Council constitution moved the centre of gravity towards the Church and the world, and this gives the doctrine of human ends its full dimensions.

Here is the text in question:

> The Church, to which we are all called in Christ Jesus, and in which by the grace of God we acquire holiness, will receive her perfection only in the glory of heaven, when will come the time of the renewal of all things. At that time, together with the human race, the universe itself, which is so closely related to man and which attains its destiny through him, will be perfectly re-established in Christ . . . The promised and hoped for restoration, therefore, has already begun in Christ. It is carried forward in the sending of the Holy Spirit and through him continues in the Church, in which, through our faith, we learn the meaning of our earthly life, while we bring to term, with hope of future good, the task allotted to us in the world by the Father, and so work out our salvation . . .
>
> However, until there be realized new heavens and a new earth in which justice dwells, the pilgrim Church, in her sacraments and institutions, which belong to this present age, carries the mark of this world which will pass, and she herself takes her place among the creatures which groan and travail yet and await the revelation of the sons of God (in the magnificent words of the Epistle to the Romans) . . . But we have not yet appeared with Christ in glory in which we will be like to God, for we will see him as he is . . . Before we reign with Christ in glory we must all appear 'before the judgement seat of Christ, so that each one may receive good or evil, according to what he has done in the body', and at the end of the world 'they will come forth, those who have done good, to the resurrection of life, and those who have done evil, to the resurrection of judgement.'[1]

I will not read you the whole chapter. These are only a few

1. *Lumen gentium* (48). All the sentences in this text are based on quotations from the New Testament. In the order in which they are quoted: Acts 3:21; Philippians 2:12; II Peter 3:13; Romans 8:19, 22; Colossians 3:4; I John 3:2; II Corinthians 5:10; I John 5:29; Matthew 25:46.

excerpts. There are many others which would be worth quoting, both in the dogmatic constitution *Lumen gentium* and in the pastoral constitution *Gaudium et Spes*. These are texts laden with biblical words of an eloquence and of an originality of expression unique of their kind. It would be necessary to draw parallels between all these passages to answer the question, 'what is the reality that we expect in faith?'

To sum it all up, I will say this:

We hope in faith that God completes and perfects his gift[1] revealed 'since the beginning'. God reveals himself to man. Consequently, eternal life finds its centre in the vision of God face to face, in St. Paul's expression, or in other words in the ultimate knowledge of God as he is and in the love flowing from this knowledge, which unites man to God in this love, which he is himself. This gift of the unfathomable trinity, Father, Son and Holy Spirit, will be incorporated in the gift of the 'new heaven' and 'new earth'; that is, in the gift of the world and man freed from the bonds of sin and death by the *reality* of the Resurrection and of the eternal adoption of the sons of God.

We confess this faith in the apostles' creed, when we say, 'I believe in the resurrection of the body and life everlasting.'

In this same creed we also confess our faith in the communion of saints.

This gift, when brought to perfection – and the revelation of it has been developing and growing deeper since the beginning – infinitely exceeds the order of the natural rights and tendencies of man. That is why it is a pure and complete gift in the full meaning of the term."

Nevertheless, what is this judgement which has been mentioned several times and which used to conjure up in men's minds the scenery and trappings of human justice, with its indictments, its pleas and its penal code?

"In his transcendence man goes to meet God, who is infinitely perfect. He halts, so to speak, on the threshold of *judgement*, which is to be understood as a need to see where he stands when finally confronted by absolute and universal truth. He understands the need for definitive justice. He also perceives, sometimes extremely clearly, the need for a complete purification when confronted with

---

1. The Creation.

the majesty of infinite holiness. All these things are the 'last ends' from the point of view of the human subject. However, in the divine intention, the full dimension of the gift transcends human sight. Perhaps the word that best helps us to understand this is the word 'communion', which suggests both the face-to-face union with the living God and the union between men finally brought into accord with the divine measure of existence and co-existence: *Communio sanctorum*, the communion of saints.

In the last analysis words fail us. Again it is the language of the Bible that hits the target; one must simply direct one's attention to each phrase, to each word of this language and, through prayer, plumb their depths."

For my part, it was the first time that I had come across the idea, or rather the shaft of light, that explains the last 'judgement' by every being's desire to 'see where he stands when finally confronted by absolute truth', in the truth of his own person, of the Universe, of God. So understood, the 'judgement' ceases to smell of the court-room. It is first of all a liberation from the doubts and deceits, from the errors and suspect obscurities, from the lies and illusions of this life, and if there is a 'court' it will not sit under the sword and scales of human justice, but under the aegis of the Gospel: 'The truth will make you free.' The 'communion of saints' will settle the rest, beginning, if I may say so, with the bill.

This old, ultramodern doctrine of the communion of saints occupies a large place in the Holy Father's thinking. It is indeed an old dogma. Its historical origin is by no means certain, but probably goes back to the earliest days of Christianity. In those times many were called to martyrdom, but they did not all have the strength to endure to the end. Some gave way, and the community kept them at arm's length for a little while. They could reduce the length of this period of exclusion by begging one of those who had survived torture to intercede for him with the Church of the catacombs: the intercessor who had survived martyrdom writing a letter requesting that the merit of his bloody witness be transferred to the failing brother, to hasten his reinstatement. These movements of spiritual capital, which later gave rise to the inflationary practice of 'indulgences', are based on the typically Christian principle of the reversibility of merit, an essential article of the 'communion of saints' whose radiant centre is Jesus Christ.

As for the divine origin of the dogma, personally I shall seek it in

Chapter 25 of St. Matthew's Gospel, to which the Holy Father had referred shortly before. Here are the operative verses:

> Then the King will say to those at his right hand, 'Come, O blessed of my Father, inherit the Kingdom prepared for you from the foundation of the world; for I was hungry and you gave me food, I was thirsty and you gave me drink, I was a stranger and you welcomed me, I was naked and you clothed me, I was sick and you visited me, I was in prison and you came to me.' Then the righteous will answer him, 'Lord, when did we see thee hungry and feed thee, or thirsty and give thee drink? And when did we see thee a stranger and welcome thee, or naked and clothe thee? And when did we see thee sick or in prison and visit thee?' And the King will answer them, 'Truly I say to you, as you did it to one of the least of these my brethren you did it to me.'[1]

Dogmas are living thoughts, and in my view the heart of this one beats in this gospel, more particularly in the words, 'As you did it to one of the least of these my brethren you did it to me.' Human acts go beyond their immediate surroundings and the social or political perimeter. Every human act passes through Jesus Christ and via him reaches others to the ends of the world. For whatever good or evil I do is done first of all to him. Between me and my neighbour, or the stranger in the distance whom I shall never meet, there is his person, whom I do not see and who is the first to gather up my tears or to receive my blows, which echo to the furthest parts of heaven. By taking my human nature, he has put me in communication with the totality of the universe, visible and invisible, of the living and the dead, and the violence which I think I am committing in the shadows makes a distant unknown angel shudder. But the smallest merit acquired through his grace will also go to the most unprovided, who without knowing me awaits my good will, whether he is conscious or quite ignorant of this spiritual reversibility, which makes the poor man the permanent creditor of the rich. Since the Incarnation human acts have infinite repercussions. That is how I envisage the communion of saints, an 'old ultramodern doctrine', of which all contemporary systems are caricatures or counterfeits, in the penitential form of collective responsibility. Human justice would perhaps overcome its grave moral perplexities if, without

---

1. Matthew 25:34–40

ceasing to enquire into the motives of a misdeed, it was inspired by the 'old ultramodern dogma' to look into its consequences. The guilty person would not perhaps become any better for it, but society would.

# V

To believe, John Paul II had said, is to enter 'the triple mission of Christ'. Now some 'missionaries' (and as Christians we are all missionaries according to the Holy Father's definition) hesitate or refuse to-day to speak openly of Jesus Christ out of consideration for their interlocutors, who may be unbelievers or adherents of other religions. Out of fear of being accused of proselytism or even religious colonialism, they object to any kind of evangelization, make it a duty to proclaim nothing to anybody and confine their activity to the 'exchange' or 'sharing' of their feelings – without explaining how they go about excluding Jesus Christ from them.

Like many converts, who are incapable of suppressing the news that has revolutionized their lives, I find it difficult to understand this kind of dumb apostolate. Is this what Vatican II prescribes?

"The missionary mandate, contained in the words of Christ himself, has only one meaning: 'Go therefore and make disciples of all nations, baptizing them in the name of the Father and of the Son and of the Holy Spirit, teaching them to observe *all* that I have commanded you; and lo, I am with you always, to the close of the age.'[1]

Vatican II harnessed itself to the work of ecumenism, that is, the unity of all Christians. It also expressed its respect and esteem for the non-Christian religions, taking principally into consideration Judaism and Islam. In addition, the Council had a good deal to say about religious freedom.

None of this contradicts the fact that the same Council confirmed the missionary activity of the Church in the decree *Ad gentes* (To the nations). Moreover, in the document *Lumen gentium* it demon-

1. Matthew 28:19–20

strated that the Church, by her nature, is a missionary Church. The missionary rôle of the Church comes straight from the mystery of the Father, who has approached us and revealed himself to us by sending his Son. Leaving the earth after accomplishing his mission, Christ remained among his people, remained in the Church through the Holy Spirit, sent in his name by the Father, in accordance with his words on the eve of the Passion. Thus the missionary mandate entrusted to the apostles is linked to the Church's most profound reason for existing. Since the beginning the Church has been a missionary body and she will never cease to be one.

Vatican II also emphasized this characteristic in its appeal to an ecumenical commitment to the unity of all Christians, as well as by pointing to all the elements of truth and all the authentic values to be found in the non-Christian religions. So far as the unity of Christians is concerned, we stand in the ranks of the confessors and disciples of the same Christ who, in his priestly prayer, asked the Father that all the disciples might be 'One'. The constant, humble search for paths to this unity certainly corresponds to the missionary vocation of the Church, if we remember that this prayer ends with these words: 'So that the world may believe that thou hast sent me.'[1]

So far as the non-Christian religions are concerned, the missionary mandate operates through a better knowledge of the 'faiths' professed. A Christian conscious of his participation in the mission of Christ, which contains the fullness of what God has wished to reveal of himself to humanity, will never stop wanting this fullness to become the share of every man. He will never stop working for this, while retaining complete respect for the convictions of those who believe otherwise. But often he will pray ceaselessly for what, as he well knows, will be not simply the fruit of man's religious thoughts, however noble, but a gift of God alone. He will leave God to be the sole judge of the consciences of his brothers who believe otherwise or do not believe at all. He will leave to God alone the exclusive right to make his truth bear fruit in minds and hearts, doing for his part in this intention all that lies in his power.

The Council's declaration on religious liberty displays a masterly

1. John 17:21

eloquence on this point, especially in the second part, entitled 'Religious freedom in the light of Revelation'."

For many observers this declaration marked the Church's break with the famous formula 'No salvation outside the Church' (which was not so terrible in any case, since no one knows the limits of the Church). The declaration reconciles every disciple's duty to proclaim the truth received from Christ and that of acting 'with love, prudence and patience' towards those in error or in ignorance of the faith, which cannot be imposed on anyone. It avails itself of the example of Christ himself, who did not wish his Kingdom to be defended by the sword or extended by force.

"Christ also defines the missionary mandate of the Church in another text, which says: 'You shall be my witnesses in Jerusalem and throughout Judaea and Samaria and to the end of the earth.'[1] Let us note the reciprocal link between the two passages, 'Teach by baptizing . . .' and 'You shall be my witnesses', a link fundamental to a genuine missionary dynamism. Even if all Christians are not called to 'teach and baptize', all, according to their own vocation, must be 'witnesses' in the measure of the gift received from the Lord. It may be a witness without words, speaking through the holiness and authenticity of a life in conformity with the evangelical spirit.

In my view, Vatican II fully confirmed these essential lines of the Church's missionary *praxis*. By putting this *praxis* in the ecumenical context, in the context of the Church's relations with the non-Christian religions, and by following the clearly understood principle of religious liberty, the Council showed that it wished to see missionary activity ripen on each of these planes, in conformity with the situation of man in the world of to-day, in all latitudes."

# VI

Better equipped than anyone else for the close combat of controversy, the Holy Father detests polemics and their summary

1. Acts 1:8

classifications. It is true that heaven has endowed him with two charismata which dispense him from becoming involved in our wretched disputes. The first is the ability to act by his presence alone, as everyone could see on the day of his enthronement when, before he had said more than three words, diplomats were to be seen weeping in their official seats – a phenomenon as rare as April showers in the Sahara. When there is a difference of opinion in the Church, he gets the opponents together, sits down at the end of the table and the problem disappears. This has been seen at certain synods which promised to be stormy and finished as peaceful sunsets, everyone having realized, under the Pope's gaze, that the person opposite also had his reasons, not all of them bad. Another gift – which also makes him the man he is – is the ability to go back to first causes, far back into history or deep into theology. The reader will have noticed more than once in the preceding pages that the Pope never hesitates to go back to Genesis or beyond and deduce consequences far ahead in the future. To speak metaphorically, we might say that he sticks one leg of his intellectual dividers on the question of the moment and the other as far as possible back into the past. Then he has only to twist the instrument for his line of thought to plant you in the middle of your final destination; the distinctions which seemed so important a moment before have been surmounted with ease and left far behind. For example, his conception of faith, which he has just explained at length, seems excellent and to me quite irrefutable; but, with the idea of redemption, it implies the notion of sin, which looks very much like being lost – a great pity for humanity. For the notion of sin is bound up with the dignity of the human being in such a way that there is more honour in recognizing a fault than in performing any action, however dazzling.

And yet, when I observed to the Holy Father that in this respect we Western Christians had the misfortune to live 'between a sinless Left', converted rather late to the views of Rousseau, and an 'unforgiving Right', which believes so strongly in sin that it sometimes gives the impression of believing in nothing else, he refused to follow me on this terrain, opened his dividers to a hundred and eighty degrees and gave me another taste of his transcendental method:

"I do not know what you mean (or rather to whom you allude) when you speak of the Christian 'Right' and 'Left'. Accordingly my reply will not be addressed to any particular people or circles; it will simply be an answer to the specific question raised.

First of all, I want to express my agreement, for essential reasons, with the assertion that the *notion of sin* is bound up with the dignity of the *human person* (I say: notion of sin, which is not the same thing as sin), just as the notion of the remission of sins concerns the whole spiritual future of the person. This observation is drawn from the very heart of the Gospel. To realize this, it is sufficient to recall the first words of Christ's call in St. Mark's Gospel: 'The time is fulfilled and the kingdom of God is at hand; repent, and believe in the gospel.' Through all the actions and words of Christ and all that his cross and resurrection tell us, one can see clearly that man always needs to repent in order to rediscover his spiritual greatness and the dignity proper to him. It was for him that Christ came, to open up the possibility of effective repentance, that is, of the remission of sins.

Here are the Lord's first words to the apostles after his resurrection: 'Receive the Holy Spirit: if you forgive the sins of any, they are forgiven.'[1] It is as if he wished to say to them, 'This is what I bring you and give you as the essential fruit of my cross, my death and my resurrection.'

Why is the notion of sin bound up with the dignity of man? Because this dignity *also* requires man to live in the truth. And the truth about man is that he commits evil, that he is a sinner. Even those who strive to eradicate the notion of sin from the vocabulary of hearts and to erase it from human language confirm this truth in different ways. To erase the notion of sin is to impoverish man in a fundamental part of the experience of his humanity.

If one wishes to eliminate the notion of sin, it is to 'liberate' man from the prospect of a 'conversion' (and hence of sacramental 'penitence'). Yet this step ends in the void, or rather burdens the subconscious with the idea of *inevitable*, and in some ways *normal*, evil. There follows the necessity to call evil not *evil* but *good*, in order to be able to yield to it even in the realm of the most fundamental moral requirements.

Christ is at the same time both merciful and intransigent. He calls good and evil by their names, without any discussion or compromise; but he also shows himself always ready to forgive. All

---

1. John 20:22–23

he does and each one of his words express his faith in man – who can 'renew' himself only by repenting, by becoming more and more man, and a free man. Paul of Tarsus takes up and launches this message with the enthusiasm of the neophyte, of the converted persecutor. And the Church, which never hesitates to call good and evil by their proper names and never ceases to forgive sins, in the last analysis serves the good of man in the deepest sense; I would even say once again in the most fundamental sense of his humanity. I tried to express a few fairly elementary ideas on this subject in the encyclical *Redemptor hominis.*

The sources of the two apparently opposite points of view which you summarize as 'sinless' and 'unforgiving' are of little importance, for they converge, and lead in the last analysis to the same result. To what? I would say: first, from the point of view of human experience, to a great anthropological danger – the imperilling in man of the very sense of his existence. Modern philosophy gives us many expressions of this danger, this peril."

The sinless, unforgiving man is such an anomaly that modern philosophy ends up by denying his existence; this is what the Holy Father had earlier called 'the death of man'.

"To what do these errors lead? The most profound answer is to be found in the words of Christ, those mysterious words in which it is asserted that all evil can be overcome by love and that every sin can be forgiven, save one: the sin against the Holy Ghost.

This sin consists for man in, so to speak, hermetically sealing his inner life against all the Holy Spirit can bring him. Now if, as emerges from the words of the risen Lord, what the Holy Spirit brings is 'remission of sins', it is clear that this remission requires man to be conscious of sin, to be aware of his liability to sin. In the opposite case man is closed, and hence not freed, not liberated from the sin that dwells in him and is aggravated because of his sin against the Holy Ghost."

# VII

So far as faith is concerned, then, of which everyone speaks without always taking the trouble to define it, we know now whence it comes and where it goes. And also what it is: the most natural thing in the world, in that it coincides with the aptitude for self-transcendence which makes us men. It is also the most supernatural thing, for it acts in us like a sort of permanent miracle. However, there remains a major obstacle on which many good wills founder, the painful objection of the heart which finds a child's tear heavier than all imaginable worlds – evil. Not moral evil: we have only to examine ourselves honestly to know the origin of that. I refer to physical evil, the suffering of the innocent, a terrible problem for the believer and a cruel stumbling-block for the unbeliever. This time I went up to the Holy Father with a brief-case full of anguished questions. Why does suffering exist? Are there sorrows which can be appeased only by the real presence of God, and which make those who have to endure them so like Jesus Christ that they can only speak of them validly to the Father in person?

"You distinguish the objective dimension, the facts, such as the suffering of the innocent, from the subjective reaction, the consciousness of evil, which constitutes, as you say, 'a terrible problem for the believer' and 'a stumbling-block for the unbeliever'. That is true. Unbelievers very often deny the existence of God because of the evil that exists in the world, and for the same reason the faith of believers is put to a harsh test. This second dimension, the consciousness of evil, is sometimes more painful than the evil itself. Of course, it is difficult to measure this sort of reality, but it can be admitted, for example, that the consciousness of the suffering of others, particularly of those close to us, is sometimes more painful than the suffering which causes it."

Compassion can be harder than suffering, for the latter has its natural limits, while compassion opens man's being to the infinite and tears him without killing him. The Pope was to give me to understand in a moment that in Christ compassion (for humanity) was an added element in the Passion.

"Speaking from experience, I can tell you that, as an adolescent, I was above all *intimidated* by human suffering. There was a time when I was afraid to approach those who were ill: I felt a sort of remorse when confronted with this suffering which I had been spared. In addition, I felt embarrassed; I thought that all I could say to the sick was only a 'dud cheque' or rather a cheque drawn on *their* account, for it was they who were suffering, not I.

There is a certain truth in the saying, 'The healthy person does not understand the invalid', although one can turn it round and say that the invalid does not always understand the healthy person either, who also suffers in a different way when confronted with the invalid's suffering.

By leading me more and more often to meet the sick, and people sick in many ways, my pastoral duties have enabled me to emerge from this period of timidity. I must add at this point that I have emerged from it mainly because the sick themselves have helped me to do so. Through visiting them, I came to realize, at first gradually, then in a way that banished all doubt, that quite unexpected relations developed between their suffering and their consciousness of it. I think I reached a peak in this domain the day I heard these words from the lips of a very sick man: 'Father, you don't know how happy I am!'

Before me I had a bed-ridden invalid who had lost everything during the Warsaw rising and, instead of complaining, this man was saying to me, 'I am happy!' I did not even need to ask him why. I realized, without his having to tell me, what must have been happening in his soul, how this sort of transfiguration could come about and above all *who* could effect it. Since then I have met in their homes or in hospitals many people tortured by pain, and more than once I was able to discern in them the traces of the same inner evolution, recognizing its different stages and variations. I have known doctors, nurses and other people in the service of the sick who knew how to clear the way for this mystical process."

He might have added, though he did not do so, that he had seen these doctors and nurses at the foot of his own bed, and that he had had personal experience of illness: after the assassination attempt of 13 May he drank at length from this bitter spring which he had not dared to approach in his youth. During his second stay in the Gemelli hospital, which a little too much optimism had induced him to leave prematurely, and whither the virus lodged in the huge blood transfusion of the day of the attempted murder had brought him back terribly weakened, emaciated, feverish, unrecognizable, he had been for over a week, so he told me, very close to death. I shall recount all this later on, since he did not speak of it on this particular day.

"What I have just said does not deal with the whole extent of our problem. How can we forget the evil that men inflict on men, the concentration camps, the tortures, all the machinery for oppressing and destroying the most human elements in man? It is very difficult to weigh the evil that is committed in the world, to enumerate the causes of the human suffering that made Christ say in the Garden of Olives: 'If it be possible, let this cup pass from me!' The chalice of Maundy Thursday, the Cross on Calvary the next day . . .

Of course, men do all they can to free themselves from evil, from illnesses, from cataclysms, from wars. These efforts are not vain. At the same time the dimensions of objective evil in the world and its subjective repercussions in man's consciousness are difficult to evaluate. The means at our disposal to-day to combat evil and suffering are admirable, as are those who lead the fight. And the Gospel is a tremendous call to action, an ever active message from the good, merciful Samaritan. Nevertheless . . .

Nevertheless, it seems as if the roots of evil lie deeper, as if evil contains a sort of mystery greater than man, one that transcends his history and his means of action. When one considers the efforts that man makes to conquer evil – especially in our day – one has the impression that his actions affect only the symptoms and do not go deep enough to reach the causes, the hidden springs of evil. It is too often forgotten that evil has not only a physical dimension but also an ethical one, and that the latter is more fundamental."

But we have come to the moment and the place where, as I said just now, passion and compassion were to meet in one unique instance of suffering:

"On the Mount of Olives, confronted with the Passion and the Cross, Jesus embraces every dimension of evil in man's heart and in the history of humanity and asks that 'this chalice' may pass from him; however, he says, 'Nevertheless, not as I will, but as thou wilt'[1] That is why this prayer is such a poignant moment in Christ's

1. On the eve of his crucifixion, on the Mount of Olives, Jesus took 'Peter and the two sons of Zebedee.' And 'he began to grow sorrowful and troubled. Then he said

mission as a whole. It is also the point to which our questions about evil in the world will continually return, evil as permitted and accepted in the eternal plan of God . . . of the Father. When our human thinking about evil turns with anxiety to this eternal plan, we come with our anguish to the garden of Gethsemane, before climbing Calvary, under the cross of Christ . . .

Gethsemane and Calvary teach us that the Son of God found himself in the same situation as any man at grips in this world with the weight of evil. He was on the side of suffering man. In that scene of agony he proclaimed to the end the Kingdom of God, the truth of a love stronger than death.

We believe that in assuming the weight of evil he conquered evil. That he conquered sin and death. *That he grafted on to the root of suffering the power of the redemption and the light of hope.* That is what he shares with every man. Those who suffer, and whom my pastoral duties have led me to meet, have borne witness to it, and still do every day before my eyes.

Christ cured the sick, restored sight to the blind, hearing to the deaf, and raised Lazarus from the dead. But to all those who suffer, from moral or physical evil, he never ceases to offer this graft of redemption, which comes from his cross and resurrection.

As I have said, it is difficult to measure the evil which is our lot on this earth. It is a mystery greater than man, deeper than his heart. Gethsemane and Calvary speak of it, and at the same time bear witness that in the history of man, in his heart, another mystery is at work, that of the Redemption, which will work to the end to uproot evil. And in this mystery not only is the day of judgement in preparation; 'a new heaven and a new earth' are also ripening, where it is written that 'justice will dwell' and that then 'God himself will wipe away every tear from their eyes, and death shall be no more; neither shall there be mourning nor crying nor pain any more.'"[1]

---

to them, "My soul is very sorrowful, even to death; remain here, and watch with me." And going a little farther he fell on his face and prayed, "My Father, if it be possible, let this cup pass from me; nevertheless, not as I will, but as thou wilt."' (Matthew 26:37–39). Mark's account is identical. Luke adds that during this hour of agony Christ's sweat became 'like great drops of blood'.

1. Apocalypse 21:4

# MORALS

# I

Sitting in a corner of St. Peter's Square in the middle of a group of Polish pilgrims, I was waiting for the Holy Father with the twenty or thirty thousand people whom the public audience assembles between the lines of grey railings every Wednesday. A few yards away a Swiss guard in his funny striped uniform was walking up and down, and the slight slope of the square made him look taller than the colonnade. On the other side of the square the buildings of the Vatican projected at different angles. The Italian way of ordering space is different from the French way. The French, who live spaciously in a not very heavily populated land, give the name 'perspective' to lines of parallels stretching away in a straight line towards an improbable meeting-point on the horizon. It is a tradition running from Karnak to Versailles. The Romans, on the other hand, pile up their buildings in an apparent disorder which has the magic effect of creating space where there seemed to be little. When the Pope had passed through the 'arch of bells', to the left of the basilica, in the white vehicle which the Mexicans first christened the *papamobile*, the streamers would unfurl over the crowd as though lifted by the wind and cheers would rise from the sea of people. Popes are always applauded; they give back to Rome, on the spiritual plane, something of its ancient temporal supremacy. There is also a second reason for the applause: Popes concentrate in their persons the maximum of legitimacy through their double investiture by God and by the Church's vote, and as a result they possess in everyone's eyes the right to be there and to speak as they do. This principle of legitimacy is so obviously alive in them that even those who challenge the papacy needs have to recognize it and content themselves with restricting its effects to the Catholic Church. The third reason, and in my view the strongest, the one that creates the excitement, is that a pope seems in the popular view – which is also mine – like the ultimate known intermediary between this world and God. He moves on the fringe of the invisible and when he stretches his arms over the crowd they do not know if he is going to heaven or coming from it. It is a very intense mystical feeling, and whether or not it is based on theology

– I do not really care – it arouses immediate veneration; and I describe it as it is, as the joyful, rowdily uninhibited result of a certain proximity to the supernatural.

Yet in John Paul II's popularity there is a further element about which I have often wondered. To speak of 'star quality' or 'superstition' is to distort the question without resolving it, and to turn to ready-made formulas about 'crowd psychology' does not help us in any way to understand how this man convinced people before he had opened his mouth, and why the world turned to him with hope when no one knew anything about him. The explanation of this phenomenon is not to be found in crowd psychology but in the psychology of John Paul II, in the exceptional unity of his personality. One might be tempted to say that he is a flawless marble, carved by the Gospel, but marble does not live; we must look further for a suitable image. We should remember what he said, at the beginning of this conversation, about his youth, when he 'received more graces' than 'battles to fight' to remain completely devoted to God. We should remember the preceding chapter in which he let us glimpse how deeply grace and faith established in him their life-giving dialogue, how the personal response to the Word of God which he calls faith can only be irrevocable when one has only one word to give, and how his spiritual life came to birth in the very depths of his being, at its very origin, as if at the moment of that first surge that carries man towards a region beyond himself where his eternity awaits him. Starting from the voluntary act of faith, John Paul's spiritual life describes its imperturbable parabola, and it is impossible to imagine anything that could deflect him from its course. In him the Gospel, the vocation and the person all form one – not a very frequent occurrence – and it is this literally nuclear inner coherence that gives him his radiance. There, I think, lies the secret of the attraction which he exerts on crowds. In this chapter on morals we shall see that morality is an integral part of this unity, just as mathematics form part of architecture.

However, although that may be the case with the Pope, it is not the same in the world. With faith in jeopardy, morality is no longer based on the commandments of God, but in the last analysis on personal judgement, corrected to some extent by the authority of the state in régimes tending in some cases towards anarchy, in others towards constraint.

State tyranny has the upper hand in the countries where, in the famous phrase defining totalitarianism, 'everything that is not forbidden is obligatory'; the West, on the other hand, is sliding towards a sort of moral self-guidance which the State is powerless to oppose by any divine or philosophical law. In the collectivist systems, the individual, reduced to the state of a molecule in the social body, cannot demonstrate a personal moral existence without risking the psychiatric hospital, the official laboratory for analysing and regenerating molecules. Where he is still free, the human being reckons to pronounce judgement himself on his own morality, in so far as he still feels the need for one, without worrying either about a God in whom he does not believe, or about his neighbour, who is directed to the ministrations of the public welfare bodies. He no longer sees himself as 'made in the image of God', and accordingly the interventions of the Church in the sphere of private morals are ever less welcomed and worse understood. Contemporary man finds himself in the situation foretold by the serpent in the garden of Eden: When you eat of this fruit, he says, 'you will be like God, knowing good and evil,' which means that you will no longer be 'images' of God but gods, and as such you will 'know', or in other words you will define and decree yourselves what is good and what is evil.

Hence the questions which I was going to put to the Holy Father: are the Church's interventions necessary and how can they be reconciled with individual liberty? Is it permissible to think that this liberty is itself founded in God, who alone can save man from total determinism? But first of all, what is the meaning of the famous verse 26 of the first book of the Bible: 'And God said, Let us make man in our image, after our likeness,' two incredibly pregnant lines rendered banal by long acquaintance, but nevertheless forming the foundation of centuries of religion? What follows from the fact that man is made 'in the image of God'? Simply a system of morality, or a permanent conflict within the human being, who, being made or, as it were, stamped in the likeness of another, paradoxically cannot be himself except in this other? The Pope replied:

"As your questions indicate, 'morality' implies a definition of man; for one cannot speak of morality without wondering *who* man is and without seeking an adequate answer to this question. The whole tradition of 'ethics', in the sense of moral philosophy, confirms this. Having meditated much on this problem during my studies, I should like to add that the relation 'morality-man' is important in both directions: what I mean is that not only is it impossible to understand or interpret morality without knowing *who man is*, but one cannot understand and explain man either without giving a precise answer to the question, 'What is morality?' These are two connected, essentially correlative realities which react on each other.

You cite the text of the first chapter of Genesis, and hence of Scripture, according to which man is made in the image of God. This text has never ceased to arouse my wonder, and the process of examining it in depth has only increased my wonder. The creation of man is described in it twice. This is explained by the origin of the book, which comes down to us from two distinct sources. The second part (from verse 29 onwards) comes from an older document than the first – the text known as 'Yahwist', since in it God is called 'Yahweh' before the revelation of this name to Moses."

This is an allusion to the episode of the 'burning bush', Chapter 3 of the book of Exodus, verses 13 and 14: 'If I come to the people of Israel and say to them: "The God of your fathers has sent me to you," and they ask me, "What is his name?" what shall I say to them? God said to Moses: "I Am he who Am." And he said, "say this to the people of Israel: He whose name is I Am has sent me to you."'

According to the specialists, this 'I Am he who Am' is a sort of commentary on the name proper to the God of Israel. Some scholars prefer to say, 'I Am he who Is', which is grammatically less surprising but metaphysically weaker. Others translate the Hebrew by 'I Am what I shall be', in reference to the changeless eternity of God, and others again by 'I Am who I Am', which has the weakness of resembling not so much a revelation as a somewhat mocking dismissal.

It should be added that the Jews never pronounce this name, obviously not to avoid a difficulty, but because, in Jewish thinking, 'to name' is already to 'appropriate to oneself' to a certain extent what one names, and this is unthinkable where God is concerned.

"In the 'Yahwist' part, man is not called 'image of God'. This appellation occurs in the first part of Genesis, verses 1 to 28, which is of later, and thus more recent, origin and is ascribed to the tradition known as 'priestly'. I spoke of it some time ago in my Wednesday public audiences.

What has struck me in the analysis of these two descriptions of the creation of man is, first, the fact that each of them demands a distinctive philosophical procedure (I pointed this out too in my Wednesday meditations). What is more, the ancient text which does not mention 'man made in the image of God' nevertheless contains a specific gloss on this designation. It shows us how man, from the start, was aware of his difference from the other living beings (*animalia*). This, so to speak, empirical realization of his 'non-resemblance' to other creatures, in the first place to creatures that were simply animate, indirectly emphasizes the fundamental resemblance specified in the first chapter of Genesis, which makes man the 'image of God'.

It is unnecessary to add that this notion has played a key rôle in anthropology and theology since the most ancient times. It is sufficient to cite the most illustrious representatives of the patristic era, such as Cyril of Alexandria, Gregory Nazianzen or St. Augustine, or the great masters of medieval theology, headed by St. Bonaventure and St. Thomas Aquinas. Since then the importance of this biblical expression has been continually confirmed. Methods differ, and so do philosophical references, but the basis of biblical anthropology remains the same.

You ask me, what are the consequences of this – a system of morality or a situation of 'permanent conflict'? Both, in my view. Morality is only possible in a personal subject, capable of thinking in absolute categories, of distinguishing good from evil – in brief, endowed with a conscience. This state of affairs, this inner situation, necessarily engenders not so much a conflict as a tension. Yes, morality implies a tension which is of a spiritual kind but is echoed throughout the complex subjectivity of the human being. Thanks to certain philosophical analyses and even more through the masterpieces of literature, one can see what a powerful sounding-box conscience possesses in the sphere of the emotions and the profoundest human feelings.

All these riches peculiar to the human being point to his transcendence as an integral dimension of his existence; by his very humanity, man is called to transcend himself. This fact, described in various ways, explains both in old and in modern language, which is particularly sensitive to direct experience, what 'in the image of God' means."

As we have had occasion to note, the Pope often appeals to the idea of 'transcendence', regarded as a certain aptitude of man to exceed his own limits and pass beyond, further or higher. This is a curious ability, the proofs of which are to be found even in the caves of Lascaux, for one cannot draw a bison without emerging from oneself and becoming the bison for the space of a brush-stroke, or in the very contemporary phenomenon of the nervous breakdown, when one is shut in on oneself and overcome by the giddiness of one's original nothingness. But in that case man is not a 'finished' or finite being, unlike the animals, which are perfect of their kind; there is a breach in him, something incomplete which opens him to the infinite and is the cause of his perpetual anxiety and dissatisfaction. If this is so, the danger of the present-day world would surely be that of making man into a finite being, either by incorporating him in a system firmly sealed against the infinite, or by closing the breach in question by various medical procedures – by treating his spiritual aspirations as bad dreams caused by biliousness, or by curing him of God with tranquillizers.

The Holy Father thought that there were two questions in my question, the first continuing the dialogue on the 'image of God', the second linking up with the first, but concerned rather with a value judgement on our age.

"In the context of the dialogue on the 'image of God, morality and tension', the relations between 'finiteness' and 'infinity' in the human subject can be explained more or less as follows: man is obviously a 'finite' being, dependent on time and space, subject to the laws of matter and of nature, but at the same time he is open to infinity. It is a question not so much of 'mathematical infinity' as of the infinite in the sense of 'absolute'. I mean that by his spiritual character man is not only attracted to true, good and beautiful things, but to truth, goodness and beauty as such. This 'opening' is the basis of the transcendence peculiar to him. It is thanks to this that man 'breaks through' his finiteness – the finiteness which is no less peculiar to him, both in the physical and metaphysical sense of the term; for man, though open to the infinite, possesses the structure of a finite being. The whole man, corporal and spiritual, is a sort of composite being.

We find ourselves here at the frontier between two languages, that of the philosophy of 'consciousness' and that of the philosophy of 'being'. The two are recognizable in your question. When you say, 'Man is a finite being,' you are speaking the language of the philosophy of 'being'. When you then ask, 'What is the cause of man's eternal disquiet,' you pass to the Augustinian level of inner experience and consciousness. I take the view that these two languages are equally indispensable to express the total reality of man.

Returning again to your way of putting the question, I should like to draw your attention to the fact that the expression 'finite being' is not employed in it in the sense which I have just described, but rather in the sense that man is an *unfinished* being, as indicated precisely by this 'fissure' in him open to the infinite. According to this view, other natures in the world of nature are in their own way 'finished beings', while man, open to the absolute, awaits his completion.

I think it is an image that corresponds to the reality of man, an image that philosophy – in one way that of 'being', in another that of 'consciousness' – expresses by the eternal dialectic of matter and spirit, in so far as these two elements together constitute man, as being and as subject.

The same image is at the basis of the Good News. It takes shape most clearly perhaps in certain passages of St. Paul which contrast the 'flesh' with the 'spirit'. If the 'spirit' is in fact this breach, this fissure, through which the human being, as 'body', has a sense of the infinite, then, according to the apostle, in this breach, in this human spirit open to the infinite, the Holy Spirit acts through Christ crucified and risen again. Under the influence of the Holy Spirit, the whole man bears fruits of holiness, good actions, salvation.

The language of St. Paul is completely original. It can be likened both to the language of 'being', as it was by St. Thomas Aquinas, and to that of 'consciousness' and inner experience, as it was by St. Augustine, Pascal, Kierkegaard and great mystics like St. John of the Cross.

However, more important than the language is the truth that it expresses: the truth about man, who is not, in Jean-Paul Sartre's phrase, a 'pointless passion', but a being whose *depth*, perceptible through this breach open to the infinite, calls out to and meets *Another Depth* and finds in it the answer to his spiritual disquiet."

That is the vision; there remains the practice. The people who govern or who manipulate others do not worry much about having to deal with such an inconvenient being, and are less concerned to keep him open than to close him up once and for all; aspirations to the infinite are not mentioned in any political programme and commerce with the Holy Spirit is not one of the features of the market economy.

"You express a fear close to my own fears about the situation of man in contemporary civilization where – to use the language of St. Paul – numerous factors contribute to the preponderance of the body over the spirit. 'For the desires of the flesh are against the spirit, and the desires of the spirit are against the flesh'[1] . . . This can be seen in the facts as well as in systems, so that two sorts of materialism can be noted, theoretical and practical. The second sort is the most widespread; the first naturally goes deeper. For the one constitutes a system or ideology closed from inside, while the other touches primarily certain spheres of action and of value judgements.

I think you conceive these two kinds of materialism as originating in such a way that theoretical materialism would give rise to practical materialism as its logical consequence. However, one has only to observe life to notice that this is not always the case."

There is not necessarily any ideological prejudice underlying practical materialism:

"The latter occurs above all under the influence of the impulses or attractions produced by material, sensual or temporal values in the whole realm of concupiscence and desire. This immediate, direct action does not necessarily imply any philosophical convictions or even the prior acceptance of a scale of values. Quite the opposite can happen, for man is divided in himself in such a way that, according to St. Paul, 'he does not do the good he wants, but the evil he does not want is what he does.'[2] It is an aspect of the problem of great importance for morality, but for the moment you have not approached it."

I spoke of the totalitarian systems which, having no other end but themselves, will not tolerate man conceiving a different one, and imprison him in a circle of captive thoughts perpetually gyrating round power. But my picture was not complete, and the Pope likes exhaustive enumerations:

"I suppose that when you speak of the danger that threatens man

1. Galatians 5:17
2. Romans 7:19

(96)

in the contemporary world you also take into account the practical materialism which appears in the West in the form known as 'the consumer society'. Various different conceptions or programmes utilise this factual materialism to convince man that he is a 'complete being', that is, a being *definitively adapted to the structure of the visible world*, and that for him this world is the sole system of reference from beginning to end, whether it is a question of the realm of thought or of the range of activities. Outside this structure, which is becoming better and better known thanks to the innumerable academic disciplines studying it, man would supposedly have no issue. He is allowed to keep the notion of infinity in mathematics, but this kind of infinity does not take into account the spiritual 'breach' which opens man to the Absolute: absolute truth, absolute good, absolute beauty, in a word, Being. A merciless war has been declared on that. The philosophy that Aristotle regarded as the 'primary philosophy' is fought by omission more than by discussion.

Thus the danger you mention certainly exists in the contemporary world. I would say that it is the danger of cutting man off from his own depths. To return to the notion of 'image of God', one could speak of an attempt to 'absolutize' this image, and this leads in reality only to the rupture of the existential link between it and its model, to alienation, to dehumanization and to engulfment in the world of things.

I would also say that it is the danger of a 'fundamental illusion', that of man imagining that, thanks to the exclusive development of material civilization, he has become increasingly the 'master' of the visible world, even of the cosmos, without noticing that at the same time he has made himself dependent on this world, that he has subordinated himself to the power of the energies liberated, that he is becoming the object of all kinds of manipulations against which he can do nothing, precisely because he has completely delivered up to the 'world' his conscience and his liberty. And the 'world' has taken possession of him."

After this harsh indictment the Pope toned it down by taking the 'world' to mean the work of God.

"Forgive me for employing language approaching that of St. John, in his gospel as well as in his letters. This does not alter the fact that I am full of admiration for the 'world' which fills the pages of Scripture from the first chapter of Genesis onwards. Nevertheless, it is also Scripture that continually exhorts man to be 'greater than the world', since he is made in the image of God.

'For God created man for incorruption, and made him in the image of his own eternity.'

It is with these words from the book of Wisdom[1] that I should like to complete my answer."

## II

Together with 'dignity', 'humility' and 'joy', *liberty* is one of the words which recur most frequently in the Holy Father's conversation. It is only fair to add that this word appears no less frequently in contemporary speeches, but those who employ it content themselves with exploiting its capacity to elate without taking the trouble to define it. For a French thinker in the late eighteenth century, liberty was 'the right to obey only the laws'. This was fair enough, but others immediately claimed that the very idea of 'law' was contrary to that of liberty, which required before anything else the abolition of the state; this is an arduous enterprise which has always ended hitherto in a reinforcement of the central power, so much so that, to put people off the scent, the central power finds itself compelled to make words say the opposite of what they mean, to call 'liberty' the obligation to obey the state, and take leave of commonsense. For sophisticated intellectuals, who want to owe nothing to God, to man or to nature, liberty is the wholly conceptual faculty of creating oneself by escaping the past and the present to subsist in an experimental, imaginary world of illusions and abstractions. For those familiar with prison, liberty simply takes the form of a door-knob. Meaning so many things to so many people, there is no longer any way of knowing what the term is supposed to denote. Many would regard liberty as the ability to do whatever one wishes; the saints would regard it rather as the additional ability to do what one does not wish, out of charity or self-denial or to please God.

1. Wisdom 2:23

So what is liberty for the Pope, who no more likes vague ideas than vagueness in the soul?

"Your question arises out of the preceding questions and answers, as though out of its native soil. It is a fundamental question for anything to do with morality. This 'fissure' or breach in being, as we have called it, which opens man to the infinite – this is liberty. Without it, man would be enclosed in the world of nature and robbed of his transcendence. He would be a 'finite' and 'complete' being, totally determined by external forces and subject to the limits imposed on animate nature, and therefore to a death without hope.

What is liberty then?

You put forward two extreme answers based on practice more than on theory, on action more than on thought. Nevertheless, a mode of action presupposes a mode of thought; we could say therefore that man is free *according to the way in which he envisages his liberty*. However, there is an inverse relation: man understands his liberty according to whether he is free – or to the extent that he strives to be free. This double meaning of the reflection indicates how far our will and our liberty are linked to knowledge.

It is true that for some men liberty is the latitude to act as they please. If, as you say, freedom for the saints is rather the power to 'do what one does not wish', it must be added that in each case it is a question of a conscious choice and of a conscious adherence to a scale of values. The saint does not act 'against' his will; he knows how to wish for more and higher things, beyond passing wishes and whims."

The Holy Father's replies are often rather dry at the start. He ploughs the question furrow after furrow, with a patience that is not afraid of testing that of the listener. Then, when he returns for the last time to his point of departure after turning over all the soil, and one feels the onset of sunstroke following this hard labour with one's eyes, the harvest of truths suddenly flowers as bright and fresh as a field of tulips:

"You ask, then, what is liberty? I too put this question to myself when I was young and I long sought the answer. While studying, while 'learning to be a man' and 'working on myself' (an expression current in Polish), I did not even notice how the theme of liberty lay at the centre of my experiences and reflections. In the last analysis it seems to me that man's liberty is *what he discerns in himself when he*

(99)

*feels responsible.* Obviously a certain discernment of liberty is bound up with this birth of awareness: 'I have the choice' (naturally within the limits of what I can wish), but it is not yet a discernment in depth. I distinguish liberty not just as a specific feature of the will, but as a property – forming the whole person at the very moment when I experience my responsibility. For it is thus, and only thus, that my responsibility is explained.

Liberty is what opens me to reality – but also what often binds me by an inner dependence: a dependence on truth. It is through this dependence on the recognized and admitted truth that I am really 'independent' – with regard to others and to things. I am dependent *on myself.* Responsibility is born with the knowledge of the truth: the truth of being, the truth of values, the truth of my relations to being and to values, the truth of the actions which I undertake.

Responsibility is not only knowledge. It comes into being at the point where knowledge passes to action. (Of course, there is also a responsibility of knowledge, for knowledge is also a form of action, involving as it does a responsibility to the truth; but we are not here concerned with that.) Well then, responsibility indicates the necessity of acting in conformity with the known truth, that is, in accord with oneself, in accord with one's conscience and, to be more precise, with a conscience formed in the truth. Responsibility so understood is another name for moral obligation.

So in man liberty is a faculty of responsible self-determination. It lies at the very centre of the transcendence peculiar to man as a person. It also lies at the basis of morality, where it appears as a capacity for choice, a capacity for numerous different choices, no doubt, but principally as a faculty of choice between good and evil in the moral sense of these terms; between the good and the evil to which conscience, an honest conscience, bears witness."

We were only half-way to our goal, but I knew my interlocutor and I waited.

"All this – conscience, truth, responsibility, liberty – forms a whole, that of human inwardness, which, although not subject to the senses, is given to us in a very intense experience. It is the experience of man and still more the experience of 'humanity', of what makes man finally and essentially man. This whole is 'composed', so to speak, of conscience, responsibility, liberty, but this 'compound' has nothing in common with material compounds.

This inner whole can be called a 'structure' but, here again, it cannot be compared with the structures known to the natural sciences. It is a structure of a different kind. In it is rooted the fact that man becomes a 'subject' and is open to the infinite, and therefore to the absolute. Kant expressed this idea in his own way when he affirmed that moral good 'is based on the categorical imperative'. I am convinced that in this sphere of moral good and evil we touch – without having to deny the contingent character of the human being – on something absolute. The Polish philosopher Wladyslaw Tatarkiewicz, who died recently, threw a good deal of light on this in a book called *The Intransigence of the Good*.

This structure or this whole of human inwardness possesses a fundamentally dynamic character. When we speak of the will, we think in the first place of the dynamic of human freedom, which belongs to every man without exception. This freedom is both a gift and a duty. Man in his freedom constitutes a task laid upon him personally. It is in this freedom, on this terrain, that he must ceaselessly 'conquer himself' and also, on another plane, conquer the Kingdom of God.

In my view, when Christ says to us, 'You will know the truth, and the truth will make you free,' he is thinking of the organic link between freedom and responsibility as well as of the dynamic of freedom whereby man conquers himself and thus turns the Kingdom of God into reality."

The corollary is that deceit is a prison. Scepticism is another. The truth reprieves the prisoner, and without the truth it is vain to dream of freedom. But then 'to be free is *to wish* and *to be able* to choose what one *must choose*, and to choose it genuinely.'

For the Christian, truth is a Person, the person of Jesus Christ, who can save him, deliver him from evil and death, and give him, beyond everything that binds him to the earth, an eternal destiny. Is it God, then, who saves us from the complete determinism which otherwise, without him, would be our lot? And if this is true, why has the Church so long seemed ill-at-ease with regard to a concept of freedom which might not exist without her; I mean which without her would certainly not contain the same promise of expansion?

"I am convinced that God is the ultimate guarantor of man's freedom. Not only in the order of causes, when we think of our origin and of the fact that, created 'in the image of God', we have been created free; but also when we test this idea in practice. This in no way implies that when he denies the existence of God man automatically loses his freedom. Obviously not. When he rejects the existence of God, he does not hereby cease in his humanity to be the 'image of God', and the act of denial that he commits is in itself a confirmation of his freedom, exactly as the contrary act is. When God created man in his own image he accepted these two possibilities in advance. He gave man the ability to accept or deny him (which happens above all with the kind of knowledge that restricts itself to 'visible' reality, accessible to the senses, whereas God is an invisible reality).

It is thus not in this sense that 'God saves man from determinism' – to use the terms of your question – since, as I have just said, the possibility of denying God is in a certain sense an elementary demonstration of man's freedom. In this case one simply sees how and to what extent God is the guarantor of human freedom.

Nevertheless, your idea that 'God saves man from determinism' is correct, but starting from another premise – not on the basis of the existence of God and the acceptance or denial of this, but on the principle that man *can think of his own freedom*.

For determinism is precisely this: man envisaging his own freedom as a function of the world and of what the world permits him. On this level determinism, of whatever school, is a denial of freedom. Either it declares that freedom is an illusion, since it undertakes to demonstrate that everything that man regards as an act of free will is in the final analysis determined, and therefore necessary; (in *dialectical materialism* freedom is no more than the recognition by man of this necessity). Or else it is in a sense the contrary: in *rationalist determinism*, freedom is a necessity dictated by knowledge. That is how the world, regarded by man as the natural field of his freedom, encourages the determinist philosophies to question this freedom, either at the level of its structures and the forces at work in them, or in the way these structures and forces are perceived.

As a denial of freedom, determinism is consequently a denial of responsibility, and therefore of morality. This 'breach' in being which reveals man's transcendence is walled up. The inner whole, the interior structure of which I spoke just now, is reduced to the reflexes of the material infrastructure, which is supposed to constitute man's only dimension. His specific and irreduceable spiritual dimension is denied; to admit this is to regard the epiphenomenon as the fundamental phenomenon of humanity."

According to the Holy Father, practice conforms with theory in two apparently very different cases.

"It can be the practice of a *totally permissive society*, in which everything is permitted precisely because the foundation of man's true freedom is denied. It can also be the practice of a *totalitarian state* where man is only a part of the whole, the property of the state, deprived of his subjective character where the laws are concerned, and the object of collective manipulation.

I think that in these two situations man, conscious of the rules and mechanisms of his existence, can discover God, or convince himself that God alone can 'save him from complete determinism.' It seems to me that man becomes more easily aware of this in the second case than in the first, in a totalitarian world rather than in a world of lax morality. Nevertheless, even in a permissive society, he eventually becomes aware of it. In both cases the transition from enslavement to freedom is usually bound up with the discovery of God.

These two systems based on determinist principles are in one way or another 'programmatically' atheist. Atheism is the guarantee of their existence and development, just as God is the guarantee of human freedom, of the freedom that we feel in the depths of our being together with the responsibility conferred on us by our freedom, as the reality of an inner autonomy in which good and moral evil demonstrate man's true dimension as a person."

The whole moral doctrine of the Holy Father is strongly centred on freedom, that curious value which we assert even when we deny it. Even when man chains himself to the determinist mechanism which makes each of his acts the ineluctable consequence of a nexus of causes on which he has no hold, and when he thinks, or wants to think, that he is himself the mere product of biology and history, that all his decisions are dictated to him by heredity or the cultural environment, in short that he is unavoidably subject, with the rest of nature, to the hard law of 'chance and necessity', he still even then gives proof of his freedom: for if he cannot avoid being determined, he becomes a determinist by his own free choice.

For the Christian, God created man free: it would be unthinkable that he should have created a being 'in his own image and likeness' who was deprived of what can make him a person; if it were so, the word of God would echo in the void and God would only ever converse with his own echo in the vast cavern of the universe. The first indication of this statutory liberty can be read figuratively in the commandment 'not to touch the tree' in the middle of the garden of Eden; for if God had not wanted man to be free there would have been no commandment, because there would have been no tree. And the whole system of relations established from the beginning between God and man implies this freedom, without which there would be munificence on one side and obedience on the other, but not love.

However, I reminded the Holy Father that my question comprised a second part in which I asked him why the Church had so long seemed ill-at-ease about freedom. This was unwise; the Pope was going to trap me.

"Forgive my frankness, but I think that before the event which you have described in your book you lived in circles where it was precisely the Church that seemed to be the enemy of freedom. These circles exist; there are many of them in the world."

It is true that before my conversion I knew hardly any more about Christianity than one can glean from Voltaire or Jean-Jacques Rousseau, who only ever saw the temporal side of the Church, and it may be that my question was redolent of the company I kept in my youth.

"Has the Church, in the different phases of her history, justified the opinion which you repeat? Some people are convinced that she has, but there is no point in crossing swords over the issue. Perhaps it is sufficient to recall the parable in the Gospel about the tree and its fruits, or rather about the fruit that it can or cannot bear.

I am persuaded that the Church has always based her mission to man on the affirmation of his true freedom and that this was always the foundation of her teaching on morality, both personal and public. More than once she has found herself forced – as she is to-day – to confront and suffer the shock of other concepts of freedom on the personal or collective level. In the atmosphere of these shocks and conflicts, the Church may have seemed, as she seems to-day, to be opposed to freedom in the eyes of those who have a different conception of it.

The Second Vatican Council did a good deal to clarify these questions. One has only to think of the declaration on religious freedom, or the famous paragraph 36 of the constitution *Gaudium et Spes* on the rightful autonomy of earthly matters.[1] Nevertheless, the fundamental problem remains, namely *the truth about freedom as such*, that is, the fundamental way to view it. In this sense it is true, as you said, that a certain 'concept of freedom' might not exist without the Church."

The conciliar definition of 'the rightful autonomy of earthly matters', which gives freedom of research its part to play, inspired me to ask another question: can the progress of science (for example, if it is demonstrated that the criminal instinct has a genetic origin) affect Christian morality in important respects?

"It is difficult to give an immediate reply. First of all, your question contains two problems which it is as well to distinguish. The first is the question whether Christian ethics undergo modifications with the progress of science; this concerns ethics as such. The second, mentioned as though in parenthesis, touches directly on anthropology and only indirectly on ethics. Let us begin with the second, which concerns the conditioning of human freedom.

In all ages Catholic ethics, or in other words moral theology, has taken into consideration this conditioning, which can have various origins. One has only to turn the pages of any manual to realize the precision with which the authors of such manuals try to distinguish 'what is intentional' from 'what is unintentional', and to what extent an act can be described as intentional. The term 'intentional' (*voluntarium*), which denotes the conscious actualization of the free will, is the key that serves to make an act responsible and so to define the responsibility of the morally good or bad character of this act. Naturally, it is only in terms of this responsibility that the good or evil is ascribed to the act and to its author.

The circumstances which change the 'intentional' (that is, *conscious* and *fully willed*) character of an act can be external. Obviously, they influence the definition of the act only to the extent

1. This conciliar text reminds us that 'created things and societies themselves have their proper values, which man must gradually learn to know, to exploit and to order', and that in this respect 'the demand for autonomy is perfectly in order.' After approving 'methodical research in all branches of knowledge, provided it is carried out in a truly scientific manner and does not override moral laws', the Council Fathers 'deplore certain attitudes (not unknown among Christians) deriving from the shortsighted view of the rightful autonomy of science,' attitudes that 'have occasioned conflict and controversy and have misled many into opposing faith and science.'

that, coming 'from outside', they condition the subject 'on the inside'. For in the last analysis it is only thus, 'on the inside', that the 'intentional' can be conditioned and above all limited. Of course, the internal, 'endogenous' circumstances peculiar to the subject himself, and to his psycho-physical structure, come into play. For example, an earthquake or an aerial bombardment causes fear, but one person may be of a more timorous character than another. We therefore have to admit that, when all due allowance is made, the first person is more seriously threatened than the second and that, as he is more subject to fear, this fact will have to be taken into account in order to judge correctly 'what is intentional' and what is not in what he may be led to do.

In conformity with these rules of thought, moral theology follows with great attention anything the science of heredity may have to say on elements limiting the liberty of the subject, both immediately and in the longer term. This will suffice to lead us to the conclusion that it is not a question of any modification to morality, but of possible changes in the moral judgement of the acts of a given person.

It is another question to know whether the progress of science, of anthropology, for example, can modify Christian ethics and morals 'in important respects', or on essential questions. Ethics and morals are linked to the recognized existence of values and to the system of principles and norms safeguarding them. Here we have to admit the fundamental immutability of these norms. The human sciences regard certain values – the dignity of man or the worth of human life – as valid, recognized facts. That is why none of these sciences could contribute to our changing the commandment of love into one of hatred or even indifference towards our neighbour. Or the commandment not to kill into one to kill.

However, various disciplines, starting with biblical studies, can help us to understand more thoroughly the particular principles of Christian morality, to see more clearly their moral rightness and to define with more precision their practical applications. In the past the problem of usury and interest in connection with the development of the economic sciences was a typical example, as is to-day the problem of responsible paternity in connection with the development of the bio-physiological sciences."

It is unnecessary to stress the importance of this last sentence. It provokes the thought that the development of the life sciences may one day lead the Church, for example in the domain of birth-control, 'to define with more precision the practical applications' of her principles.


# III


It is a fact that the liberty of conscience rightly demanded under the name of 'religious liberty' by the Second Vatican Council has a tendency these days to turn against the Church in the countries where she can still exercise her magisterium: the liberty that she demands for believers, mindful of those regions of the world where it is denied them, is demanded in turn of the Church by the faithful. Showing at the most a polite interest in the hierarchy's directives when they do not quite simply reject them as unwarranted and misplaced, they are increasingly inclined to form their own judgement on this or that aspect of morality – whether it be to tighten up or to relax its requirements. The Christian's religious autonomy is displayed in indifference and even a growing aversion to confession, which introduces the confessor as an untimely third party in conscience's debate with itself.

Hence my question to the Holy Father: must the Church intervene in the intimate life of Christians?

"Your question implies another more fundamental one which concerns the very essence of morality; not of 'ethics' but of morality as such, in the concrete, existential sense. Now morality – 'that which is moral' – is an essentially intimate, inward affair. Problems of morality are always, for the person concerned, problems of conscience and will (attitudes, choices); it is in conscience and attitude that the 'inner man' is expressed.

Of course, morality has also an outward, and as it were visible, dimension, perceptible from outside by reference to the objective norms of human conduct. Nevertheless, this fact – the existence of this outward dimension – in no way affects the previous fact, namely that morality is a matter of conscience and of decisions by the inner man.

Christ taught morality. The Gospel and the other books of

the New Testament show this quite clearly. We know that the Decalogue, the ten commandments of the moral law of the Old Covenant, was confirmed by the Gospel, which tells us that, of the two commandments to love God and to love one's neighbour, the first is 'the greatest' and the second 'like the first'.

When he taught morality, Christ took into account the two dimensions – the external, and hence social, even public, dimension, and the inner dimension. However, in conformity with the very nature of morality, of 'what is moral', he attached prime importance to the inner dimension, to the rectitude of the human conscience and will, otherwise known as the heart.

When he elucidates the doubts of his disciples on the ritual precept to wash one's hands before eating, he utters some significant words: 'What comes out of the mouth proceeds from the heart, and this defiles a man. For out of the heart come evil thoughts, murder, adultery, fornication, theft, false witness, slander. These are what defile a man; but to eat with unwashed hands does not defile a man.'[1] One can find many similar passages, especially in the Sermon on the Mount.[2]

In teaching morality, the Church strives to act in the same way. To teach morality is to mould the inner side of the human being: to illumine conscience in the light of the truth, to strengthen the will so that it chooses the good and grows strong in it as in good works. In the context of this teaching there is a great deal of room for encouragement, admonitions and reminders. If the Church did not act like this, would she not betray her master? Can she not be *mater et magistra* even in the most intimate recesses of man's heart if Christ entrusted her with this task?"

Thus the difficulty or objection indicated in the preamble to this chapter disappears: the Church does not intervene in man's debate with himself as an 'untimely third party'; she is the appointed intermediary in the dialogue between the conscience and Christ.

"But to answer your question more precisely, it is only fair to add that Catholic ethics are not simply a collection of norms, command-

1. Matthew 15:18–20
2. Matthew 5–7: chapters of moral instruction that have all passed into proverbs; they are too long to be quoted here. The first of these chapters begins with the beatitudes ('Blessed are the poor in spirit') and ends with these words: 'You, therefore, must be perfect, as your heavenly Father is perfect.'

ments and rules of action; they also comprise exhortations and advice drawn from the Gospel and addressed to the conscience, that is, to the inner man. Moreover, there are norms directly concerning *exclusively* inner acts. The Decalogue already contains two commandments beginning with the words 'You shall not covet' and consequently not aimed at any external act but simply at an inner attitude, in the first case with regard to 'your neighbour's wife', and in the second with regard to other people's goods. Christ put even more emphasis on this. His words in the Sermon on the Mount, where he calls the look that covets a woman 'adultery of the heart' were for me the point of departure for long reflections on the specific character of gospel morality in this domain. But that is not all. We know that the Sermon on the Mount also speaks of good actions 'such as prayer, alms, fasting, which the Father sees in secret'."

John Paul II's 'long reflections' led to a homily which aroused world-wide interest, was misunderstood and provoked very ill-informed comments. It forbade this 'covetous look' even in conjugal relations. What, people said, can one not desire one's wife without incurring guilt from the standpoint of Christian morality? A little attention would have sufficed to avoid errors of interpretation which people were perhaps not always sorry to commit. Covetousness is not desire; it is a form of possessive greed in which the heart plays little part and which makes the other into a mere object to be appropriated. The Pope thinks that there is no exception to the respect which beings owe each other, even in marriage, in fact especially in marriage, which is after all something better than a collection of bad habits shared between two people. It was possible on this occasion to estimate the true worth of some people's repeated protests against the male's sly contempt for 'woman as an object'.

The fact remains that Christian morality is often considered restrictive, especially by those who do not practise it, while others, having robbed it of its supernatural function, construct out of it a meritorious but joyless Christianity. If the rôle of Gospel morality is not to forbid us what we could legitimately claim but to give us much more that we could reasonably hope for (the 'Kingdom of Heaven'), can one prove that it is a liberating force? Is it this morality which builds the person?

"When you say that Christian morality 'is often considered

restrictive,' I discern in this observation the echo of different opinions and different systems of thought about morality, in the first place about Christian morality, no doubt, but indirectly about morality in general.

I want to emphasize right at the beginning of this reply that since my youth, since the time when these subjects gave me food for thought, I have always considered and continue to think that Christian morality is a *demanding* one.

This term – demanding – is important because it answers the two questions which you put to me after your initial remarks: first, can one prove that Christian morality is liberating (and not constricting)? And secondly, is it this morality which builds persons – and I would add, which builds *real* persons?

There is no doubt that there is an essential difference between the term 'restrictive' and the term 'demanding'.

It is true that some people find Christian morality 'constricting'. Everyone is more or less tempted to call it that when the will comes up against its demands. Man finds in the very principles of Christian morality the root of this opposition to his will. Christian morality often confronts him with demands which he would prefer to avoid, even if he hesitates to reject them altogether. At such moments he takes the view that Christian morality is cramping, that it fetters his free 'ego'.

Here we must take a step further and ask the question: is this not a feature common to all morality? Is there a system of morality of such a kind that man is never restricted by it, and that his will never rebels? Would such a morality that involved no conflicts still deserve the name of morality?

During the few years of my life that I was able to devote primarily to philosophical work, I studied more closely the thought of Kant and Scheler on the relation between duty and value in what is 'moral'. I came to the conclusion that morality in its dynamic structure – the newspapers would say 'operational morality' – concentrates on values, and first of all on moral value itself, which is inconceivable without *duties*. There is no morality without obligation. What is more, the subject (the 'ego'), contemplating the truth of the value, that is, the good that it represents, expresses himself by a judgement in the first person – 'I must' – in which the subject, in the name of the recognized truth of this value, binds himself or puts himself under an obligation. We have to know then if the obligation becomes *ipso facto* synonymous with 'constraint' or 'requirement'. I am convinced that for all Christian morality the second term is the right one, although in practice man has a tendency to prefer the first."

Many people to-day think that 'the law should follow morals,' which scarcely helps a society to improve itself. The same persons often think that young people want an accommodating morality: easy paths sloping gently in the direction of their inclinations. The Pope shares neither the first view – as we have just seen – nor the second.

"During my meeting with the young in the Parc des Princes which you recalled at the start of this conversation about morals, I had to answer many questions. I was asked in particular what are the Christian principles governing the union between man and woman. People said: 'In questions of a sexual nature the Church has a rather intransigent attitude. Why? Are you not afraid, Holy Father, that young people will move further and further away from the Church?'

This is how I replied: 'You ask me what principles the Church teaches in the domain of sexual morality. Seeing that these principles are difficult, you express the fear that young people, for this reason, will turn away from the Church. I reply: If you think of this question deeply, going right to the heart of the problem, I assure you that you will realize only one thing, which is that in this domain the only demands made by the Church are those bound up with true, that is, responsible, conjugal love. She demands what the dignity of the person and the basic social order require. I do not deny that they are demands. But that is the essential point, that man fulfils himself only to the extent that he knows how to impose demands on himself. In the opposite case "he goes away, sorrowful," as we have just read in the Gospel. Permissiveness does not make men happy. The consumer society does not make men happy. It never has done.'

I said all this with profound conviction. To judge by the reactions of my listeners, they seemed to hear my reply with satisfaction."

I can testify that in fact the 'reactions' of young Christians are not always those that one would be tempted to expect from them, to judge from what one reads in the (adult) newspapers. Mingling one day in the big audience hall in the Vatican with six thousand

European students who had done me the honour of asking me to give the closing speech at their congress, I was surprised to hear them give a long ovation to . . . the sacrament of penance, the benefits of which the Holy Father had just emphasized. That day, at the end of the audience, the applause, in the form of repeated 'three cheers', lasted for about a quarter of an hour. John Paul II patiently beat time with the sole of his shoe. Six thousand young enthusiasts for penance! I did not expect that, but I was wrong.

"I had not wished to moralize or simply to be the mouthpiece of the 'system' before these young people. Christian morality asks a great deal. It can even put demands which one can sometimes honestly find too elevated. Apart from those in question at the Parc des Princes – which underlie the reproach nowadays addressed to Christian morality of being 'restrictive' – what are we to say about this Gospel injunction, 'Love your enemies, do good to those who hate you,'[1] or about this one, 'If anyone strikes you on the right cheek, turn to him the other also'[2]? Confronted with such demands, one has to say to oneself frankly, 'They are beyond my capacity.' But to say this does not mean that they are *restrictive*. It means: *I appeal to something more than my capacity*, I appeal against myself.

I think we can now try to give a composite answer to your question. The key is the way we understand human freedom. If freedom is the ability 'to do anything I wish' (or rather, 'anything I fancy'), then it is clear that, confronted with freedom in this sense, not only Christian morality – the principles of conduct contained in the Gospel and taught by the Church – but any human system of morality can be considered restrictive. My neighbour's freedom is then an irritation and a threat to mine; that is what makes Sartre say, 'Hell is other people.' On the other hand, if freedom (as I pointed out earlier and as I am profoundly convinced) is expressed in responsibility, that is, in the perception of the truth about human dignity – that of others and also mine – then Christian morality will seem 'liberating' in the inner experience of those who apply it conscientiously and honestly. This saving truth helps us to understand the human person and consequently to mould it in conformity with its destiny.

1. Luke 6:28
2. Matthew 5:39

I admit that in taking this path man must accept a certain risk. But if we admit that moral value constitutes essentially a 'difficult ideal', we cannot wish things to be otherwise. One cannot wish freedom to consist purely and simply in the latitude to act as one wishes. Such a use of freedom might seem at first 'liberating', but subsequently it always turns out to be enslaving. Moreover, it is normally egotistical and anti-social.

How shall we sum up the discussion? I think that the attitude of the young people who took part in the meeting in the Parc des Princes and reacted as they did to my answer bears witness to the rightness of their intuition about the meaning of human freedom, about what is meant by 'to be truly free'."

# IV

John Paul II puts great hopes in young people, just as he loves children, and while he was speaking a picture shone insistently in my mind's eye. During a ceremony in St. Peter's Square the Pope, walking along the barriers, noticed a little girl lost in the crowd. She was passed over the railings, the Pope took her by the hand and walked back alone with her along the line of red carpet that led to the throne. Suddenly we were in a fairy story: Bernini's colonnade was a forest of tree-trunks robbed of their branches, the Holy Father in his ample robes, his mitre glittering in the sun, was a legendary king and the little girl a sister of Tom Thumb. When he arrived at the throne the legendary king raised her in his arms so that she could be seen from further off, and her parents ran up from the back of the square and received her from his hands. A delightful picture interleaved among the pages of my memory. I know that there are graver subjects, pitiless conflicts of abstractions and interests which steep the world in blood, and I was soon to have occasion to speak of them with John Paul II; but I cannot help it if the little events of daily life touch me more than those of political life, if the few moments of frightened loneliness of a little girl separated from her parents move me more than one of those battles which I know only by hearsay, if the panic of Joseph and

Mary looking for their child in Jerusalem conveys more to me than a treatise on the human condition.

However, the incident in St. Peter's Square suggested a question to me. Since the notorious 'Families, I hate you'[1] uttered by a man who cultivated his faults with as much care as a gardener cultivates his roses, one or two generations of moralists have made demoralizing assertions which fail to stand up to Chesterton's robust and serene assertion: 'The family is a cell of resistance to oppression.' This aspect of the family does not seem to be very clearly perceived by the theorists. I asked the Holy Father what he thought about this.

"Chesterton's words are beautiful. Beautiful and true. Moreover, they are shrewd – and demanding. For the family to be, as he asserts, 'a cell of resistance to oppression', it must be a community of great maturity and depth. When I say, 'it must,' I mean that a moral obligation subsists. To speak of the family as a 'cell of resistance to oppression' is to indicate its moral value and at the same time to define its proper structure – and in the last analysis to rely upon the spiritual maturity of the persons involved. When this is missing, the man or the woman is liable to see in their indissoluble union only a constraint to be broken.

The family – much more than any other social community – has an essentially personal structure. Each of its members has his own importance, not owing to any given function, or to the resources he procures or anything else, but simply because he exists, because he is a 'person', because he is 'this particular person'. That is why the family, more than any other form of human contract, deserves the magnificent description of a 'communion of persons', which indicates the depth and intensity of the mutual relations, as well as the depth and strength of the resulting interpersonal ties. If in a family (supposing that it is morally mature) each member, and therefore each individual, has his own importance, this cannot create a climate of individualism – nothing is less characteristic of a family that develops healthily. The fact that man has an existence 'for himself' obliges him to live also 'for others', as we read in the beautiful words of *Gaudium et Spes*: 'Man can fully discover his true self only in a sincere giving of himself.'[2] Thus the 'communion

1. André Gide.
2. *Gaudium et Spes*, 24

of persons' is much more than a bond between people; it signifies existence, life, action based on the principle of reciprocal giving – the reciprocal gift of humanity.

In a family, every being is important because of *what he is*, because he *exists*. The gift of humanity from each to each is, so to speak, the starting point in the family, and also its duty. The more each member of a family knows how to live for others, the clearer it is that for this family that member is important because he *exists* and because of *what he is*. Even when it cannot be said that 'he knows how to live for others', the fact remains that he belongs to this family and that he counts because he exists, he counts *for what he is*, even though in that case he is causing suffering – which itself demonstrates this truth. It is less obvious in communities which take a more 'neutral' stance, which are less sensitive to the human person. Some years ago I wrote a little treatise on the family as a 'communion of persons', largely inspired by the passage in *Gaudium et Spes* which I have just quoted."

I wondered if by any chance it was he who had written this passage in *Gaudium et Spes* but, knowing his discretion I did not ask him. It probably was not; otherwise he would not have described it as 'beautiful'.

I asked him if what he had just said was not also true of the parish, which can be regarded as a sort of extension of the family and sometimes suffers from the same attempts at dismemberment.

"If the parish is a community which embodies in a way 'the local Church', then between it and the family, conceived as a 'community of persons', a relationship exists, a profound cohesion and co-responsibility. For the Church also is a 'community' – see the classic passages in *Lumen gentium*, for example, paragraphs 14 and 15 – and from the most ancient times the family was called the 'domestic church' or *ecclesiola*. So much can be said very briefly about the family–parish relationship, without going into details of structure and function. One can add that the family needs the parish and the parish needs the family. You say yourself, rightly, that the parish is a kind of extension of the family; it is thus to some extent an enlarged family, or a community of families. If this is the case, everything must be done to help the family to 'feel at home' in the parish, and the parish in the family. It is an old and tested principle of pastoral care, and a method as well, since the very principle indicates how to put it into practice."

Another question had been bothering me for a long time. In the West, many people to-day think that baptism should be put off until the age when free will can operate in full knowledge of the facts, or at least until the age of legal majority. This was formerly the point of view of atheist families in which the question of religion still arose through habit, heredity or environment. I can still hear my mother saying that after my birth, whenever the question of baptism was raised (though it was not very clear, given the religious diversity of my ancestors, whether baptism would have led me to Catholicism, a Protestant church or the Synagogue) my father, a steadfast unbeliever, insisted that I would choose my religion 'at the age of twenty', if I ever experienced the need for one. However just and tolerant such a principled attitude may have been in a resolute atheist, it always seemed to me – since I was baptized – false and *unjust* when adopted within a Christian Church. A healthy rationalist mentality may prefer a political party to accept only adult members, even though the party may have a 'youth movement' with only a hazy grasp of party doctrine. But a Church does not recruit adherents; it receives from God children whom it is responsible for introducing to the life of grace; the Church exercises stewardship, if you like, not ownership. As for the 'full knowledge of the facts' required, if one had to await this to enter the Church, no one could ever call himself a Christian.

In short, should infants be baptized?

"I shall answer you by pursuing the reflections embodied in my preceding answer. If the family 'feels at home' in the parish and the other way about, this becomes particularly apparent at the key moments in the life of both. One of those moments is certainly the sacrament of marriage itself, whereby the family in fact begins as a 'domestic church'. The sacrament of baptism is another. It is a function of the birth of the children, which makes the couple into a real family.

You want to know if infants should be baptized? The Church answered this question long ago and her response of days gone by also coincides with the discovery of the parish by the family and of the family by the parish. It was and still is a *response of faith* – joined to Christian practice rooted in faith and arising out of faith.

We know that it was not the primitive answer. It came with time, when a tradition of Christian life had been formed in the Church as well as in the family. Before that, baptism was administered mainly to adults. This required a certain spiritual preparation, based on suitable evangelization, initiation and catechesis. Hence the institution of the *catechumenate*, of which we still find traces in the liturgy, especially in Lent. For in the first few centuries this period of Lent was devoted particularly to the intensive instruction of converts. From the liturgical point of view, the 'paschal (or Easter) vigil' was the most suitable moment for baptism, the sacrament of birth into a new life in Jesus Christ. Even to-day it is difficult to understand the liturgy of this Easter vigil except in relation to this 'resurrection' through baptism to the life which is in Christ. This life which *is*, since it was made manifest in his own resurrection. Let us recall the force of St. Paul's words when he says that Christ rises and reveals this life in him which is more powerful than death. Through baptism, man is buried in the death of Christ, to rise with him from the death of sin to the life of grace.[1]"

It is clear that the baptism of pagans converted to the Gospel was an adult baptism; but as soon as Christian families were formed children were baptized. It was later, in the much decried 'Constantinian' period, that baptism was often delayed, partly because of the rigours of public penance.

The Holy Father had already often used the word 'mystery' – and was to use it again; it is a word to which not everyone ascribes the same meaning. A mystery should not put us off, but lead us on; it is not, properly speaking, something hidden; on the contrary, it is something revealed, but revealed all at once as against the successive steps required by normal cognitive processes. Mystery is an object of contemplation for the believer – who is neither more nor less baffled by it than the nuclear physicist who observes that a particle may explode simultaneously both in space and *in time*. A Dominican whose name I have forgotten – but not his spiritual genius – said that a mystery 'is a thing obscure in itself that illuminates everything else'; it is an invisible source of light to which the contemplative mind is exposed.

"It is certain that our ancestors in the faith put their baptism at the very centre of the paschal mystery, against the background of the magnificent catechesis of St. Paul's epistles.

However, it is not difficult to understand that as Christianity acquired a more complete social expression, *as the Church found*

---

1. Romans 6:3–11; Colossians 2:12; 3:1–3

*herself more at home in whole families*, and families as such in the Church, people began to prefer making this entry through grace into the divine adoption (which gives Christ the 'multitude of brothers' of whom St. Paul speaks) as soon as possible. Christian parents wanted their children to pass without delay 'from death to life', that is, from original sin to sanctifying grace, and to become sons of God in Christ. They wanted their children to participate as soon as possible in the life of God himself and at the same time in the life of the Church, the body on which Christ bestows all the gifts of his redemption. When they presented their children for baptism, they undertook to complete by education in the family what in earlier days formed part of the catechumenate – and what is still obligatory in adult baptism.

You ask, 'should' infants be baptized? I answer by recalling how we have come to baptize babies. What was decisive, and is still, was practice, the *praxis* born of a living faith. But we also find in this practice the answer to the question, 'Why' should infants be baptized? For without this answer the custom would not have taken root. The answer is that parents have the right to share with their children what they consider a very great good, a supreme good. When Christian parents present their children for baptism so soon after their birth, they show their wish to share their greatest good according to the light of faith, just as through faith they find themselves at home in the Church and find the Church in their family, the *ecclesiola*.

Christian parents do not always see these problems in the way they once did. They do not always assume quite consciously, and with the requisite responsibility, their rôle as catechists and educators, a rôle of the first importance for their children; they do not see how it is precisely the family that should be the subject of the catechesis, which is at the same time the spreading of the Gospel. From this point of view the last synod of bishops effected a sort of rediscovery of the family, by indicating the importance of conscientiously and responsibly continuing this practice. The Synod pointed to the need to base the practice on the Christian family's self-awareness as a 'Church in miniature'."

In this connection everything starts with marriage, an institution which is still valid in spite of all the attacks to which it is subjected by 'thinkers' (some of them, alas, in the clergy), who depict marriage as a sort of prison in which two unfortunate people condemn themselves to act out until death supervenes a sort of variation on Jean-Paul Sartre's *Huis clos*, hell no longer being 'other people' but simply 'the other person'. These wretched caricatures in no way prevent marriage, founded on mutual respect and a total commitment, from responding simultaneously to the instinctive and idealistic elements in human nature; it is a way of returning to the Garden of Eden, and growing old together in it is a gentle and moving experience quite beyond the grasp of those who decry this 'gamble on innocence'.

Nevertheless, under the influence of a permissive Western society (which no longer understands that fidelity itself acts as a grace) and the dangerous proliferation of individual cells it causes (I really think that the expression most often heard on television is 'I personally' preceding the enunciation of an opinion), some young people, unaware of their own weakness and of the strength that the sacrament of marriage could give them if they had the humility to ask for it, consider it pointless to marry; they live together in a 'trial' union that at the best leads only to the administrative bliss of regularization. Others hesitate about the depth of their feelings and fear failure and the difficult lot of divorced people. I asked the Pope whether any change in the Church's attitude to marriage and divorce could be expected.

"The sacrament of marriage is deeply rooted in God's Revelation and man's vocation. We come back here to the beginning, to these words of Genesis, 'Male and female he created them,' on which is based the vocation of these 'two' to unity 'in the body', a vocation linked to the immemorial blessing of the Creator that served as a prelude to the birth of the new man.

But that is not all. Marriage has the structure of a covenant, the same covenant by which God entrusted himself to man, expecting in return an analogous confidence in faith. This covenant reaches its summit in Jesus Christ. To express it, St. Paul cites the analogy of marriage according to the Old Testament: the faithful love of man and woman united for their whole lives. United by a mutual faith. Conforming to the same analogy, the prophets admonished and punished Israel for its infidelities to Yahweh – the God of the Covenant. Marriage is genuinely and deeply rooted in Revelation.

And in man's vocation. I come back once again to the constitution *Gaudium et Spes*. If what we read in it on the subject of man is true – and I consider that it is true – then marriage has no meaning except as a real covenant between persons, an unbreakable covenant.

Since man, 'the only creature on earth that God has wanted for [man's] own sake . . . can fully discover his true self only in a sincere giving of himself,'[1] marriage corresponds to the vocation of man conceived in its integrity. I am using the term 'integrity' here both in its 'personalist' sense and in its ethical sense, which are in any case inseparable. The sacrament of marriage is based on this sort of conception of the vocation of man as a responsible person.

You tell me that these young people, confronted with a vocation so understood, should be aware of their weakness and that sometimes, unfortunately, things turn out quite differently. Be careful not to generalize! It is true that man should at all events experience a certain fear before the size of so great a task. He should ask himself: shall I be equal to it? Such a fear corresponds to his inner truth and proves that he measures correctly the decision to be taken. It can also be a humility that has nothing to do with lack of courage.

It is good that the young should be humble before their love. That makes it clearer that their love is a real gift and that they will be a mutual gift to each other; that is better than seeing them cocksure and presumptuous.

Marriage – like the priesthood – requires a *humble magnanimity* and a mutual confidence which implies a source deeper than purely human feeling."

He went on, as usual, to demonstrate his idea.

"The sacrament by which man and woman, who are in fact its dispensers, swear 'love, honour and fidelity' to each other until death, tends towards the humble magnanimity on which the true dignity and vocation of spouses is based. The sacrament of marriage, like every sacrament, is a sign of the action of Christ, a sign of the grace to which one must entrust oneself, for it is more powerful than the weaknesses endemic in the heart of man, threatening the love, honour and fidelity of married life.

The Church is aware of these weaknesses; she tries to understand them in each case and strives to obviate them. That is how Christ used to act. At the same time, she cannot renounce her faith in redeemed man, she cannot renounce the conviction that, for all

1. *Gaudium et Spes*, 24

man's weakness, he '*can* do all things in him who strengthens' him.[1]

This also touches the problem of the indissolubility of marriage, on which Christ's words are certainly lucid, but no less categorical for all that."

I was to obtain no further enlightenment on this particular point. The Pope directed me to the Sixth Synod of Bishops, which presented him with a long series of propositions and asked him 'to make himself the interpreter to humanity of the Church's lively solicitude for the family'. This suggestion was at the origin of an 'apostolic exhortation' of John Paul II on the 'tasks of the Christian family', numbering from 67 to 232 pages according to the edition. I direct the reader in my turn to this text, which deals at the end, in a spirit of pure evangelical charity, with all the grounds for divorce. I shall quote only this recommendation: 'With the Synod, I warmly exhort pastors and the community of the faithful to help divorced people who have married again. Let everyone act, with great charity, in such a way that they do not feel cut off from the Church, for they can, and indeed must, as baptized persons, share in her life.'

But what about women? Although for pious Christians the greatest of created beings – the Virgin Mary – was one of them, and although they have played a substantial part in the history of Revelation, people ascribe to the Church a certain mistrust in regard to them and see the proof of this in the fact that they are denied the priesthood (although some contemporary theologians are inclined to confer it on them). Here too, I asked the Pope, was any change likely?

"The same question, differently phrased, was put to me in the Parc des Princes. Allow me to reconstruct that question, although in different words, and the answer incorporated in my long allocution to the young people. Here is the question, so far as I remember it: 'Will the Church always be governed by men? Will women always have a secondary rôle?' Linking this question to another one on 'the present rôle of laymen and especially the young in the Church', I answered in these terms: 'Learn to know Christ. Never stop learning to know Christ. In him are truly to be found unfathomable treasures of wisdom and intelligence. In him man,

1. Philippians 4:13

weighed down by his limits, his defects and his sins, really becomes a new man, a being *for others* and the glory of God, according to St. Irenaeus, Bishop of Lyons and martyr. The experience of two thousand years teaches us that in the mission of the whole People of God there is no difference of principle between man and woman. Both, in accordance with their own vocations, become this *new* human being who lives *for others* and is therefore the *glory of God*. Although it may be true that it is the successors of the apostles, and hence men, who govern the Church from the hierarchical point of view, there can be no doubt that in the charismatic sense the influence of women is no smaller; perhaps it is even greater. I beg you to think often of Mary, the Mother of Christ.'

I don't think that the reply I gave then corresponds exactly to your question, for the reason that it stops where you start! Nevertheless, in whatever way the question is put, one cannot get away from the fact that the apostles alone heard the words 'Do this in memory of me' at the Last Supper, when the Eucharist was instituted. There was no woman among them, although there were many of them among Christ's followers. It is at this point that our thoughts turn particularly to the unique woman who yet had a primordial right over the body and blood which Christ handed over to the Church as the sacrament of the new and everlasting Covenant, as a symbol of the sacrifice on the cross which was to be ceaselessly renewed under the species of bread and wine. When the Church adores the Eucharist, does she not salute the body 'born of the Virgin Mary, immolated on the cross for men'? In the constitution *Lumen gentium*, we read that 'she suffered profoundly with her only begotten son and associated herself with his sacrifice with all her mother's heart.'

Here we find the fullest expression of what is usually called 'the priesthood of the faithful'.[1] At the summit of this priesthood stands Mary, without rival.

However, the Church has never anywhere attributed to her the priesthood received at the Last Supper by the apostles as a 'service' and 'hierarchical functions'. No, Christ did not introduce his Mother into the hierarchical structure of the Church, which was based on the apostles. When this Church was born to an auton-

---

1. The faithful, too, participate in the priesthood of Christ as continuers of the Old Covenant and a 'people of priests' in accordance with the vocation of Israel.

omous life, at Pentecost, Mary was present, but only as one of the women who prayed and awaited the coming of the Holy Spirit. At the same time, in spite of, and perhaps because of, all this, it is in her and in no one else that the Church sees her most perfect model, as is affirmed by the same constitution, *Lumen gentium*, on the word of the Fathers of the Church.

Thus the exaltation of a woman, the Virgin of Nazareth, in the work of salvation and the exceptional devotion given to her by the Church – teaching summed up comprehensively in the constitution *Lumen gentium* – do not nevertheless form an argument in favour of the 'priesthood of women' advocated to-day in certain circles; on the contrary, they would be the most serious argument against it.

At the same time there is absolutely nothing in the Church's position to suggest any sort of inequality, which would be quite alien to the Gospel and to tradition. It would contradict the whole economy of Revelation and the Redemption. The special elevation of woman in the person of Mary is the proof of this. Christ's behaviour to women, which is so striking in the context of the mentality and manners of the age, bears witness to it. In the documents of Vatican II we find many a passage showing how much the Church is concerned with the dignity of woman and with the equality of her rights – when this equality is *correctly interpreted* – in the modern world. I emphasize 'correctly interpreted', for I have had more than one opportunity to realize how erroneously this question can be understood and how often, on the pretext of equality, woman has her rights infringed. But that's another question."

I think the Holy Father was alluding indirectly to laws that claim to liberate, such as the legalisation of abortion, but are in fact only male laws, passed to free men rather than women from their scruples and responsibilities.

"What I have just said is not unconnected with the priesthood of women. For it cannot be denied that this question has risen into prominence, not against the background of Revelation and tradition, but against that of a certain kind of civilization and mentality. In principle, this kind of civilization is not opposed to Revelation or to Christianity. The documents of the last council (especially *Gaudium et Spes*) show that clearly enough.

However, this compatibility of principle is not the decisive factor. The ministry of the Eucharist was from the start, at the very moment of its institution, too personal an act of Christ's to allow us to neglect the smallest aspect of it.

It is true that he did not say, 'I forbid women to do what I am doing,' but at the particular moment when he instituted the Eucharist it was in fact only to the apostles that he said, 'Do this in memory of me.' He could have decided otherwise. On this point he was perfectly free. And it was precisely on this point that he was free: more than once he defended the right of women to approach him and follow him.

What are we to say, then? What is the conclusion? The fact that at that decisive moment Christ acted in this way is a sufficient indication and one that binds us in conscience. The Church abides by that without any intention of belittling woman. The fact that she alone can be a mother, and not man, is not a sign of any inequality between them either. It is in the order of nature. It is the same with the order of grace and the charismatic order, where the gifts are different."

John Paul II put forward another argument on this subject.

"When the Church abides by the tradition of ordaining only men, I believe, in company with many theologians, that she retains for herself the character of spouse which is so deeply rooted in all biblical ecclesiology, especially in the letters of St. Paul.

According to this magnificent analogy, Christ, bridegroom of the Church, bestows on his spouse, the Church, the gift of the redemptive sacrifice, the gift which has the Eucharist as sacrament. So he who celebrates the Eucharist, that is, he who by the power of, and in the place of, Christ offers his own bloodless sacrifice, must be able to express that there is a gift from the bridegroom to the Church, his bride.

Thus the tradition of ordaining only men, observed just as faithfully by the Eastern Church as by the Western Church, seems even more profound than the 'historical' circumstances of the institution of the Eucharist. The Church keeps its life-giving mystery. She stands facing Christ like the bride before the groom.

Without losing sight of the Mother of God, who is her model, and whom she imitates as a mother, for she too wants to be a mother."

In John Paul II's private chapel, high above the altar, is a big crucifix; and under one of the arms of the cross, on the side of the heart, in the supposed position, as it were, of the *stabat mater*, there is a small icon of Our Lady of Czestochowa. The Holy Father's devotion to Mary is well known. It springs from the Gospel, of course, but it owes a good deal to a small book lost or forgotten for a century and a half, the *Traité de la vraie dévotion à la Sainte Vierge* by Louis-Marie Grignion de Monfort, written about 1700.

"The reading of this book was a decisive turning-point in my life. I say 'turning-point', but in fact it was a long inner journey which coincided with my clandestine preparation for the priesthood. It was at that time that this curious treatise came into my hands. The *Traité* is one of those books that it is not enough to 'have read'. I remember carrying it on me for a long time, even at the sodium factory, with the result that its handsome binding became spotted with lime. I continually went back to certain passages. I soon saw that in spite of the book's baroque style it dealt with something fundamental. As a result, my devotion to the Mother of Christ in my childhood and adolescence yielded to a new attitude springing from the depths of my faith, as though from the very heart of the Trinity and Jesus Christ.

Whereas originally I held back for fear that devotion to Mary should mask Christ instead of giving him precedence, I realized in the light of Grignion de Monfort's book that the situation was really quite different. Our inner relation to the Mother of God derives from our connection with the mystery of Christ. There is therefore no question of the one preventing us from seeing the other.

Quite the contrary: 'true devotion' to the Virgin Mary is revealed more and more to the very person who advances into the mystery of Christ, the Word incarnate, and into the trinitarian mystery of salvation which centres round this mystery. One can even say that just as Christ on Calvary indicated his mother to the disciple John, so he points her out to anyone who strives to know and love him."

The Pope was referring to this episode in the Gospel: 'Standing by the cross of Jesus were his mother, and his mother's sister, Mary the wife of Clopas, and Mary Magdalene. When Jesus saw his mother, and the disciple whom he loved standing near, he said to his mother, "Woman, behold, your son!" Then he said to the disciple, "Behold, your mother!" And from that hour the disciple took her to his own home.'[1]

"'Perfect devotion to Mary' – that is how the author of the

1. John 19:25–27

treatise puts it – that is, the true knowledge of her, and confident surrender to her, grows with our knowledge of Christ and our confident surrender to his person. What is more, this 'perfect devotion' is indispensable to anyone who means to give himself without reserve to Christ and to the work of redemption. Grignion de Monfort even shows us the working of the mysteries which quicken our faith and make it grow and render it fruitful. The more my inner life has been centred on the mystery of the Redemption, the more surrender to Mary, in the spirit of St. Louis Grignion de Monfort, has seemed to me the best means of participating fruitfully and effectively in this reality, in order to draw from it and share with others its inexpressible riches."

The spiritual writers of the time of Grignion de Monfort were not all alike, but they all wrote rather in the style described by the Holy Father as 'baroque', in reference to the epoch. Grignion de Monfort's 'baroque' style was to provide John Paul II with the opportunity to give us an attractive thought on freedom.

"My devotion to Mary modelled on this pattern – I have only given you a brief glimpse of it to-day – has lasted since then. It is an integral part of my inner life and of my spiritual theology. It is well known that the author of the treatise defines his devotion as a form of 'slavery'. The word may upset our contemporaries. Personally I do not see any difficulty in it. I think we are confronted here with the sort of paradox often to be noted in the Gospels, the words 'holy slavery' signifying that we could not more fully exploit our freedom, the greatest of God's gifts to us. For freedom is measured by the love of which we are capable.

That, I think, is what the author wanted to show us. I should add that my extremely personal and inward spiritual relation to the Mother of Christ had merged since my youth with the great stream of Marian devotion which has a long history in Poland and also many tributaries. Yasna-Gora[1] has borne witness to this down the centuries, only recently in the years 1956–1966 and subsequently.[2]

1. Yasna-Gora ('Clear Mount') is the citadel of Czestochowa, the last point of the Poles' resistance to the Swedish invaders in the seventeenth century. From this point the country was reconquered.

2. Those were the years of a novena commemorating the conversion of Poland which the Polish Church made the point of departure for another reconquest, a moral and spiritual one.

I should like to mention in particular the Marian sanctuary of Kalwaria Zebrzydowska, near Cracow and Wadowice, where I was born, a sanctuary which is so dear to me and which I visited so often in my youth, and later as priest and bishop. I can tell you that, in the manner of devotion shown by the people to whom I belong, I found there what I had discovered in the treatise."

One last point: a certain kind of misunderstood psycho-analysis, which leads good Christians to treat their faith as disease, sees in the cult of Mary an oblique way of devaluing other women by comparing them with an inaccessible model. The Pope is not of this opinion.

"These attempts at would-be Christian psycho-analysis applied to Marian spirituality and even Marian dogma do not tally with my experience. My conclusions are quite the opposite: as far back as I can remember, devotion to the mother of Christ has helped me to show consideration for woman and has only increased my respect for her mystery."

# V

We read in St. John's Gospel, Chapter 4:

[The Lord] left Judaea and departed again to Galilee. He had to pass through Samaria. So he came to a city of Samaria, called Sychar, near the field that Jacob gave to his son Joseph. Jacob's well was there, and so Jesus, wearied as he was with his journey, sat down beside the well. It was about the sixth hour. There came a woman of Samaria to draw water. Jesus said to her, 'Give me a drink.' For his disciples had gone away in to the city to buy food. The Samaritan woman said to him, 'How is it that you, a Jew, ask a drink of me, a woman of Samaria?' For Jews have no dealings with Samaritans. Jesus answered her, 'If you knew the gift of God, and who it is who is saying to you, "Give me a drink," you would have asked him, and he would have given you living water.' 'Sir,' the woman said to him, 'you have nothing to draw with, and the well is deep; where do you get that living water?

Are you greater than our father Jacob, who gave us the well, and drank from it himself, and his sons, and his cattle?' Jesus said to her, 'Every one who drinks of this water will thirst again, but whoever drinks of the water that I shall give him will never thirst; the water that I shall give him will become in him a spring of water welling up to eternal life.' The woman said to him, 'Sir, give me this water, that I may not thirst, nor come here to draw.'

Jesus said to her, 'Go, call your husband, and come here.' 'I have no husband,' the woman answered him. Jesus said to her, 'You are right in saying, "I have no husband"; for you have had five husbands, and he whom you now have is not your husband; this you said truly.' The woman said to him, 'Sir, I perceive that you are a prophet. Our fathers worshipped on this mountain; and you say that in Jerusalem is the place where men ought to worship.' 'Believe me, woman,' Jesus said to her, 'the hour is coming when neither on this mountain nor in Jerusalem will you worship the Father. You worship what you do not know; we worship what we know, for salvation is from the Jews. But the hour is coming, and now is, when the true worshippers will worship the Father in spirit and truth, for such the Father seeks to worship him. God is spirit, and those who worship him must worship in spirit and truth.' The woman said to him, 'I know that Messiah is coming (he who is called Christ); when he comes he will show us all things.' Jesus said to her, 'I who speak to you am he.'

Just then his disciples came. They marvelled that he was talking with a woman, but none said, 'What do you wish?' or 'Why are you talking with her?' So the woman left her water jar, and went away in to the city, and said to the people, 'Come, see a man who told me all that I ever did. Can this be the Christ?'

This passage from the Gospel of St. John (4:3–29) is not only a literary masterpiece that with rare economy of means calls up in the imagination a picture full of grace and sunshine; I find it astonishing not only for the boldness of the teaching it contains: it has always aroused my curiosity because of the behaviour adopted by Christ, who in this episode seems to take liberties, dare I say, with his own rules. He says in fact to the Samaritan woman, 'You have had five husbands, and he whom you now have is not your husband,' yet he entrusts one of his most beautiful messages to this woman who is in an irregular situation with regard to his own teaching about marriage. I certainly would not go so far as to say that there is a contradiction between what Christ says and what he does, but I think it is permissible to note that with him the law always gives way to charity, to the love of human beings; and thinking of certain strict attitudes – for example, to divorced persons who are not allowed to receive communion – I wondered, or rather I asked the Holy Father, whether the Church was not too often afraid to imitate her master.

"I think you are combining two questions that are not as directly connected as you suggest. It is true that, speaking to the Samaritan woman, Christ entrusts to her, as you say, one of his most beautiful messages. This does not alter the fact that he says to this woman who had every reason to think that he did not know her: 'You have had five husbands, and he whom you now have is not your husband.' He thus calls the sin by its name, as he was to do still more explicitly in the episode of the woman taken in adultery whom people wanted to stone. Christ speaks to her in the same way as he does to the Samaritan woman, and what he says and what he does then is again 'one of his most beautiful messages'. The reaction of the woman's accusers is still more eloquent than his words. He says to them, 'Let him who is without sin among you be the first to throw a stone at her.'[1] No one dares to do so. In this case Christ expresses himself less in words than in this reaction of consciences; one sees how deeply he examines them, how he touches the most secret nerve of these men's moral sense. That is the message, and it is shattering. Yet, at the end, he says to the woman whom he had just saved from being stoned, 'Go, and do not sin again.'

Thus in both episodes the encounter with sin gives Christ an opportunity to reveal the sources of eternal life, the sources of grace, and to show that love is stronger than sin. But there is no indulgence to sin in either case. Christ simply indicates the path of conversion. His mode of action points always in the same direction.

With the Samaritan woman he transgresses only Jewish customs and thus a 'usage'; he converses with a woman, which provokes the disciples' surprise (rabbis did not do this); and he addresses a

1. John 8:7

Samaritan, which does not fail to surprise the woman herself (the Jews didn't do it!). As a good shepherd, Jesus seeks the lost sheep and speaks to it. This is quite in accord with the pastoral practice of the Church and there are no 'strict attitudes' to prevent him from doing so.

On the other hand, Christ does not renounce any point in the Decalogue (what is called and what you doubtless call in your question the 'Law'). There is not a single commandment that 'gives way' to love. On the contrary, all the commandments *find their accomplishment in love* – and this accomplishment does not involve the renunciation of any of them: not an *iota* will pass away until all is accomplished.

It is thus that Christ, in the spirit of love, reproaches the Samaritan woman with her sin, and she understands him perfectly. What is more, not only is she inwardly contrite but she admits in public 'all she has done'. Then she brings her compatriots to Jesus, as the man who has 'told her everything'. One may thus say that Christ 'pardons', forgives sins, 'on the usual conditions', which are contrition and the promise of conversion.

To anyone who takes the teaching of Christ seriously, the so-called 'strict attitudes' of the Church seem very kindly. In the last analysis they all concern acts, while Christ, each time, touches the depths of the human being – his heart. We know, in particular through the Sermon on the Mount, that this is equally true of married life and the way in which the man treats his wife. We have already spoken of this.

To return to your question, in my opinion, if the Church has to fear not 'imitating' Christ sufficiently, it is certainly not in the sense of being 'strict' where he was 'indulgent'. No, Christ was demanding. But he had such power to penetrate consciences that the very people who came to know his demands felt touched by love. In this the Church can never imitate Christ enough. But she will never cease to imitate him; she will never cease striving to do so."

So the contradiction which I thought I had glimpsed between Christ's words on marriage and the distinguished rôle of messenger allotted to the Samaritan concubine does not exist. I had lost my case. But I noted, in the Holy Father's verdict, the expected pastoral element which requires love to accompany and even to determine the moral demand, so that the sinner – and there is no need to recall that we are all sinners – cannot doubt the one in becoming aware of the other.

Yet many Christians are ready to confront the Holy Father with St. Augustine's famous words, 'Love and do what you like,' which take the place of moral teaching and sometimes even civil law for many a person. And one can understand, of course, that he who loves cannot err, since he inscribes himself in the heart of the divine economy. But many people ingenuously turn St. Augustine's remark upside down and, because they do as they wish, imagine that they love.

Can one ever be sure of loving?

"Naturally it's a question of knowing what 'love' means. If it means, as you said, 'to inscribe oneself in the very heart of the divine economy', then, loving like that, 'you can do what you like'. You *can*, for the power, the capacity to love, and hence the will are already firmly attached to good, rooted in the divine economy of salvation and grace, the source that liberates the good in man.

Can man, you ask, be sure that he loves? Can he be sure that his will is rooted in good, in the economy of salvation and grace? He can be sure that God wants him to love truly. He can be sure that God will not refuse him his grace, that he desires his salvation. In other words, in the great drama of existence, man, placed between good and evil, can be assured that God wants good to triumph in him, and, through him, in the world. Christ is the surest guarantee of this divine will to save. Christ crucified and risen again; the Christ who pardons, the eucharistic Christ. By looking at this Christ or, as you say, 'inscribing yourself in the divine economy' and taking root in it, man can be sure of love as a *gift of God*.

Can he be sure of himself? St. Paul replies: 'Work out your salvation with fear and trembling.' With these words he describes exactly how man 'can be sure of his love' – by striving and working for it without respite, by praying for this intention and by doing everything 'to really inscribe himself in the heart of the divine economy'."

If there is 'no greater love than to lay down one's life for one's friends', we are bound to think at once of Father Maximilian Kolbe, who at Auschwitz took the place of a condemned companion and died for him.

"It would be difficult indeed not to cite this great figure, not to marvel at this triumph of good over the ramifications of evil, at this conspicuous fruit of the paschal mystery, this triumph of man which was at the same time clear evidence of Christ's victory in man, and of that of the spirit over the body, in the total sacrifice of this body. And it must be said too, in the light of Father Maximilian's spirituality, evidence of the victory of Christ through Mary, through the Virgin Immaculate.

Did Father Kolbe know that such would be the end of his life? That this would be the meaning of those 'two crowns', white and red, that he had wished for in days gone by?"

It is said that, as a child, Maximilian Kolbe, thoroughly upset by a remark of his mother's ('whatever are we going to do with you?' or something like that), had run to the church and knelt at the feet of the Virgin Mary, who had given him the choice between two crowns, one white, denoting that he would remain pure, the other red, indicating that he would die a martyr. He had asked for both.

"I don't think he knew, but I have no doubt that he prepared himself for the test which was to be the last of his life. He never ceased to prepare for it, without knowing what it would be, or where and when it would take place. What happened in the end seems to go beyond not only the foreseeable but also beyond human strength. Yet Father Maximilian went that far; he was not unequal to the test. 'I can do everything in him who gives me strength,' says St. Paul. Father Kolbe is not the only one who has proved in his person the truth of these words.

This is how I shall answer your question, 'Can I be sure of loving?' I shall answer: I can, in fact I must, do all I can to 'inscribe myself in the very heart of the divine economy' – without worrying about 'my love'. It will mature of its own accord. And if one of those tests beyond human strength occurs, then one will have to pray even more urgently, like Christ in the garden of Gethsemane."

Nevertheless, we had not yet finished with the remark 'Love and do what you like' so readily employed almost everywhere, in and out of season, and out of context. The Holy Father picked up a book to make the author of the maxim give evidence himself.

"It is obviously very dangerous to quote St. Augustine's maxim without reflection, neglecting the rest of his thought. One realizes this if the words *Dilige et fac quod vis* are put in their context. They are to be found here, in the commentary on John's letter to the Parthians:

> The Father gave up Jesus Christ, who was also given up by Judas. Is this not one and the same action? Did God the Father betray him as well?
>
> Far be it for us to think that, you will say. But it is not I, it is the apostle Paul who writes to the Romans: 'He did not even spare his own Son, but gave him up for us all', and to the Galatians, 'Thus the Father gave him up, and he has given himself up.' What, then, distinguishes the Father giving up his Son, and the Son giving himself up, from Judas, Jesus' disciple, who gave up his master?
>
> The difference is that the Father and the Son acted out of charity, Judas out of treason . . . God proposed to himself the salvation and redemption of our souls. Judas had only the price of his bargain in view . . .
>
> It is therefore the difference in intentions that here makes the difference in the acts. One single fact is involved; but if we judge it by the intentions that produced it, we love it or condemn it . . .
>
> Such is the power of charity. You can see that it alone establishes a difference, a real distinction in human actions. The only thing that establishes this difference is the root of charity. A large number of actions can be good in appearance, and yet not proceed from charity. So observe this very brief commandment: 'Love, and do what you like.' You keep silence? Do it out of love. You speak out? Let charity dictate your words. You reprove a brother: do it out of love. You think you should spare him? Let this be from love, too.
>
> Have love rooted deep in your heart; it can only produce excellent fruit.

I think that St. Augustine has explained adequately how one can and should interpret his words."

Charity – love – is infallible. But who still listens to it? Who can recognize its voice?

So ended this conversation about morals. I had left aside many questions dealt with by the Holy Father in his public statements, doctrinal allocutions or encyclicals; I had asked those which one does not usually have the opportunity to put to him and which worry many people. That is why, for example, noting that these days we live a strange moral existence composed of a bad collective conscience and individual blamelessness, I asked the Holy Father if the obscuring of the notion of sin, which has long borne witness to the nobility of the human conscience at grips with its ideal, was not in the last analysis a net loss, not for confessors made redundant, but for humanity itself. I reverted to this point before passing on to another subject in the dialogue.

"I have already answered you, but I shall complete my reply.

The notion of sin gives a definite meaning to the evil in the heart of man, in his acts and in his history. Why? It defines it on the basis of the whole inner truth of man in relation to his intelligence and will, in relation to his conscience. At the same time, in this same notion of 'sin', evil is defined by reference to man's relationship with God. It is defined at this level, at this depth.

But that is not all. The evil in man's heart, in his acts, in his history, is defined in the notion of sin by reference to *God's relations with man*.

It belongs strictly and organically to the context of Revelation.

It is defined in the context of the mystery of the Creation and the Redemption.

It is defined by the parables of the prodigal son[1] and the grain of wheat[2].

It is defined by the event of the Cross and of the paschal night.

It is defined by the death of the Son and the love of the Father.

That is why the notion of sin, in the light of the Gospel and faith, is inseparable from the worth of man, from the dignity of man, and I would even say, from the greatness of man. It doubtless bears witness to this *a contrario*, but also by a cry of obvious poignancy.

1. Luke 15:21–24. 'The son said, "Father, I have sinned against heaven and before you; I am no longer worthy to be called your son." But the father said: "Let us eat and make merry; for this my son was dead, and is alive again; he was lost, and is found."'

2. John 12:24. 'Unless a grain of wheat falls into the earth and dies, it remains alone; but if it dies, it bears much fruit.'

The Church proclaims, with Christ, the whole truth about sin, not primarily to accuse man, but to bear witness to Love, which desires and forms his supreme dignity."

# THE
# CHURCH

# I

In the last century the Popes still reigned over states of moderate size, coloured yellow by the geographers and cutting across the Italian boot at the level of the knee. They were small, generally easy-going sovereigns whose subjects would have gladly applied to themselves the medieval saying 'It's pleasant to live under the crozier.' These earthly possessions were supposed to guarantee the material and political independence of the Church, an advantage accompanied by the major drawback of involving two systems of morality, that of the Gospel, which requires us to pardon our brother seventy times seven times, and that of the state, which tends to be rather less long-suffering.

In 1870 the troops of Victor Emmanuel entered Rome and put an end to this temporal reign. The Papal States were reduced to a few plots scattered about the Eternal City and its surroundings and, in the main, to the few gilded acres of Vatican City. There were people who feared for the prestige and power of the Holy See, but something quite different happened. Peter's See, freed of its temporal encumbrances, rose at once to its true height, and the papacy regained a hundred-fold in spiritual authority what it had lost in political power.

But another danger immediately loomed up, that of a complete sacralization which would 'disembody' the person of the Pope and keep him out of range of the faithful, who would in future see him only as a sort of icon exhibited from time to time on the balcony of St. Peter's between a pair of plumed fans. It is a fact that from then onwards the Pope was scarcely seen except at the vanishing point between two lines of cardinals, and provided one turned up at the crack of dawn in white tie and tails, black waistcoat and patent-leather shoes. This stranglehold of protocol began to relax under John XXIII, who soon tired of living besieged in the Vatican and allowed himself a few sorties, which Paul VI extended to Jerusalem, India and America.

Little by little, from Pope to Pope, so to speak, I have witnessed the disappearance of the most surprising attributes of Roman pomp. I often wondered whether they had not been invented by those sly geniuses, the princes of the baroque age, with the express purpose of dismissing Christianity to the realm of Mesopotamian legend – an impression strengthened by the twisted bronze pillars of the St. Peter's baldachin, the taurine look of certain broken pediments, and the vaguely Asiatic decorum of the baroque ceremonies. In the Romanesque and Gothic architecture of Northern Europe the whole scriptural cast of characters rush to the doors of the cathedral to welcome the passer-by and engage him in conversation. The façade is animated and voluble; some give news of paradise, others rise up from hell to leer down from the capitals of columns. The baroque style is less familiar; its saints in their loggias no longer converse with the earth; theirs is a play full of clever lines; they are going to act it before you, with tremendous talent; you'll see, just look at the inspired actors who make the marble billow round them with their great dramatic gestures and ecstatic leaps! The ecclesiastical paraphernalia long in use in the Church belonged to the same aesthetic, in which the 'mystery' tended towards stage-craft. Thank God, we have not seen for many years the fans which waved on a level with the Holy Father as he sat raised upon the *sedia gestatoria*. The appearance of the Pope on this floating chair which rolled from side to side amid a storm of photographer's flashes had something moving and frightening about it. Paul VI still used it, from necessity; his fragile constitution made him vulnerable, and immersion in the crowd would have immediately washed him away.

Since then the *sedia* has disappeared and with John Paul II ceremonial has become even more sober. On Wednesdays he comes slowly down the central aisle of the big public audience hall with its luminous ceiling, on foot, lingering at the upper bays, where the least good seats are situated, grasping as many as possible of the hands stretched towards him, thumbs down, like beaks hungry for food. The seats of honour in the first few rows take less of his time; the people there have a chance of meeting him elsewhere. He is essentially, as he has told us, and it is quite obvious, a pastor.

In one century the papacy will have moved from the sort of protesting absenteeism which followed the invasion of the Papal States to the mystical exaltation of its function, and from the punctilious observance of etiquette to pastoral informality. And it was precisely to the pastor that I wanted to put my first questions about the Church. It is very difficult to determine when, under what influence or as a result of what inner revelation the Church emerged from the fortress where she was sitting tormented by siege fever at the end of the nineteenth century to realize one day that the crowd of atheists which she had thought ready to invade her was occupied elsewhere and that there was no one below the ramparts. It may be that the First World War, by mingling believers and unbelievers in the same suffering, radically modified the mentality of Catholics with regard to atheists, their brothers in misery, and led the Church to abandon certain too rigid positions and to embark upon a process of evolution that was even more psychological than doctrinal. The Second World War, by effecting in the West a regrouping of the anti-nazi moral forces, in which Christians were strongly represented, was to accelerate the process still further by diverting it, as a natural consequence of the success of the resistance to Hitler and of the hopes to which it had given rise, in a political and social direction which brought the Catholics of the world closer together while drawing them away to some extent from their spiritual bases. Vatican II was to draw the lessons of this period with an 'updating' which made it possible to observe that, when all was said and done, Christianity was a new idea in Europe, for the reason that it had never been applied anywhere – politically, that is.

However, as one can never know where a process of evolution will finish, even when one thinks one knows where it started, it is quite impossible to perceive the end of this historical sloughing-off process of the Church. Some people remain shut up in their dogmatic castle and refuse to parley with the world; these are the 'integralists'. Many others have taken advantage of the policy of 'openness' to sneak off on the quiet and they are to be seen less and less in church. Others again follow, in a generally half-hearted fashion, the directives of their bishops, who do not all possess the same conception of what they – all – term evangelization. Among the most active advocates of evolution, a few have gone astray and turned into Marxist fellow-travellers, while some devote themselves enthusiastically to theological or ideological research, without so far bringing back any unassailable truths from their long exploration. Finally, there are people who try to carve out a new path in modern societies, a steep and sometimes dangerous path: these are the practitioners of what are called 'liberation theologies', although they have no precise theological form. There is one country where all these tendencies in Catholicism co-exist and sometimes come into violent confrontation; this gigantic country, which in the year 2000 may alone represent half of Christendom, is Brazil. We were talking about it one day when John Paul II said: 'The Church is on the side of the poor, and that is where she must stay.'

Does being 'on the side of the poor' mean, as some 'liberation theologians' think, that the Church must take into account the class struggle? If this is not the case at all, and if the Church rejects the principle which forms the basis of Marxism rather than of Christianity, how will she make herself understood and obeyed by the rich? And if all mediation fails, if moderation ends only in the evasion of justice, in what circumstances and in what limits can rebellion be permissible?

For the first – and last – time in this conversation the Pope was to reply with a sermon.

"The simplest thing would be to recall, if not completely at any rate in part, what I said during my pilgrimage to Brazil, in that 'continent of a country', and particularly in the poorest quarter of Rio de Janeiro, the *favella* Vidigal. This will help us to get to grips with your questions.

Wondering how to present myself to the inhabitants of this country that I was visiting for the first time, I felt that I should begin by citing the teaching of the Beatitudes.[1]

Among you, I said to them, the poor are numerous. The Church in Brazil wants to be a Church of the poor. She wants to bear witness to the first Beatitude.

The poor in heart are those who are most open to God and to the 'wonders of God'. Poor, for they are always ready to accept this gift from on high which comes from God himself. Poor in heart, for, conscious of having received everything from God, they live in gratitude and think that 'everything is a favour'. They are the

1. The reader will be aware that the Beatitudes, according to St. Matthew's Gospel, are the eight diptychs of the Sermon on the Mount. The first is the most famous: 'Blessed are the poor in spirit; the kingdom of heaven is theirs.' This is sometimes translated, 'Blessed are the poor in heart.' One can also say 'The poor of the spirit', which would then be the Holy Spirit. This mystical interpretation is extremely rare. In Luke the beatitudes are only four in number, and the first speaks simply of 'the poor'.

people of whom Jesus said that they are meek and that their hearts are pure, that they hunger and thirst after justice, and weep, that they are peacemakers and persecuted in the cause of right. Finally, they are the merciful of whom the same Beatitudes speak.

And it is true that the poor, the poor in heart, are the most merciful of men. Hearts open to God are thereby open to their brothers, ready to share everything, ready to take in the widow and the orphan. They always find one more corner in their tiny dwellings, a piece of bread, another place at their humble tables.

Poor but generous. Poor but magnanimous.

I know there are many of them in Brazil, among you who listen to me. And elsewhere.

Does this mean that the words of Christ about the 'poor in heart' make us forget social injustice and neglect the concrete problems of daily life? These can change, take different forms and vary in intensity from one country to another, from one continent to another: at bottom they remain the same.

The words of Christ do not mask social problems in any way. On the contrary, they make them converge towards that central point, man, the heart of man, face to face with God and with other people.

Doesn't this Beatitude imply a warning and an accusation? Doesn't it mean that those who are not poor in heart exclude themselves from the Kingdom? Will Christ not say one day, 'Cursed be the rich', closed to God and to their neighbour?

'Meek and humble of heart' himself, Jesus is capable of speaking roughly to the evil rich.

All over the world the Church wants to be a Church of the poor by adopting the whole content of the Beatitudes, especially that of the first, which she wishes to teach and to put into effect in imitation of Christ.

She wishes to draw from the Beatitudes all that concerns man, every man, the poor man and the rich man; everyone has to hear in the first Beatitude what is addressed to him personally . . .

She reminds the poor, those who live in poverty – like the people of the *favella* Vidigal – that they are particularly close to God and his kingdom.

The Church asks those who live in abundance to avoid spiritual blindness, to resist with all their strength the temptation of the power of money. The Beatitude about the poor should constantly nag them like a permanent demand and prevent them from barricading themselves in the fortress of egoism and sated sufficiency.

If you have much, remember that you must give much! That you must think how to give, how to organize social and economic life so that it tends to more equality and does not dig abysses!

If you are educated and occupy a position at the top of the social hierarchy, do not forget for one minute that the more one has, the more one must serve. Serve others. Otherwise you risk departing from the Beatitudes, especially the first. One can be rich and poor in heart, when one never ceases to make a gift of what one has and of what one is, when one never stops serving.

The Church of the poor, which speaks to each and every person, is the universal Church, the Church of the mystery of the Incarnation. She is not the Church of a class or a caste. She speaks to us in the name of truth. Now the truth is realistic. It takes account of everything that affects us, of every injustice, of every tension, of every struggle. The Church of the poor does not wish to serve those who provoke tensions and conflicts. She admits only one single combat – for truth, for justice. Wherever good is at stake, she is behind those who are employed in promoting truth and justice. She fights with 'the sword of the word', sparing neither encouragement nor warnings, sometimes severe ones, following the example of Christ. She can be firm in denouncing the consequences of lying and evil. In this evangelical struggle the Church of the poor does not wish to serve ephemeral political ends or to take part in battles for power. She is very much on her guard against letting herself be manipulated.

Thus she speaks to every man in particular but also to associations, institutions, and social and political groups. She puts awkward questions to political systems, she is interested in social and economic structures, in her own way, which is that of the Gospel, aware of the progress of the human sciences and never deviating from the Spirit who guides her.

She speaks in the name of Christ, and also in the name of man. She expresses herself like this:

You who have the power to decide the fate of the world, see that in your country man's life is more human and more worthy of him! Do all in your power to narrow the abyss between the small number of the too rich and the huge numbers of those who live in poverty. Do all in your power to prevent this abyss from growing wider, to ensure that social equality is gradually achieved and that an unjust division of goods is succeeded by a juster one.

Do it in the name of every man, your neighbour and compatriot. Do it in the name of the common good. And for yourself.

The only social structures that are justified are just ones, those that ceaselessly tend towards greater justice. They are the only ones open to the future. A social system that has no care for justice undermines its own future.

Take account of your past, scrutinize the present, and on this basis build the future of your community, of all of you without exception!

All that I have just said figures in the Sermon on the Mount, in that first Beatitude which contains everything: 'Blessed are the poor in heart, for the Kingdom is theirs.'"

This long quotation, springing from one single sentence in the Gospel, answers several questions of 'social policy'. There remained the question which I had asked.

"I have just read almost in its entirety the address I gave in the *favella* Vidigal of Rio de Janeiro, where Cardinal Araujo Sales was very keen to take me. But have I answered your question? In part, I think. We still have to define 'in what circumstances and in what limits rebellion can be permissible'.

The social ethic of the Church gives you your answer. In the first place it tries to penetrate the whole historical complexity of the various social situations . . . and all the human and social complexity of historical situations. The word 'rebellion' (in the sense of revolution) is not typically evangelical. What is really evangelical is the word *metanoia* or 'conversion': the Church strives to act in this sense, while remaining fully conscious of the double inner and social dimension of the term.

Holy Scripture, both through the mouths of the Old Testament prophets and in the letters of the apostles,[1] speaks very strongly

1. For example, in the epistle of St. James 2:6. 'But you have dishonoured the poor man.' Or 5:4–6. 'Behold, the wages of the labourers who mowed your fields, which you kept back by fraud, cry out; and the cries of the harvesters have reached the ears of the Lord of hosts. You have lived on earth in luxury and pleasure . . .'

against injustice and against all exploitation of man by man. In the liturgy these words are called to mind especially during Lent, which invites us every year to be converted. Is this an adequate basis for 'reinterpreting' the message of the Gospel and the mission of the Church in revolutionary terms?

Of course, when she proclaims the need for conversion in accordance with the demands of justice and fraternal love, when she insists on the social dimension of conversion, the Church goes halfway to meet any aspiration to greater social justice. She lends her support to everything that *really serves* to achieve greater justice. In this respect John XXIII spoke in a very significant way.[1]

However, what one might call (if one must use this term) the 'revolution' of the Gospel possesses its own dimension, a deeper, more fundamental and more universal dimension that any historical form of socio-economic revolution. This dimension appears constantly in the Gospel message, most clearly in the Sermon on the Mount, in the eight Beatitudes, in the revelation of the command to love our enemies. No 'key' supplied by any revolution in history could serve as an authentic interpretation of what one might call the 'Gospel revolution', which is, at bottom, conversion, *metanoia*.

In this connection, and from a certain point of view, the idea of the 'poor in spirit' is a key idea.

The Church of the poor passes through the revolutions of history and is often persecuted by them; but she survives by the power of her crucified and risen Saviour to take up again ceaselessly, like true leaven, her task of transforming man, a transformation that the Gospel nowhere calls revolution. Nevertheless, it brings an increase in justice and peace into history, for the extension of the Kingdom of God.

In different forms, the Church of the poor is present in the midst of all the peoples and all the nations of the world."

Christianity has a peculiarity which is not always recognized, probably because it is too obvious: the individual person is of infinite importance to it, and just as salvation is the work of one individual, of 'the man called Christ', so, unlike systems which

1. In *Pacem in terris*, 161, 163

operate through the mass and material weight, according to Christianity one single being who changes can change the world.

# II

This conversation about the Church was not to follow any logical order – but what conversation does? When the Holy Father spoke of 'the Church of the poor', which consists of people, not ideas, I thought of the priests who with their various vocations – from the purely contemplative life of the Carthusian to physical commitment to the poverty of shanty towns – have the common point that they have all been *ordained*, and I wondered what makes a priest to-day, in the midst of the general desacralization. Of course, one can maintain that this desacralization began in one sense on the day that Christ, by pronouncing the words of the first consecration of the bread and wine ('Take and eat all of this, this is my body given up for you'), allowed everyone to absorb God, thereby abolishing the fear bound up with the idea of 'sacred', which keeps people at a distance, and opening the era of the 'holy', which on the contrary attracts people. But since the idea of 'holiness' also seems to be in process of being lost, what has become of the priest?

It seems that in our day there is hesitation about the nature of the priesthood, just as there is discussion about ecclesiastical celibacy. Hence two questions to the Holy Father; on the last point, is it reasonable to think that the priest is a man who lives alone so that others should not be alone? And on the first point, why must one be consecrated to repeat (in the Mass) the breaking of bread, and in what way is the priestly function fundamentally distinct from all others?

"Let me link my answer to the preceding one. While it was a question there of 'the Church in the light of the eight Beatitudes', we are concerned now with 'the Church which *is ceaselessly born* of the Eucharist', for it is to this sacrament that we must turn if we wish to deal with the nature of the priesthood, which, whether it be ministerial or hierarchical, is closely connected with it. The words

'Do this in memory of me' immediately followed those of the institution of the Eucharist, in the upper room.[1]

The Church lives on the Eucharist and through it is ceaselessly reborn. And thanks to it she is fulfilled in a quite particular way: the Eucharist is the zenith towards which everything in the Church rises and converges. When you question me on the subject of the priesthood, you approach this dimension of the Church-Eucharist, its innermost, most sacral and most sacramental aspect. And it is above all from the Eucharist that the Church draws this character.

The priesthood exists because Christ *left in the Church, in the Eucharist,* his sacrifice, the sacrifice of his body and blood which had become for the first time, under the species of bread and wine, at the Last Supper, food and drink for his disciples. When he gave the apostles this food and this drink he expressly indicated the body and blood of his immolation on the cross. He said, 'This is my body which is given up for you', and, according to Matthew, 'This is my blood, the blood of the new testament which will be shed for you in remission of sins.' He was speaking of the sacrifice of the new and eternal testament, of which he is the sole priest.

He who offers the sacrifice of the new and eternal testament is priest of this new and eternal testament, and it is precisely Christ who is such a priest, as we see it wonderfully explained in the epistle to the Hebrews.[2] He is the sole priest of his own sacrifice, of the sacrifice of Gethsemane and Calvary, offered to the Father by the Son stripped of himself and obedient unto death.

At the same time he is the priest of the Upper Room, 'priest for

1. At Jerusalem, the cenacle in which the apostles celebrated the Passover with Jesus on the eve of his Passion is, according to tradition, the upper room of a dwelling on the hill of Sion known to-day as the 'tomb of David' (which is supposedly located in the lower storey). The Eucharist or 'act of thanksgiving' is a mystery of a depth and complexity which still give work to theologians – and joy to mystics. The source is to be found in the first letter to the Corinthians 11:23–25; in the Gospels of St. Matthew 26:26–28, and St. Mark 14:22–24, and this passage from St. Luke 22:19–20, describing the last meal or 'Last Supper' of Christ with his apostles: 'And he took bread, and when he had given thanks he broke it and gave it to them, saying, "This is my body which is given for you. Do this in remembrance of me." And likewise the cup after supper, saying, "This cup which is poured out for you is the new covenant in my blood."'

2. Hebrews 7:23–24. We read there in particular: 'The former priests were many in number, because they were prevented by death from continuing in office; but he holds his priesthood permanently, because he continues for ever.'

ever according to the order of Melchisedech', the mysterious King of Salem (an old name for Jerusalem) who went to meet Abraham with bread and wine.[1] The tradition enshrined in the ancient Eucharistic prayer of the 'Roman canon' sees in Melchisedech's gesture a sign pointing towards the perfect sacrifice. In the Upper Room Christ made the bread and wine sacramental signs of the sacrifice which he was to offer the Father the next day with his body and blood."

Before we go any further, one misunderstanding must be cleared up. The notion of sacrifice is quite alien to the contemporary mind, especially in so far as it embraces the idea of reparation or redemption. What, people will say, there is a God so greedy for vengeance and sacrifices as to forget his own precept to pardon seventy times seven times? If he is like that, how does he differ from the cruel gods of paganism who were only appeased by blood, and what is this 'justice' that swoops down from the height of eternal perfection on a weak, unarmed being? This caricature has been accepted in the end by innumerable minds as an obvious truth, so much so that even churchmen themselves often hesitate to-day to employ the word 'sacrifice', which has lost its spiritual meaning. Well, it is not true to say that the sacrifice of Calvary was required for the sake of justice, which would have been satisfied with just one of Christ's tears over Jerusalem. The slightest familiarity with the Gospel teaches us that justice's share in the divine work was nothing compared with the part played by mercy, which is another name for love. The truth is that sacrifice, that is, the total gift of oneself, is the ordinary mode of being of the Holy Trinity.

"So then, the Upper Room is the place where Christ made his own sacrifice into the sacrifice of the Church. He bequeathed it to the Church as the most magnificent gift of his bridegroom's love. By associating with this sacrifice all those who constitute the Church, he associated them at the same time with his sacrifice and made of them a 'Kingdom and priests' for his Father. So that all can participate in the sacrifice of redemption Christ said to his apostles, 'Do this in memory of me.' This was giving them the power to

1. Genesis 14:18–19. 'Melchisedech, the king of Salem, brought out bread and wine; he was priest of God Most High. And he blessed him and said, "Blessed be Abram by God Most High, maker of heaven and earth."' The patriarch's name, Abram, 'exalted father' was changed by God a little later to Abraham, which seems to mean 'father of a multitude'. The Gospel calls paradise 'Abraham's bosom'.

renew his sacrifice sacramentally, by telling them how they should do it.

And when they did it, the apostles did not act simply in his name, but through the effect of an extraordinary assimilation to him who alone is the dispenser of it, that is, priest at his own sacrifice; it was thus that they became likewise dispensers and priests of the sacrifice in the sacramental order.

It is impossible to offer this sacrifice without being a priest. To celebrate the Eucharist, it is not enough to reconstruct the historical event of the Last Supper; the indispensable element is the priestly character of the celebrant. To acquire this character, one must be ordained or consecrated. This consecration is necessary to enable the Church to be *born of the Eucharist*, to enable her to live as the body of Christ celebrating the memory of the death and resurrection of the Lord.

I repeat here the apostolic tradition and the tradition of the Fathers of the Church, which you will find in all the documents of the Church's magisterium, down to and including Vatican II."

What the Pope had just said about the ministry of the sacraments obviously did not mean that he had forgotten or minimized the priest's two other ministries, that of the Word and the pastoral ministry, which he exercises himself with such zeal, as we know.

"The priesthood is a constituent element of the life and accomplishment of the Church. It constitutes a special vocation and a well-defined service in the community of believers, of all those who, through baptism, share in the paschal mystery of Christ, and so in the sacrifice inseparable from his priesthood.

The priestly ministry is 'from them' and 'for them', exactly as the epistle to the Hebrews says: 'Chosen from among his fellow men and made a representative of men.'

So far as priestly celibacy is concerned, you used just now a very significant formula: 'The priest is a man who lives alone so that others should not be alone.' That is really a beautiful description and I want to thank you for it.

I think it is a particular, but very fair, formulation of Christ's words concerning both celibacy and religious profession. Christ speaks of celibacy 'for the sake of the Kingdom of heaven', a succinct expression which hides a formidable load of different meanings. Celibacy is a way of life which a person chooses consciously and spontaneously in order to *serve* the affairs of the

'Kingdom', and above all to bear specific testimony to this Kingdom as the final reality and yet one already present in the world.

Now to bear witness to the Kingdom of God, to bear witness to it by the symbol of celibacy, that is, by the symbol of *expectation*, expectation of the unique Bridegroom and expectation of Love, the source of all true love, means in fact 'to live alone so that others should not be alone', it means bringing close to them the presence of God, 'he through whom all are alive'.[1] It is to make this God present by the symbol of my life, my choice, my existence."

# III

The Church of to-day puts much emphasis, in the name of the Gospel, on politics, justice and the social institutions, which leads us to the question that Christians have often asked: 'Has the Gospel any temporal effectiveness?' It is a grave question for the Christian conscience and presents enormous difficulties. In fact, the Gospel establishes a system of direct relations between God and the human being, so direct that the system is set forth mainly in the second person – 'Thou shalt love God', 'Thou shalt love thy neighbour as thyself' – and rarely in the third person. Now God may have the right to say to one of his children, 'If some one takes thy tunic, let him have thy cloak as well,' or 'If a man strikes thee on the right cheek, turn the left cheek also,' but it is obviously difficult to draw up a code of civil law on the basis of this divine moral perfection; I can always do as I like with my own cheek, but it would be a strange law that allowed me to do as I liked with my neighbour's too.

Is it possible to infer a policy and, if need be, social institutions from the Gospel?

"This kind of question reminds me of the conversation between Christ and Pilate. Jesus of Nazareth, accused of wishing to make himself king, at first replied to his judge in the negative: 'My kingship is not of this world; if my kingship were of this world, my

1. Luke 20:38

servants would fight, that I might not be handed over to the Jews; but my kingship is not from the world.' Pilate rightly observes that an affirmation is included in this denial. He therefore asks for the second time, 'So you are a king?' Christ then replies in the affirmative: 'You say that I am a king. For this I was born, and for this I have come into the world, to bear witness to the truth. Every one who is of the truth hears my voice.'

I think the connection between these words and those of *Gaudium et Spes* is clear: 'The Church, by reason of her rôle and competence, is not identified with any political community nor tied to any political system. She is at once the sign and the safeguard of the transcendental dimension of the human person.[1]

These two declarations, one by Christ before Pilate, the other by the Church in 1965, do not cover the same ground. The Council states that the Church as a community has no political character, that she is not a state. Before Pilate, Christ denies that his power is political. Nevertheless, although the fields of application do not coincide, they touch each other closely. Political power falls by right to political communities; the Church, a community established by Christ, does not aspire to such power. As the Council says, she is not tied to any political system. In this precise sense, 'politics' does not correspond to her nature, her principles or her end. The 'Kingdom' which is realized in her 'is not of this world.' A Church which identified itself with the state would cease to be itself. It would cease to be a Church. The experience of two thousand years confirms that this spiritual frontier has never anywhere been crossed. In spite of various forms of dependence of the Church on the state or of the state on the Church, and in spite of the existence of the 'Papal States', the Church has always remained the Church. The definition established by Christ has proved stronger than all the trials of history."

This reply was dictated to the Pope by his personal picture of the Church. I can already hear the cries of objection. For the last two or three centuries the Church's compromises with the established order, of whatever kind, have been one of the most frequent commonplaces of anti-clerical polemics, which have contrived to sound so convincing that many good Christians to-day regularly beat their breast, or rather their mother's breast, summoning her to

---

1. *Gaudium et Spes* 76:2. The preceding quotations come from St. John 18:36–7.

show contrition at last and to recognize that she brought dishonour on herself with the Roman Empire, with all the monarchies of Europe and with the nineteenth-century bourgeoisie. People no longer even take the trouble to give examples, so wide, evidently, is the choice from Constantine to Richelieu, from the colonization of South America to the confusion of powers in the old Papal States. Let us not deny the weaknesses, but must we exaggerate them? Richelieu was a churchman, but he was no more the whole Church than St. Francis of Sales or St. Vincent de Paul was; a king took him as a minister, but no one ever took him as a confessor. It is not true that the Church identified itself with the nineteenth-century bourgeoisie. The parish priest went to the farm and the castle, but he was seldom to be seen in the home of the Voltairean, atheistic bourgeois, who would have scarcely tolerated someone coming to talk about the Gospel in his shop or his factory, even in the mildest terms. Is it true that the conversion of Constantine inaugurated an era of triumphalism and of a confusion of powers disastrous to the purity of the Church? When Constantine recognized Christianity[1], he did not subject the Church; he subjected the Empire to a law superior to that of the state, a law whose first effect was to forbid him to deify himself as his predecessors had rarely hesitated to do. Caesar was no longer God, and that was no small event. Far from being confused, the temporal power and the spiritual power were definitively separated in law, even though they may have joined forces more than once in fact. The Pope was perfectly justified in saying 'this frontier has never been crossed'; it is erected at a very high level and in this sense is inviolable.

"Let us return to our parallel. The second part of the reply to Pilate and the declaration of the Council seem to agree more closely: to *bear witness to the truth* and to *safeguard the transcendental dimension of the human person* are one and the same thing. For man expresses and puts into effect the transcendence proper to him by his relation to the truth. This transcendence shows his 'royalty'. It is a question of a universal dimension affecting every man and consequently all men.

Christ is King in the sense that in him, in his witness to the truth, is made manifest the 'royalty' of each human creature, the

1. Christianity was the principal beneficiary of the Edict of Milan (313) on religious liberty.

expression of the transcendent character of the person. That is the heritage that belongs to the Church.

Your question touches on the problem of 'the Church and politics'; hence my reference to Christ's reply to Pilate. However, we have not come to the end of the question. You ask me if one can deduce a policy from the Gospel, since the contemporary Church, in the name of this very Gospel, puts so much emphasis on politics and social justice. Although Christ's reply to Pilate may not exhaust this question, the light it throws on it is indispensable to us in a domain of the first importance for the witness that we must bear to the truth – and therefore to the transcendent character of the human person. This domain is politics."

The Holy Father remarked that the very term 'politics' is, to say the least, ambiguous.

"According to the Aristotelian tradition, politics coincides more or less with social ethics. For modern man, it is more a technique of government, a thoroughly utilitarian technique, as is shown by Machiavelli's notorious treatise.

In the first case politics would also signify social justice. In the second case it would not.

When the Church pronounces on political affairs she does so in conformity with her mission to teach, which deals in principle with questions of faith and morals. She supplies each time the appropriate interpretation of the moral law explicitly contained in the Gospel or confirmed by it.

In this sense the Church teaches social ethics while leaving to the competent persons the actual task of governing, and while continually expressing her pastoral and magisterial concern that the technique or art of governing should not be simply a method of retaining power, but should serve social justice, that is, the common good of the members of the body politic. Social justice and the common good are closely related notions, since both denote a system of social relations that preserves the transcendent character of the person while respecting his basic needs.

Hence the frequency with which the Church adopts a definite position; this corresponds to the double need for fidelity to the Gospel and fidelity to man. The Church has the duty of bearing witness to the truth, like Christ before Pilate. If we mention that dialogue once again, it is to emphasize that the Church must have a profound awareness of the Kingdom 'that is not of this world' in order to be able to pronounce clearly and decisively on the affairs of this world, where man must not lose his transcendence: but in order to meet it, to confirm it – as well as to make man conscious of it and to reveal it to him – it is necessary *to bear witness to the truth*."

I had asked, 'Can one deduce a political policy from the Gospel?' The Pope had replied that the policy of the Gospel was the transcendence of man. The human person is formed by the relation of this transcendence to the truth which, according to Christianity, is itself a person – the person of Jesus Christ. The man who bears witness to the truth bears witness at the same time for himself. A policy 'deduced from the Gospel' would thus have the principle and purpose of continually making possible this witness, which is the foundation of the person.

# IV

Upset no doubt at having missed, they say, so many 'historical turning-points' (the 'turning-point' of the Renaissance, the 'turning-point' of the French Revolution and, for some people, the turning-point of Marxism, among other twists and turns in the career of Western societies), Christians are more and more tempted to immerse themselves in history, that divinity of modern times, to the detriment of all transcendence and all contemplation. If the function of adoration were not carried out in monasteries and by a few old ladies in what active parishes remain, it would be forgotten. But is it not a vital necessity for the human soul?[1]

"I note that after 'faith' and 'morals' the main theme of our conversation is now the Church. That is why I have been trying to bring out a fresh aspect of the Church from each of your questions. Thus we have discussed in turn 'the Church of the Beatitudes', 'the Church of the Eucharist' and, just now, 'the Church of the

1. I know that the word 'soul' has been erased from the vocabulary of modern thought, for reasons which escape me. To me, the soul is that part of us that quivers at the name of Jesus Christ. Apart from faith and hope, let us say that the soul is what, in man, hesitates to die.

Kingdom' or, if you prefer, 'the Church and politics'. This time I cannot perceive any central formula or rather intuition. However, an idea occurs to me which could guide my answer. Remember the course of the last Council: to me, it is an eloquent and significant fact that the *first* subject debated and the *first* document completed was the *Constitution on the Liturgy*. On the other hand, the *last* subject for discussion and the *last* document passed was 'The Church in the Modern World', and consequently the Church in time and history.

If this memory prevails, perhaps the very course of the Council's work can give us an indication which will enable us to make our way towards a correct reply."

Just as one takes a turn round the garden before going to the office, so the Pope is not averse to walking round a question before stepping into it.

"Your remarks are bound to make one think. More than that, they are bound to make one feel worried, worried about *what is going on in man*. You rightly ask the question, 'Isn't prayer, contemplation, a vital necessity for the human soul?' Its decline in the human being, in society, is distressing not only for the vitality of the Church but also, and above all, for man himself. One cannot but be worried by the atrophy of the sense of transcendence, by the indifference to all the challenges issued to us by the absolute, and by our confinement in immanence, or rather by our subjection to the transitory?

You ascribe all these phenomena to an 'immersion in history', 'that idol of modern times'.

For my part, I don't think that history is opposed to transcendence. Properly understood, it would be more a means of demonstrating it, as I think I have already said."

But there are different ways of understanding history. There is the history that one tells, the history that is written in an invisible book that we shall only read at the end of time, the history of which one can say, like Shakespeare speaking of life, that it is 'full of sound and fury, signifying nothing', the history of the historians and the history that claims to recapitulate everything, including God.

"One must distinguish between 'history' and 'historicity', and still more between history and 'historical materialism'. As for history as such, in my view it is one of the dimensions of man's transcendence and does not imply at all that his existence has a purely 'horizontal' character. Provided, of course, that we correctly define the relation of man to history, that is, that we base history on the full truth about man, a truth that takes account of all the vital and lifegiving necessities of the human soul. History so considered does not result in materialism or atheism – or even horizontalism. History is not responsible for the reduction or alienation of what is essential in man.

I say this while taking account of the specific character of Christianity as a religion. Christianity is not a religion of the 'pure Absolute' or of the 'solitary Absolute'. The God in whom we believe is a living God, and also the *God of history*. We do not meet him only above history, above the transitory flux of the world of men: he is a God who has entered history, a God who has committed himself to the history of man, in the midst of the drama of humanity. He has taken this drama 'on himself', if one may put it like that. That is why he became 'a stumbling block to the Jews' and 'folly to the Gentiles', as St. Paul writes to the Corinthians.

Far from accepting the 'history as an idol' of which you speak, Christianity proclaims and professes the presence of God in history.

He is also a God who gives the history of man its innermost and most definitive meaning. *The history of salvation* is the only dimension of the history of man in which the future does not let itself be held back by the past but 'absorbs' it, by putting it on the road to the age to come, by making it into the subject-matter of the future. One can learn much on this subject by reading the documents of the last Council and the books of theologians such as Urs von Balthazar or Mouroux."

In short, through the programme in Genesis ('Subdue the earth'), the expectation of the Messiah and the hope of men's salvation, Judaeo-Christianity was the first to give a meaning to history, which in pagan thought had none.

"We could have entitled this part of our dialogue 'the Church and History', but that would not satisfy me completely. I should prefer 'the Church of the commandment of love', a title which I am going to try to justify.

You are right to deplore the fact that in certain circles the need for adoration, prayer, contemplation is disappearing. To keep a balance, it would be as well to add that at the same time, in other places and circles, we are witnessing the discovery of prayer and a rebirth of the inner life. These are processes which are sometimes symmetrical, sometimes meet, or are unaware of each other. Yet both are developing. Perhaps they even act on each other, by pulling in opposite directions, as in a tug of war.

The need to pray and worship is born in man as a response of faith to the word of the living God, as the expression of his meeting with this God who addresses himself to him, who has manifested his love for him precisely by entering history.

In the act of Christian worship, the point of departure is usually the abasement, the annihilation of God, his 'condescension', his cross, the Eucharist. The meeting with the God of love in the immensity of the universe would not be so overwhelming as it is in the Eucharist, the cross – or the manger of Bethlehem.

That is why your question seems to me to be concerned above all with the right approach to the commandment of love. For if it is true that we must respond with love to the Love that has chosen human history in which to reveal itself, and that we do it by loving and serving our brothers, it is also true that we cannot love and serve by love if we do not root ourselves by means of worship in the greatest love of all. It was thus that Christ arranged things, by uniting in his commandment the love of God above all else, and the love of man on the human plane.

I pointed out just now that the Council had providentially begun its labours with the constitution on the liturgy and concluded them with the constitution on the Church in the Modern World: this was a clear indication that the renewal could only be fashioned correctly by following the correct approach to the commandment of love."

# V

I mean to come back later to the connections between Christianity and 'history', which sometimes looks like a comedy liable to turn out badly, while the Judaeo-Christian religion would turn it into a paradoxical tragedy with a happy ending. For the moment I felt like that curious predecessor of Aristotle of whom the latter said amicably that 'he had succumbed under the weight of the question which he had raised.' How we had moved from history to the catechism I don't really know, or rather I know perfectly well. A global vision of the world and its destiny presupposes a doctrine, a body of teaching, and this teaching is disseminated to-day by different paths – the magisterium of the Church (from the encyclical to the Sunday sermon), Christian schools, where any remain, the printed word, audio-visual methods and, at the grass roots, by Christian families – who often rely on the catechists.

So far as catechisms are concerned I have seen all sorts, speaking all sorts of languages. Handed over to private enterprise, religious instruction shows considerable variations from one country, one region or one district to another. One hears loud congratulations that to-day's catechisms no longer proceed as the older ones did by question and answer, which had in particular the disadvantage, so people say, of calling more on memory than on intelligence. Perhaps a change of method was indeed necessary, but since the answers have disappeared as well as the questions, the new manuals add mainly to the reader's perplexity. Opinion polls regularly prove that Christians are less sure of what they believe than of what they do not believe.

I asked the Holy Father if it would not be a good idea to define for everyone those elementary truths of the Christian faith on which neither compromise nor bargaining is possible.

"The Church and catechesis is a fundamental subject. Here we are following in the footsteps of the last but one synod of bishops, in which I took part when I was Archbishop of Cracow. Behind me I had Cardinal Luciani of Venice, who became John Paul I. It was in October 1977. To my mind, this synod formed a sequel to that of 1974 on evangelization. A synthesis of the gains made by the synod of 1974 is to be found in Paul VI's exhortation *Evangelii nuntiandi*, while the exhortation *Catechesi tradendae* summarizes the work of the following synod. These two synods and exhortations reflect the pastoral thinking of the Council and provide the indications necessary for its application to the life of the Church. Catechesis is without any doubt the fundamental dimension of the 'self-realization' of the Church. It is a method of evangelization, its path for centuries. The documents of the tradition bear witness to this since the most ancient times, continually adding to the varied experience of days gone by the thoughts and efforts of the epoch.

In a sense, the document *Catechesi tradendae* contains the answer to your question, a richer and more exhaustive answer than any that I could give you at the moment.

The exhortation *Evangelii nuntiandi* emphasizes the general principle that the Church, as a community, is responsible both for transmitting and for receiving the Gospel: 'As evangelizer, the Church begins by evangelizing herself, by a constant conversion and renovation, in order to be credible when she evangelizes the world . . . After being evangelized, the Church herself sends out evangelizers . . .' As for the exhortation *Catechesi tradendae*, it provides means to this end: 'No one in the Church of Jesus Christ', it says, 'should feel dispensed from receiving catechesis. In fact it is very much indicated for those called to work as pastors and catechists; they will perform these tasks all the better if they can go humbly to school with the Church, the great catechist as well as the great catechumen.' These principles fix the responsibilities so far as the content of the truths taught is concerned, and at the same time open the way to every initiative. Naturally the responsibility for the content of the truths taught belongs in the first place in the Church to the pastors, and thus to the bishops, the bishops' conferences and the Holy See."

The Church is not perfect. For some time she has been more keenly aware of the need to evangelize herself, and the consciousness of this obligation is at the root of a multitude of experiments and explorations which sometimes provoke admiration, sometimes amazement, and on which it is too early to pass a final judgement.

"If it is a question of 'recalling' the basic truths of faith, one can only cite the Credo of the People of God published by Paul VI for the nineteen hundredth anniversary of the martyrdom of the apostles Peter and Paul. In this domain I do not see any difficulties. What is doubtless more difficult is the problem of a post-conciliar catechism of the whole Church, in so far as a catechism includes not only 'definitions' but also a certain way of explaining the truths of the faith and the principles of the Christian life resulting from a particular theology. As it happens, theology is at present in a phase of wide-ranging research to which the Council itself made a remarkable contribution. One has only to recall John XXIII's famous allocution at the opening of Vatican II."

In that inaugural address John XXIII invited the Council fathers to work 'joyfully and fearlessly' at the updating – *aggiornamento* – of the Church's dialogue with the modern world. He thought that the Christian truths could be expressed to-day in a different way from before – an idea or suggestion which led to a large number of initiatives and quite a few mistakes.

"Moreover, with the Council came the opening of the ecumenical era, the problems of which were bound to influence catechesis. Finally, thanks to Vatican II and the synods – especially that of 1974 on evangelization – the episcopate of the universal Church acquired a new awareness of the relations between the Gospel and culture, as well as of the multiplicity of the cultural contexts in which the local Churches must evangelize and catechize.

All this only pleads in favour of the unity of catechesis and of a special effort to effect this unity; but it shows clearly enough how this unity can only be the fruit of plurality.

Is this unity possible? I think so. In fact it is indispensable."

Considering these differences in culture, to which so much importance has been attached lately that people venture to speak of the doctrinal 'imperialism' or 'colonialism' of the Roman Church, which is deemed to impose her outlook on peoples brought up in other intellectual climates, I said to the Holy Father that although I was born into a family that lived near Belfort, where camels and palm-trees are rare, I had no hesitation in adopting the story of the carpenter of Nazareth, and had learned with pleasure that I should be invited one day to leave my cultural environment for 'Abraham's bosom'. But the Holy Father picked up the phrase 'private enterprise' which I had employed, not without malice, I must admit, on the subject of the catechism.

"If this 'private enterprise' of which you speak were to signify the denial or elimination of the Church's hierarchical responsibility, obviously one would have to put a question mark against it, if not a full stop.

But if this 'private enterprise' signifies an extension of the number of persons actively engaged in catechesis (owing, for example, to the inadequacy or absence of religious teaching in the schools), an extension willed and directed by responsible persons and authorities who watch the content, quality and methods of catechesis, then this 'private enterprise' is to be welcomed and encouraged.

The family and relations have always rightly been regarded as the first catechists. To-day, when one takes account of the not always very happy diversity of this basic family apostolate, the devotion of volunteers, lay people for the most part, ready to assume the immense duties of catechesis, is a good sign of the times. We know what the missionary work of the Church owes to them. I myself am very happy to meet these lay catechists on my visits to the parishes of Rome.

'The harvest is plentiful,' says the Gospel, 'but the labourers are few.'"

# VI

I suggested to the Pope that Christians should dismiss the sort of inferiority complex which they cultivate with a morose pleasure based on panic when confronted with what they call 'the mentality of modern man', which is not necessarily all that much better or more original than that of the cave man.

If the apostle Paul had felt the same concern to make himself acceptable at any price, and if he had accommodated his message to the mentality of the Athenians of his own time, who had as little taste as our contemporaries for mysticism, would there have been a Christian religion?

"St. Paul had a keen sense of the evangelical message which he was going to deliver to various different peoples, to the Jews as well as to the Greeks. He knew that the truth which saves comes from God and not from the world. The consciousness of this was no hindrance to him; on the contrary, it helped him to adapt this message to its recipients. Witness his meeting with the Athenians and his speech to the Areopagus: Paul strives to adapt himself to the mentality of his audience. He begins with a sort of *captatio benevolentiae* by praising the piety of the Athenians; after which, having tackled the subject from their own point of view, as it were, he speaks of the altar erected 'to an unknown god' and what he says conforms with the ideas of the Stoics. He cites some poets: Cleanthus' hymn to Zeus and the poem of Aratus. It is only his last sentence on the Resurrection that his audience finds unacceptable."

I think it would be useful to quote here the essentials of this passage from the Acts of the Apostles, which begins with a humorous comment on the inhabitants of the city of Athena, the goddess of Reason.

Now all the Athenians and the foreigners who lived there spent their time on nothing except telling or hearing something new.

So Paul, standing in the middle of the Areopagus, said: 'Men of Athens, I perceive that in every way you are very religious. For as I passed along, and observed the objects of your worship,[1] I found also an altar with this inscription, "To an unknown god". What therefore you worship as unknown, this I proclaim to you. The God who made the world and everything in it, being Lord of heaven and earth, does not live in shrines made by man, nor is he served by human hands, as though he needed anything, since he himself gives to all men life and breath and everything. And he made from one every nation of men to live on all the face of the earth, having determined allotted periods and the boundaries of their habitation, that they should seek God, in the hope that they might feel after him and find him. Yet he is not far from each one of us, for "In him we live and move and have our being"; as even some of your poets have said, "For we are indeed his offspring." Being then God's offspring, we ought not to think that the Deity is like gold, or silver, or stone, a representation by the art and imagination of man. The times of ignorance God overlooked, but now he commands all men everywhere to repent, because he has fixed a day on which he will judge the world in righteousness by a man whom he has appointed, and of this he has given assurance to all men by raising him from the dead.'

Now when they heard of the resurrection of the dead, some mocked; but others said, 'We will hear you again about this.'

"Of course, in spite of this, the apostle does not alter the content of his preaching, which is the Gospel of the Risen Christ; in this central point of his message he does not try to 'adapt himself to the mentality' of his audience; he tolerates their mockery without

1. The idols to be seen all over the city; they had much irritated Paul, as we are told a little earlier in Acts.

ceasing to be the witness of the paschal mystery . . . Yet it is the same Paul who wrote:

'For though I am free from all men, I have made myself a slave to all, that I might win the more. To the Jews I became as a Jew, in order to win the Jews; to those under the law I became as one under the law – though not being myself under the law – that I might win those under the law. To those outside the law I became as one outside the law – not being without law toward God but under the law of Christ – that I might win those outside the law.'[1]

Since the time of Paul the principle of adapting the Gospel message to its recipients has remained the golden rule of all missionary activity. People often object that in the past the Church, with her 'Western' mentality, has not always managed to adapt herself enough to other mentalities and cultures. Take China, for example, and the story of the famous Father Ricci and the Jesuit missionaries.[2] Nevertheless, today, as in the past, this practice demands a good deal of discernment. And more than once, in her missionary work, the Church has had to accept a setback like Paul's before the Areopagus. Christ had foreseen such failures and had foretold them to his disciples. In addition, he taught them to look on themselves as 'unworthy servants' and asked them to confine themselves to acknowledging, when their mission was crowned with success, 'We have only done what was our duty.'[3]

I am replying to you as if the subject of your question were 'the Church and the apostolate'. That is what you were thinking of?"

It was indeed. But I had begun by deploring Christians' 'inferiority complex' in face of 'the mentality of modern man', as if the heirs to Christianity, laden with spiritual riches, had anything to envy in the hovels in which contemporary ideologies lock up their prisoners.

"You understand this 'mentality', which according to you gives some Christians complexes, as a sort of inner synthesis that we meet in the men of to-day, especially in the context of certain civilizations. This synthesis can be expressed in many ways; for

1. I Corinthians 9:19–21

2. The Jesuit Father Ricci would have liked the evangelizers of China to turn themselves into Chinese with the Chinese, like Paul with those 'outside the law'.

3. Luke 17:10

example, by putting the emphasis on progress as an end in itself, on the absolute priority of science and technology, or again on a conception of freedom that excludes the recognition of any authority at all. It would form the basis of a presumed 'superiority complex', since there would be an 'inferiority complex' among the Christians.

Well now, I think that Christ teaches us many things. He teaches us love, including love of our enemies; he teaches us humility before God, before men and before the universe; but his teaching excludes both inferiority and superiority complexes. Complexes of this sort accord neither with love nor with truth.

A real scholar never sees himself as superior to other men, but as a servant of the truth. He is full of humility in his research; if he were not, he would never discover anything. The great artist has the same attitude to the art which he serves.

Humility always goes hand in hand with magnanimity, and magnanimity with humility.

A complex, of whatever sort, denotes a certain lack of authenticity."

These last two sentences provide a good summary of John Paul II's chivalrous view of human nature.

"What should be the Christian's attitude to his age, and thus to 'the mentality of modern man' or 'the contemporary mentality'? *Gaudium et Spes* gives a simple but detailed reply to this question. This constitution of Vatican II was called 'pastoral' for profound reasons, and in particular because it tells us what the Christian's attitude should be to the age in which he lives. While rejoicing at the real successes of his epoch and taking part in them, and without abandoning a healthy critical spirit or forgetting the threats of which this age is full, the Christian must constantly 'bear witness to the hope that is in him'. I think that this form of relation to one's time – whichever it may be, not just our own time – can be regarded as evangelical, a way of identifying oneself with the time in which one lives.

Yes, of 'identifying oneself', for after all it is our own contemporaneity that is involved! There is something here of the divine *kairos* which Providence grants us.

So then, an attitude of identification in accordance with the Gospel, but without any complexes."

The *kairos* to which the Pope alluded is the 'acceptable time' mentioned by St. Paul in his second epistle to the Corinthians (6:2): '"At the acceptable time I have listened to you, and helped you on the day of salvation." Behold, now is the acceptable time; behold, now is the day of salvation.'

The first two lines of this quotation are themselves a quotation from the eighth verse of chapter 49 of Isaiah. As a result of the constant presence of Christ among us, every time is a *favourable time* for the grace and good news of the Gospel.

# VII

In my view, the supreme beauty of Christianity is one of the principal reasons for the world's incomprehension and hostility. I sometimes wonder if we understand it ourselves. 'Familiarity with the divine' often makes us insensitive to the avalanche of grace and illumination which the Church never tires of shedding over us and which we too often allow to go to waste. For example, the sacraments, which accompany the Christian from one end of his life to the other: baptism ensures that he is treated like those royal children who were sometimes married off before they had attained the age of reason; penance ensures that he can be born again at any moment from his own ashes; and the Eucharist enables him to prepare now the transfigured flesh of his resurrection. Do we still have any idea of the nature, origin and scope of these living signs of a solicitude which is never rebuffed and never despairs?

The Pope pointed out that if it was a question of remedying the ignorance of numerous Catholics in this domain, then priests, pastors of souls, bishops, whole episcopates, the apostolic see and the council had already answered me. Recommendations about a catechesis appropriate to the sacraments had not been lacking:

"I think that during the course of my life great progress has been made in this respect. I say this obviously on the basis of my own experience, which is naturally tied to specific places and situations. So I shall proceed by way of my own personal experience for, when account is taken of certain understandable limitations, it is through that experience that I see the specific dimension of the problem, the sacramental dimension of the life and existence of the Church, even though your question, as you have phrased it, does not demand so much!

So I shall answer you in accordance with what I have experienced, going back to my youth and even to my childhood. It has always been clear to me that the Church was the place where the sacraments are dispensed and received. From my first years at primary school, preparation for first confession and first communion taught me that a sacrament 'is a visible sign of invisible grace, instituted for our salvation'. That is how the catechism put it. Independently of this formula but certainly in accord with it, I lived the sacraments – confession, communion – as things very closely linked to Christ, touching man in the depths of his being and binding his conscience in particular. So much for the two sacraments which I have just mentioned. As for baptism, I only understood its real meaning later, thanks mainly to the liturgy of Lent and Easter. I realized then that everything that in the early days of the Church belonged to the catechumenate had been postponed until after baptism in the life of later generations.

My first visits as a young bishop to the parishes of my diocese were a decisive experience, one almost as intense as the youthful experiences of which I have already spoken to you.[1] These visits took place according to the traditional ritual, but also following certain usages peculiar to my country. It was an event of great importance in the life of the parishes. I soon realized that although the object to be attained is multiple, one must lay as foundation and put into effect *the common experience of the sacramental dimension of the Church*. From this point of view, it was not simply a question of an awareness of the Church as dispenser and beneficiary of the sacraments – an awareness strongly impressed on me since my first confession and first communion – but of something more, namely that the Church lives through the sacraments the life which is most properly hers, and which is at the same time that of the community and that of each person in this community."

For a moment I had had the impression of plunging through

1. At the beginning of this dialogue. In particular, the discovery of the philosophy of being.

undergrowth in the footsteps of the Holy Father, as he hacked out a path with a billhook. But I knew my guide. I awaited the clearing, and here it was:

"Thus Christ is constantly present and always extremely active by the power of the cross and the paschal mystery. And the Church, thanks to this ever active power of her Lord and Bridegroom, becomes truly *his body*, a mystical and at the same time very real body. The sacraments give the Church reality as the body of Christ."

This doctrine of the 'mystical body', which links up with that of the 'communion of saints' discussed in the previous chapter, is essential to the Christian vision of the Church. It is obviously difficult to summarize. For all theology since St. Paul, *the Church is the body of Christ*. The word 'body' is to be taken here both in the sense of 'organism', since it is the same life that flows in it, and in its social sense, since it is a question of a community. *The unity of this Church is perfect*, whatever the rents in it, for nothing can prevent a body from being one even in its wounds; and this unity *is the fruit of charity*. The doctors of the Church have built enormously on these foundations. Perhaps the modern spirit will note particularly in this doctrine of the 'mystical body' the fact that it delivers the human being from its solitude, that the human being stops being incarcerated in its 'ego', and that the doctrine abolishes all the obstacles that this 'ego' normally puts in the way of communication. The difference from the totalitarian systems is that the latter claim to arrive at the same unity by alienating individual persons, while according to Christian teaching it is by being fully themselves through the grace of Christ that people are able to communicate with others: there is no better means of communication than love.

"During this new phase in my life (I was already a bishop, although it was before the Council), I will not say that my awareness of the ecclesial dimension of the sacraments became predominant, but it certainly strengthened in a remarkable way my old conviction that the sacrament was above all 'holy' and 'personally sanctifying', while the Church was only the place where this sacrament is given and received. Thus prepared, I entered on the period of the Council, which helped me to verify my personal experiences, to deepen them, to confirm them and to consolidate them. I speak in this way because at the Council the bishops did not only exercise their magisterium; for them it was a real 'school of the Holy Spirit'. I tried to express this in a study written after the conclusion of Vatican II.[1]

*The table of the word of God* and *the table of the Eucharist*: this admirable patristic image, recalled and made topical by the Council in the constitution on the liturgy, indicates the essential paths of the eternal plan of salvation, a mystery, says St. Paul, hidden in God since the beginning of the world, embodied by the ineffable sacrament of the Word of God made flesh by the action of the Holy Spirit in the womb of the Virgin of Nazareth, to flower in the Church and to become in it the life of souls and the growing plenitude of Christ.

Christ leads the Church by the power of the Holy Spirit and simultaneously acts in her by the power of the Word and of the sacraments. Thus it is that the Church, as we read at the very beginning of *Lumen gentium* 'is in Christ like a sacrament, that is a sign and instrument of the intimate union with God.' The 'Sacrament of the Church' is completely rooted in the 'Sacrament of Christ'. The Word acts in her – the Church – in view of the sacraments: it is in them that she attains her full efficacy in the saving action of Christ himself.

Your question apparently did not go so far, but it seemed to me impossible to reply to it without going that far. For in fact all these dimensions of 'sacramentality' are revealed to our faith in the Word of God in a conjoined and coherent way, although this revelation can occur gradually, as I tried to show by the example of my own life.

In the light of this experience it seems to me of capital importance that Christians should have in the first place a deep awareness of the sacrament as a 'holy' sign and one that 'personally sanctifies' through the power of Christ. Then all the rest will be revealed to them in a, so to speak, organic way. The right path seems to me to be that of conscience and experience. Although the 'ecclesial' dimension of the sacraments is essential, we cannot stop there. The Church constantly receives the Word and the sacraments of Christ as the bride from the bridegroom, but she must also *constantly give herself to Christ*. This must be affirmed and confirmed in the conscience of every dispenser of the Word and the sacraments, but

1. *Aux sources du renouveau*, Editions du Centurion

also in the faith of each of those who participate in the sacraments, by receiving them in the 'Church'."

# VIII

The meetings early in the morning at the Holy Father's Mass were the most exciting ones. Usually I was so afraid of being late that I allowed myself over an hour for a trip that takes ten minutes by car, for fear of a mechanical breakdown. The result was that I arrived at St. Peter's well before dawn, when the huge basilica was still outlined in grey against the black of the sky, and I would look twice every minute at the great clock on the façade. This church is so majestic that it slows down the steps of those who approach it, and so beautiful that it ennobles those who visit it.

That day I noticed a priest on a bicycle pedalling hard towards an unknown destination, with much squeaking of rusty gear-wheels, like a night-bird afraid of being caught in the daylight. I thought of that huge congregation of humble servants of the Church, most of them imprisoned in such poverty by the stinginess of Christians that the 'worker-priest' with his minimum guaranteed wage, can pass for a rich man compared with the suburban curate whose minimum is well below the statutory minimum. Yet all those not slowed down by the breviary are in a hurry. Where are they hurrying? It looks as if the world is escaping them. In the West, statistics register a continual decline in religious practice, and if churches are ever less frequented, one may doubt whether this is so that people may worship better 'in spirit and in truth', in accordance with Christ's wish at Jacob's well.

To-day, with man so distracted from God, what is the most urgent task for priests and for laymen ready to commit themselves? I passed through the Bronze Door of the Vatican thinking these thoughts. The answer came after Mass, with coffee in the Italian style.

"None of your questions has made me feel so keenly the beauty of this great cause, both gift and duty enclosed in the doctrine of Vatican II on the People of God. It is a marvellous chapter, for which we are indebted to the collegial effort of the bishops called to pass on the word of the Spirit to the Church of our time. If the truth that dominates this chapter is indeed the word of the Spirit on the People of God, this truth can only be read with the appropriate key. And this key is provided by the word 'participation'.

The People of God is obviously a community, a huge universal society progressing through history, but if this 'people' is 'of God', it is not for human or social reasons, or because of a dynamic or activity peculiar to the societies of this world of men . . . but simply and solely because of participation; it is 'of God' to the extent of, and because of, its participation in the mission of the Son of God, become the Christ; it is 'of God' to the extent that Christ acts in it and expresses himself through it: priest, prophet and king.[1] Its participation in this triple mission of Christ constitutes the sole basis and the sole justification for this people – that is, the Church – to be called 'of God'. So if I had to define the real subject of your question, I would say that it is concerned with the Church as multiform, differentiated participation in the mission of Christ, priest, prophet and king. This participation constitutes the Church as people invested with a mission, and everyone is concerned in this mission. Every Christian participates in his own way; he is unique and irreplaceable in the mission which the Church has received from Christ. Each one of them has his personal vocation, and the different vocations are paralleled by different gifts, as St. Paul says of gifts and charismata in his epistle to the Corinthians. The multiplicity of gifts and vocations can be compared with that of the organs in a body. The Church, people of God, is a body, the body of Christ. This analogy also comes from St. Paul, writing to the same Corinthians. Here is the passage:

For just as the body is one and has many members, and all the members of the body, though many, are one body, so it is with Christ. For by one Spirit we were all baptized into one body – Jews or Greeks, slaves or free – and all were made to drink of one Spirit . . . The eye cannot say to the hand, 'I have no need of you,' or again the head to the feet, 'I have no need of you.' On the contrary, the parts of the body which seem to be weaker are

1. It will be as well to avoid any misunderstanding. Royalty here has no connection with the exercise of a sovereign power; it is awarded to him who conquers and dominates not the earth, but sin.

indispensable . . . If one member suffers, all suffer together; if one member is honoured, all rejoice together.

The body lives by the Spirit and the grace of adoption, which in Christ makes us sons of God. And it lives by fulfilling the mission entrusted to it by Christ, thanks to the multiplication of gifts and vocations which mutually complement each other and are all necessary to each other.

Vatican II, which was an 'ecclesiological' council, said much about the vocation of priests (although this may have been less clearly noticed) and on the vocation of laymen.

I think that the most urgent duty for both – and this is equally true for religious orders and people living according to evangelical counsels – is to *rediscover oneself* fully in this conciliar vision of the Church as People and Body, and to identify oneself with it as deeply as possible.

One could call Vatican II the Council of the identity of Christians – of each and of all."


# IX

For some time the idea has been growing among Christians that perhaps their divisions are not irremediable and that if to-day there were still what may roundly be called 'wars of religion', they would not be waged among Christians, who would usually find themselves in the same camp, that of the defence of man against racist, materialist and totalitarian ideologies. Will they continue to remain at the foot of the same cross, each clutching a piece of Christ's cloak like the soldiers of Calvary, or will the feeling of danger which threatens them all, them and their faith, be strong enough to unite them until love does? Sometimes this tendency to unity which exists in all the Churches seems to make decisive progress, and an active reconciliation – I mean one that is not simply the result of a politely shared doctrinal indifference – seems near, raising great hopes. But sometimes, too, ecumenism seems to be no more than a noble idea, rather like Esperanto, which everyone praises and no one speaks. The difficulties should certainly not be underestimated. For example, it is clear that everything that brings the Catholic Church closer to the Protestants takes her further from the Orthodox Church, and *vice versa*. Yet she has taken this road and will not turn back. What are then, for the Catholic Church, the conditions of a properly understood ecumenism?

"In reply to your previous question, I told you that Vatican II could be called the Council of *the identity* of Christians, when one took account of their different vocations and of the gifts which correspond to these in each and all. The question which you ask me now provokes me to enlarge the meaning of this identity beyond the circle of the Catholic community and to give it an ecumenical dimension. The Council took note of the truth that Christians can only have their full identity in union with the Church. This union having been broken during the course of the centuries, they can only recover their Christian identity by a sincere and lively effort at unity. It cannot be otherwise in face of the unity of Christ, although St. Paul, confronted with the divisions already tending to appear in his own time, was led to ask, 'Is Christ divided?'[1] This question has not ceased to be topical; it returns from age to age as the fruit of our weaknesses, which go with the human condition. However, through all these generations of Christians divided in the course of the centuries, the indivisible unity of Christ has never ceased to launch the 'challenge of unity'. The Gospel of St. John never tires of recalling these words of Christ: 'Father, that they may all be one!'[2]

This challenge and this prayer of Christ echo particularly in the consciences of Christians of our generation, or rather of contemporary generations, for ecumenical initiatives began some years ago. John XXIII was the man who made Christ's appeal for unity the programme of the Church, first by the creation of the Secretariat for Christian Unity and then by the Council.

You ask me what are the conditions for a properly understood ecumenism? The answer is to be found in Vatican II's decree on the restoration of Christian unity. What had been a particular inspiration of Pope John has become through the Council a mature

1. I Corinthians 1:11–13. 'For it has been reported to me by Chloe's people that there is quarrelling among you, my brethren. What I mean is that each of you says, "I belong to Paul," or "I belong to Apollos," or "I belong to Cephas," or "I belong to Christ." Is Christ divided?'
2. John 17:21

word of the Spirit which the Church awaited and which she welcomed with joy."

This decree is obviously too long to be quoted in full here. After declaring that the division of Christians 'is openly opposed to the will of Christ, that it is a scandal for the world and that it forms an obstacle to the holiest of causes, which is evangelization', it fixes the Catholic principles and rules of ecumenism in the pleasant language of good will. For my part, I remember in particular an invitation to go beyond 'the visible limits of the Catholic Church', too often regarded in days gone by as an impassable frontier beyond which the empire of exterior darkness began immediately.

"This does not mean that the ecumenical road is free of obstacles. The Council decree says expressly what you have just noted yourself, namely that 'what brings us closer to the Protestants takes us further away from the Orthodox.' We Catholics realize that, as do our Orthodox and Protestant brothers. But the language of the Spirit is stronger. It never ceases to prick our consciences to keep taking different steps: not only to meet in prayer for unity, but to bear witness wherever possible to unity and in unity, and to surmount obstacles, both those existing in a mentality marked by centuries of divisions and separations, and the more important ones, which stem from doctrine and theology. All this is in progress. The very realization that, in spite of everything, what unites us is stronger than what divides us and deeper than what separates us obliges us to look deeper: this means a big effort of research; it means a theological dialogue; it means prayer and contemplation."

My question incidentally expressed a certain fear, which comes quite naturally to mind, that the desire to attain the end at any price would lead the partners in the ecumenical dialogue to one of those compromises that are known in political congresses as a 'combined motion', in which all the different tendencies merge in indifference.

"There is no question of moving towards a 'compromise'; the aim is a meeting in truth, made possible by good will and by love. In the last analysis, the union of Christians can only be a mature gift of the Holy Spirit, accepted by the intelligence, the heart and the will, and translated into acts from year to year. There are centuries and centuries to catch up.

Thus 'the Church on the road to the unity of Christians' is a new and difficult reality, but one full of promise. In following this path, the Church correctly deciphers the signs of the times; in following this path she must make big demands on herself, hold firm in humility and charity, be inspired with evangelical boldness and, I would even add, arm herself with a heroic hope, for 'nothing is impossible to God.' Ecumenism is not only 'a noble idea', as you say. It is a great test of faith, hope and charity, a step towards 'what is possible to God' and what sometimes seems impossible to man."

In this spirit, John Paul II said to the Jews, Moslems and non-Catholic Christians of Portugal:

"Whatever our religion may be, the witness of faith in God unites us. We are called to proclaim religious values in a world which denies God. Our witness, our example can help those who seek him . . . To bear witness to one's faith is to contribute to the good of our neighbour, to the common good of humanity. Abraham, our common ancestor, asks us all – Jews, Christians, Moslems – to follow the path of mercy and love."

# X

A pope is always impressive. I was to catch sight of five of them. Pius XI was a soldier of the faith caught between two world wars and solidly armed to meet all dangers. He had published two thundering encyclicals against totalitarian régimes which he named explicitly and did not hesitate to condemn outright. A white and stocky figure with a flashing pince-nez, he was like a ball of energy in the marbled halls of the Vatican. His successor, Pius XII, was a sort of Roman Melchisedech. On the balcony of Castel Gandolfo, blessing the crowd, he looked like a Ravenna mosaic detached from the wall. In his pontificate the papacy attained a degree of prestige which almost excluded any contact with the affairs of this world. With John XXIII there was a brusque transition from gaunt hieraticism to cordial rotundity. He immediately because known as 'good Pope John'; people were delighted to see that the Church, after a long sojourn on the level of symbols, was ready to be embodied once again in convincing plumpness. John was the Pope of the Council, of the *aggiornamento* and of peace. Although his reign was short he left an abiding memory. Paul VI succeeded him without much discussion: ever since his modest start in the offices of the Secretariat of State, everyone knew that he was the best candidate. He was a sophisticated intellectual, but very strong on doctrine; the breadth of his intellect formed a contrast with the fragility of his attachment to the earth. He was entrusted with the tiller just when one of the roughest storms that had ever shaken Peter's bark was breaking out, and he steered as one must in such cases, tacking so as not to capsize, but without ever losing sight of the guiding star that he was probably the only one to see fleetingly between the clouds. Each of these Popes had his own clear, distinct and necessary mission, whether it was resistance to ideological oppression, exaltation of the priesthood, opening up to the world or navigation amid reefs. Even the meteoric passage of John Paul I was clearly indispensable to lead the Sacred College to break with the tradition of Italian Popes, as though by the salutary effect of that gift seldom requested of the Holy Spirit and known as the fear of God. One can say that in a way John Paul I gave us John Paul II, who has been, in my view, from the very first day, the Pope of unity – of unity rediscovered, or on the way to being rediscovered, after a period in which one felt the visible architecture of the Church totter under obscure internal pressures, aggravated by the powerful hurricane of a historical change that did not spare any institution or any system of values in the free world. I sincerely think that we were threatened with having as many Churches as continents, countries – or intellectual parishes. The inflow of the peoples gathered together by John Paul II has consolidated the edifice and its unity has been underpinned.

Thus when I asked John Paul II what was his prayer for the Church of to-day, I already knew the answer.

"Of course, I pray ceaselessly for the Church, I pray for her various concerns; I have always prayed for her intentions and I do so even more to-day in the light of my ministry in the Roman see of Peter.

However, all that I myself could say or that any one of us could express in his own way in a prayer for the Church – under the dictation of the human sequence of the affairs of this world, with its needs, fears and aspirations – will only ever find its true dimensions in the prayer of Christ himself, as recorded by St. John in his Gospel immediately before his account of the Passion.

In the first place it is a prayer for the disciples:

'Holy Father, keep them in thy name, which thou hast given me, that they may be one, even as we are one . . . I do not pray that thou shouldst take them out of the world, but that thou shouldst keep them from the evil one . . . sanctify them in the truth.'

Further on, Christ moves from prayer for the disciples to prayer for the Church to come:

'I do not pray for these only, but also for those who believe in me through their word, that they may all be one; even as thou, Father, art in me and I in thee, that they may also be in us, so that the world may believe that thou hast sent me. The glory which thou hast given me I have given to them, that they may be one even as we are one, I in them and thou in me, that they may become perfectly one, so that the world may know that thou hast sent me and hast loved them even as thou hast loved me. Father, I desire that they also, whom thou hast given me, may be with me where I am, to behold my glory which thou hast given me in thy love for me before the foundation of the world. O righteous Father, the world has not known thee, but I have known thee; and these know that thou hast sent me. I made known to them thy name, and I will make it known, that the love with which thou hast loved me may be in them, and I in them.'[1]

A poignant prayer. It reaches the ultimate depths of the mystery of the Church, which lies in the unity which the Son forms with the Father in the Holy Spirit. Thus we read in *Lumen gentium* that the whole Church appears 'as a people united in the unity of the Father, the Son and the Holy Spirit'. Here we have the depths of knowledge and the depths of surrender: the depths of love. From these depths are born the mission and the witness; from them are drawn light and strength for the new life of men in the world, in the midst of the world – from them rises the glory to come.

Our daily prayers for the Church do not go so deep. None of us could pray like that of his own accord, although we know that in the last analysis we only ever express in our prayers what Christ

---

1. John 17:11, 15, 17, 20–26

expressed in his. His prayer remains the measure of all ours, the fertile soil whence they all spring and bear fruit. We approach closer to this soil and touch it most surely when we celebrate or participate in holy Mass; that is perhaps why in St. John's Gospel Christ's priestly prayer forms a sort of introduction to the Passion and the Resurrection of Easter. To pray for the Church is to revive constantly in oneself awareness of the paschal mystery."

# XI

The fresh clouds piling up over the world, the threats of every sort weighing on the human person and aiming to constrain him or to make him disintegrate, give one the feeling that Christians will soon have to bear witness:

"This hour of witness continually draws nearer to Christians. Nearer to all and to each of them. That is why the words 'Keep watch' are so often repeated in the Gospel; it is through vigilance that the Church is herself, the Church of Christ which not only 'has come' but 'is to come'. The hour of witness approaches for every man at every moment, as it arose for Peter in the courtyard of the high priest."

The episode is well known. Peter, who had followed Jesus when he was dragged off by the guards to the high priest, was warming himself at the brazier by the porter's lodge when he was recognized and denounced three times. Three times he denied that he knew the Jesus of whom they spoke. At the third denial the cock crew, as Jesus had foretold. Then, says the Gospel, Peter remembered 'and wept bitterly'. One may say that at that moment the Church was dead. She too was to rise again on the third day with Christ's question to this same apostle: 'Peter, do you love me?'

"We have to bear witness in many ways and in many circumstances. Christ's appeal for vigilance is constant, and if the circumstances in which the witness is required are not clear to us, they can be for those of our brothers or sisters in the secrecy of their minds and hearts.

Yes, the Church is a Church of vigilance and of witness, both for every Christian and every community. For one can, in fact one must, see the truth of the Church in all her communal dimensions. From the start, the community of Jerusalem had to bear witness, then so did all the others during the course of the centuries, in the context of the great Roman empire. When Constantine's decree came, that did not mean that the time of trial was over. The hour of witness has struck one day or another in various parts of the world throughout the history of the Church. The baptism of blood has been repeated, in one place or another, at different epochs. For example, I am thinking at this moment of the Church in certain Asian countries, where the harvest of martyrs seems no less abundant than in the time of the Roman empire. If we look to-day at the map of the world, we can indicate without difficulty where and how the hour of witness arrived for this or that Church.

But the call to bear witness does not always take the same form. It does not always or exclusively mean the bloody or bloodless persecution of the Church, of religion, of believers. There are other situations where to bear witness does not consist so much in defending the Church herself, her mission, her institutions and her members, as in *opposing* social, economic and political injustice, and in defending life and morality in legislation.

If the Church failed in this duty of opposition where it is necessary, she would not be faithful to her prophetic and pastoral mission; she would not be interpreting, as it must be interpreted, Christ's call to vigilance . . . And this call should also put us on our guard in a quite special fashion against the excesses of unrestricted freedom and against this morbid hunger for material goods which reduces social relations to exchange and consumption.

So I share your conviction that the hour of witness is approaching for Christians. I think that one can say this in every age. We must be aware of it. We must be aware of times and places, not only so as to understand and to know, but above all so as to keep watch together. To be with those who suffer and who, in different ways, accept the challenge and take responsibilities . . . In the midst of all these trials we must continually see to the essential point: to remain a *Church that loves*!"

Nevertheless, if any Christian can be called upon to bear witness to his faith at any moment in his own life or in that of his community, if the Church all through her history has never been dispensed for one single day from bearing witness, is it not paradoxical that so many Christians to-day refuse to proclaim their faith for fear of being accused of proselytism? – and I am not thinking only of the lukewarm and the doubtful but of those responsible for convincing others.

"I shall answer you briefly. The Church of our time must be conscious – and she is conscious – that her irreplaceable mission, her fundamental duty to humanity and the world is and will always everywhere remain spreading the Gospel. 'Woe to me,' once said the apostle Paul, 'if I do not preach the Gospel!' The Church of every age must repeat the same words to herself and fear the same 'woe'. I think that the Church of our time has understood this in a quite special way and has expressed it in the pontificate of Paul VI. The Second Vatican Council was nothing other than a *magna charta*, a great charter of availability, for the preaching of the Gospel to the world of to-day. The teaching of the Council was subsequently translated into the language of concrete evangelization by the synod of bishops of 1974, and afterwards by the exhortation *Evangelii nuntiandi*.[1]

Such then is my reply to the question suggested to you by certain remarks current about proselytism, and this reply is the Church of evangelization.

But to preach the Gospel does not only mean proclaiming that Jesus is the Christ; it also means continually fashioning the history of man by drawing on the unfathomable riches of him 'who for our sake became poor, so that by his poverty you might become rich.'[2] To preach the Gospel is to work in union with Christ; is to work without respite to make man rich in Christ."

1. In which one may read these significant lines: 'The man of to-day does not want masters, but witnesses, and if he accepts masters, it is because they are witnesses.'

2. II Corinthians 8:9

# THE
# WORLD

# I

This century is one of the most murderous in history. It has been wading through blood since its birth and it has not yet reached its end. There is little consolation to be found in the fact that in olden times the slaughters were just as numerous and only caused fewer deaths because there were fewer people in the world. This kind of observation only comforts statisticians.

To-day, there is not a region of the world without its focus of war, disturbances, tensions or terrorism. On top of the ideological conflict between East and West, there is the profound antagonism between North and South produced by economic inequality, post-colonial bitterness and mutual incomprehension. The relations between peoples are based on the will to power and self-interest, which is not new; what is new is that for the first time the world possesses the means to destroy itself and to yield to the lure of annihilation to which religion alone can prevent it from succumbing. Religion seems to doubt itself and so does science, while degraded ideologies are reduced to mere repression. Fear of a universal conflict is gradually mounting: man has imprisoned himself in history and does not dominate it. He has believed in humanism, in progress, or in all sorts of metaphysical idols which have crumbled one after the other into dust; now he no longer believes in anything and awaits no enlightenment or compassion from some 'other' spiritual realm. Yet in the midst of his nausea he still sometimes feels a sort of painful aspiration to a 'something other' which he is incapable of naming and which he often seeks from various more or less suicidal techniques or mystiques.

Hence my first question to John Paul II about the world. Has the moment not come to speak to men about God in plain language, without empty psycho-sociological detours and without watering down doctrine in order to save a fraction of morality at the expense of Christian joy?

"St. Paul answered this question a long time ago when he wrote to Timothy: 'I charge you in the presence of God and of Jesus Christ who is to judge the living and the dead, and by his appearing and his kingdom: preach the word, be urgent in season and out of season . . .'[1]

These words of Paul, 'be urgent in season and out of season' mean that we must always and everywhere speak of God, bear witness to him before men and before the world – not only because such is the mission and the vocation of the disciple, but because this is the deepest need of man and the world: the world and in particular man in the world have no meaning outside God.

If one employs a still more objective terminology, that of the philosophy of being, one could say that the world and man exist to the extent that 'He who Is' 'is', to use the words of the book of Exodus.[2] This is a truth of every age; it is forever topical, but sometimes assumes a particular acuteness. Is this the case with our epoch?

I should like us here to keep the necessary sense of proportion essential in any observation on the state of the human conscience. I suppose that your view, 'Man has believed in humanism, in science and in all sorts of metaphysical idols,' concerns certain circles in the contemporary world. If all men were concerned, we should then have to say that they are concerned in very different ways. It could be that those who have most completely lost faith in these ideals are those who had professed that faith most ardently; it is in them that faith seems to fail most completely.

I understand that, according to you, this 'secular faith' meant to eliminate religious faith. It was to lead man to believe in the world without restriction, and to think that his existence in this world – with all that it could offer him – formed his sole, total and definitive destiny, that the whole meaning of his life was included in this one dimension. To speak the language of existence rather than that of knowledge, it was a question of acting in such a way that man abandoned himself and entrusted himself totally to the world, to achieve in it his ideals of humanism, science and progress.

According to you, this would-be secular, 'lay' faith is in the process of collapsing in our contemporaries: in which case there would be a particular need, possibly even what one might call a chance and an excellent opportunity, to speak of God, to bear witness to God, in a simple, clear fashion, 'without empty detours'.

1. II Timothy 4:1–2
2. See p. 92

According to St. Paul and his letter to Timothy, this need never ceases. The truth must be proclaimed 'in season and out of season'. And if this is more than ever necessary to-day, it is not so much because man has lost his faith in Progress, Science and Humanism as because it is necessary to help him, precisely, *not to lose* this faith in humanism, science and progress (which I am deliberately writing this time without capitals, although these could perfectly well be employed for my purpose). With or without capitals, humanism, science and progress speak to us of man, they bear witness to him and make manifest his transcendence in comparison with the world. In them and through them man can fulfil himself 'as the only creature on the earth that God wanted for itself'. These are the words used in *Gaudium et Spes*. And that is why the book of Genesis describes man as 'the image and likeness of God', as we have seen.

Consequently, if the situation of man in the modern world – and especially in certain circles of civilization – is such that his faith is collapsing, let us say his secular faith in humanism, science and progress, there is surely occasion to announce to this man the God of Jesus Christ, the God of the covenant, the God of the Gospel, quite simply so that he can rediscover the fundamental, definitive meaning of his humanity: the actual meaning, that is, of humanism, science and progress, so that he may not doubt and may not cease to see in them his earthly task and vocation.

All the more if it is true, as you say, that 'in the midst of his nausea, man feels more than ever a painful aspiration to a "something other" which he cannot name' and which he seeks where it does not exist.

In the same letter, after exhorting Timothy to proclaim the word 'in season and out of season', St. Paul writes: 'For the time is coming when people will not endure sound teaching, but having itching ears they will accumulate for themselves teachers to suit their own likings, and will turn away from listening to the truth and wander into myths.'[1]

Paul wrote that in the very early days. Twenty centuries later we find the same phenomenon recurring. The cultural context is different, but the phenomenon is the same."

However, 'humanism, science, progress' are only the different

1. II Timothy 4:3

articles of the credo of Reason, which was elevated into a divinity by the men of the French Revolution, who erected a statue to it in the Place de la Concorde in 1793. It is true that the cult of the 'goddess Reason' did not last long and did not rise from any point of view to the rank of a national holiday, as its founders hoped. It was none the less significant and it was of that – among other things – that I was thinking when I spoke to the Holy Father of 'metaphysical idols'. Reason has been worshipped for some time by incredulous people who finally believed in a lot of things and whom the unhappy state of the world has led to observe that reason does not always suffice as a basis for wisdom. But – and this was my question to the Pope – how is it that men, rational creatures, show such inability to order their lives, their relations and their acts reasonably?

"Yes, why does man, a reasonable being, act in an unreasonable fashion? It is a basic question and a fascinating problem of ethics and existential anthropology. An age-old question, too. I think it occupies a large part of world literature. And it never ceases to gnaw at man day after day, for at every step he comes up against this deep-seated contradiction. He trips and falls on it time and again.

What an eloquent coincidence there is between Ovid's line, 'I see the better, yet I turn to the worse' and St. Paul's heart-breaking words:

> We know that the law is spiritual; but I am carnal, sold under sin. I do not understand my own actions. For I do not do what I want, but I do the very thing I hate . . . I can will what is right, but I cannot do it. For I do not do the good I want, but the evil I do not want is what I do. Now if I do what I do not want, it is no longer I that do it, but sin that dwells within me. So I find it to be a law that when I want to do right, evil lies close at hand. For I delight in the law of God, in my inmost self, but I see in my members another law at war with the law of my mind and making me captive to the law of sin which dwells in my members. Wretched man that I am![1]

Thus we are dealing here with a problem as old as the world and of a universal nature. To introduce the answer supplied by the

1. Romans 7:14–15; 18–24

Christian faith I shall start by quoting a concise passage from *Gaudium et Spes*. It is the chapter devoted to the dignity of the human person and it opens with these words: 'Believers and unbelievers agree almost unanimously that all things on earth should be ordained to man as to their centre and summit. But what is man? He has put forward, and continues to put forward, many views about himself, views that are divergent and even contradictory. Often he either sets himself up as the absolute measure of all things, or debases himself to the point of despair. Hence his doubt and his anguish.' After recalling the teaching of Scripture, according to which man, created in the image of God, is capable of knowing and loving his creator, and has received power over all earthly creatures, to rule them while glorifying God, the same conciliar constitution makes this remarkable diagnosis: 'Although set by God in a state of rectitude, man, enticed by the evil one, abused his freedom at the very start of history. He lifted himself up against God, and sought to attain his goal apart from him. Although they had known God, they did not glorify him as God, but their senseless hearts were darkened, and they served the creature rather than the creator. What Revelation makes known to us is confirmed by our own experience,' and it is true that the evidence of human experience and the voice of Revelation meet here admirably, as is shown by the convergence between the words of Ovid and those of St. Paul which I have just quoted.

What does experience say, then, confirmed, interpreted and elucidated by Revelation and the Christian faith? This, which we find in the same Council document:[1] 'When man looks into his own heart he finds that he is drawn towards what is wrong and sunk in many evils which cannot come from his good creator. Often refusing to acknowledge God as his source, man also upset the relationship which should link him to his last end; and at the same time he has broken the right order that should reign within himself as well as between himself and other men and all creatures. *Man therefore is divided in himself.*'

That is certainly the trouble. These words are exceptionally eloquent: man is torn.

Note that it is not simply a question of the dialectical contradiction between 'reasonable nature' and 'unreasonable action', but of

1. *Gaudium et Spes* 12:13

the actual state in which man finds himself, of his inner situation, confirmed and amplified by outward experience, the experience of the world: he is divided between what he does without wishing it and what he does not do while wishing to. What is in him is not so much a contradiction as a disproportion.

Our conciliar text goes on: 'As a result, the whole life of men, both individual and social, shows itself to be a struggle, and a dramatic one, between good and evil, between light and darkness.' It would be appropriate to add here that this struggle between good and evil confers on human life the character of a test. It is a moral test; hence its specific beauty. To a certain extent the test gives a meaning to our existence; in it we glimpse the call of Christ to realize the Kingdom of God on this earth."

What had just been recalled by the Council and by the Pope was the doctrine of original sin, over which religious teaching to-day occasionally slides with serpentine caution. Yet this sinful condition has gone on from the beginning of the world, from generation to generation and from one man to the next. It is the cause of the rent that everyone can observe in himself and which leaves him divided between the good that he loves and the evil that he does. The only people who escape this rule are those so sunk in error that they think themselves perfect, like the pharisee in the parable, or imagine that no one could be better, like Jean-Jacques Rousseau in his *Confessions*, summoning his peers to the Last Judgement and challenging them to produce one single personal file more honourable than his own. Apart from this kind of aberration, the common rule is certainly that of the rent, as cruel as a wound that Christ alone can heal by faith.

But he came into the world, 'and the world did not accept him.'

He said: 'I am the way, the truth and the life.' The world neglects this way, denies the truth and destroys life. What can it expect?

"To start with, one small remark. The words of Christ that you have just quoted have given rise to different interpretations. The history of commentaries on this text shows that the Greek fathers, and with them St. Ambrose and St. Leo, saw in Jesus the *way* and the *truth* leading to eternal *life*. In the view of Clement of Alexandria, Augustine and most of the Latin fathers, Jesus as *way* leads to eternal truth and eternal life. Thomas Aquinas and the medieval commentators saw Christ as *way* in so far as he was man, *truth* and *life* in so far as he was God. That is also the view of some modern scholars like Lagrange. Others say: Christ is way, that is, truth and life. The notion of *way*, essential here, means that Christ alone is the mediator of salvation, the norm and model in the moral sense and *access* to the Father. He is way as the Father's revelation to men, and therefore as incarnate truth: through knowledge of this truth man reaches *life* – or Christ again. Christ is thus *way* and at the same time the end of this way; it is to him that it leads.

Now you say, 'The world neglects this way, denies the truth and destroys life.' And you added, 'What can it expect?'

This question has already received its answer. First of all, when Jesus, on the fortieth day of his life, was taken to the temple in Jerusalem for the rite of purification, the old man Simeon greeted him with these words: 'Behold, this child is set for the fall and rising of many in Israel, and for a sign that is spoken against.'[1] Yet these words of Simeon only herald the answer. The essential answer to your question is also to be found in the Gospel: it is the Cross.

In the Cross the words of Simeon are completely accomplished.

All through human history it is the revealing sign of the contradiction with the world which has accompanied Christ since the beginning.

You said that the world neglects this way, denies the truth and destroys life. The assertion is correct, but only in part. For it is a fact that at the same time Christ, through the Cross, has remained in the world and dwells there always. He dwells there forever. *Stat crux dum volvitur orbis*: the world turns, the Cross remains. And that is not all. For if the Cross fixes the world's repulsion for 'the way, the truth and the life', the fact remains all the same that in this same Cross, in it and in it alone, this same world is always accepted by God as the site of the Kingdom, the truth and the life of which Christ is the way. Inside the world which rejects him, Christ builds his kingdom which transcends the world.

Thus your question about what the world can expect receives its answer. It is to be drawn from the revealed Word, in the depths of the divine economy. It is obviously the response of faith. It comes not from the world, but from the heart of the Gospel."

1. Luke 2:34

# II

Behind us sinks the contemplative world of the Middle Ages, whose religious and cultural waves have washed up as far as our day, bringing us a sense of the intelligibility of the world, a moral sense, an intuition of universal harmony and hope of an eternal destiny for the human being.

All these spiritual blessings come to us from God, whose presence at the centre of man's thoughts acts as an irreplaceable principle of unity and communion.

It is the remains of this world centred round the cathedral which are in the process of disappearing, and it is vain to attempt to snatch them from the night of history.

Before us a new world gradually appears, based no longer on the contemplation of God but purely on a system of dialectical relations. It is in a sort of gaseous state, still devoid of perceptible structures. In the transitional period in which we stand to-day we have lost the intellectual and moral supports of the world that has passed away, and the world that is in process of formation does not yet offer us any firm hold; we are walking on the water, and this demands something which is in short supply – faith.

I asked the Holy Father if this view of things was correct or false.

"Your picture is beautiful and true, but – shall we say? – localized. I mean that it has its place in the thought of every Western man, of every European. It is very suggestive. As I listened to you, I could see in my mind's eye the beauty of the medieval cathedral, around which human life was moulded: 'the contemplative world of the Middle Ages . . . a sense of the intelligibility of the world, a moral sense, an intuition of an eternal destiny for the human being', and so on. It's true, we all carry this picture in us, we have grown up with it and it lasts, it continues to live in us in a certain way.

Nevertheless, it is only a partial picture, alien to a person from North or South America, and even more to an African, an Oriental, a man from the continent of Asia.

When the Council had to tackle the subject, 'The Church in the world of to-day', it had to be admitted that this 'human world' is made up of numerous different worlds, which, while close to each other, are from many points of view very distant from each other. However, this did not prevent the Council from defining 'the situation of man in the modern world' in a coherent and convincing way.

What is this world towards which we are moving?

I think that since the Council 'the situation of man in the modern world' has changed again, although the changes that it has undergone are situated in the context of one and the same era.

The nature of this world towards which we are moving – and which you see as 'devoid of structures' and still 'in a gaseous state' – proceeds from the unknown future which we confront.

We have reason to fear this future. We have reason to fear that the countenance it will unveil will be more terrible than all we know of the past.

You say that we are walking on the water, like Peter, whom Christ had ordered to leave his boat and walk across the waves to him.[1] But although faith is indispensable for walking on the water, we must constantly seek a form of faith adapted to a world that is being continually renewed, and not one adapted simply to a past that we have left behind for ever. It would in any case be difficult to identify ourselves with this world of days gone by, although we may admire it. We should find it difficult to live in a 'pre-Copernican' world, a 'pre-Einstein world' . . . or even a 'pre-Kantian' world.

I think the Council fulfilled its task in showing a face of Christian faith adapted to the world of to-day. And to the world of to-morrow.

But among the conciliar texts there is one which should not be forgotten: 'The Church also maintains that beneath all that changes there is much that is unchanging, much that has its ultimate foundation in Christ, who is the same yesterday, and to-day, and forever.'[2]"

1. Matthew 14:28–31. 'And Peter answered him, "Lord, if it is you, bid me come to you on the water." He said, "Come." So Peter got out of the boat and walked on the water and came to Jesus; but when he saw the wind, he was afraid, and beginning to sink he cried out, "Lord, save me." Jesus immediately reached out his hand and caught him, saying to him, "O man of little faith, why did you doubt?"'

2. *Gaudium et Spes*, 10

The reader will have noted the sentence about the world to come which could very well present a face 'more terrible than all we know of the past'; and even now we can see some of its features distorted by violence or livid from a sort of 'deathly plot' which makes us into people pitiless to unborn children, favourable to premature euthanasia and ready to lend an ear to every plea in favour of suicide, in conformity with the words of Scripture: 'They have made a friend of death'. Over all this floats an atomic threat whose destructive power is estimated at 4.5 tons of old-fashioned explosive per inhabitant of the planet. From a human point of view, this world, which reason does not suffice to bring to its senses, is travelling towards its destruction rather than towards glorious accomplishments.

Has it got one last chance of escaping the logic of death in which it is gradually being enmeshed?

"The world in which we live is deeply scarred by sin and death.

Your picture underlines the present extreme tension of the powers of sin and death, and the grave threats hanging over a world which, in spite of all the conquests of human genius, contains everything necessary to accomplish its own destruction. This world runs the risk of becoming an inhuman world; our century has furnished many reasons to fear it.

But at the same time it is a world redeemed; a world in which a love more powerful than sin and death has been manifested. This love is always present in it and never ceases acting in it.

This love is the *ultimate reality*.

Not only does it reveal the prospect of a fullness of life and goodness as the final end and meaning of the existence of man in God, but even in the world, *this* world, this love never ceases to transform the hearts and acts of man – of living man, of sinful man.

Our world is situated in time. It never ceases to tend to its end. But as long as it exists, this love, which is also merciful, will work tirelessly to make this human world ever more human.

I often answer you by referring to the Council. The phrase 'make this world more human' is repeated several times and in numerous similar forms in the constitution *Gaudium et Spes*, which is known as a pastoral constitution. To the best of my knowledge of the history of Vatican II, it was John XXIII who had the idea of rounding off the Council's magisterium with the constitution on the Church in the modern world.

I participated later in the preparatory work for this constitution. I think that in many a passage it reflects the situation of our world which, possibly as never before, looks both powerful and weak, capable of the best and the worst. It sees an opening towards freedom or servitude, progress or decline, brotherhood or hatred. These words are to be found in *Gaudium et Spes*. So are these: 'Man is growing conscious that the forces he has unleashed are in his own hands and that it is up to him to control them or be enslaved by them.'

So speaks the Council. If it is otherwise, if man does not realize, if he does not become sufficiently aware of what we have just said, that is, that the right deployment of the forces that he has set in motion *still* depends on him, then the Church's duty is certainly to remind him of it, never to relax her efforts to make this world 'more human'. And to bring closer to us the reign of justice, truth, freedom and love – this is and always has been part of the very essence of evangelization. Such are also the views of the pastoral constitution of Vatican II, an idea born in the heart and mind of Pope John in the last few months of his life."

Intelligence and pessimism form a depressing but solid combination. Discernment usually brings with it more tears than joy. Such is not the case with the Pope. The clarity of his judgements is well established, and yet his 'optimism' strikes all those who meet him (what there is left of mine is based solely on his presence at the head of the Church). Why? He had really replied already to this question in the preceding paragraphs: his mind constantly takes account of the totality of history – not just the fragment of an age that we are in the process of living through – from God's creative act to the final accomplishment of human destiny, from Genesis to the New Jerusalem, where love will at last be answered with love. He does not read history by episodes, a practice which invariably tends to the observation of failures. He takes it as a whole, last ends included, as Revelation invites us to read it, and he pushes its horizon back to the sun of ultimate truth, which for him illumines even the darkest stretches of humanity's slow and painful progress from this world, where it dies, to the next, where it will live.

I knew this, but I put my question all the same. Reading what he was to say, people will possibly be tempted to think that he missed the point. This was not so at all. His reply was that of humility, and it was dictated to him by his absolute confidence in the word of Christ. His 'optimism' is a brotherly variant of his act of faith.

"I have long liked to meditate on these words of Christ to the apostle Peter: 'Strengthen your brethren.' Luke alone reports them. We do not find them in either Matthew or Mark, who confine themselves to predicting Peter's denial and to describing this denial itself, which is recounted by all four evangelists. We read in Luke these words of Christ, uttered, it seems, in the night of Gethsemane or possibly on the road to the Mount of Olives: 'Simon, Simon, behold, Satan demanded to have you, that he might sift you like wheat . . . When you have turned again, strengthen your brethren.'[1]

I have often thought of these words, and even more of their whole context.

Christ says, 'Strengthen your brethren' to a man who had by no means shown himself to be strong, although he was sure that he would never disappoint his Master. Christ says to him, 'strengthen' them, and immediately afterwards responds to his firm assurance with the announcement of the disappointment that he is going to cause him. For Peter says, 'Lord, I am ready to go with you to prison and to death,' and Christ replies, 'I tell you, Peter, the cock will not crow this day, until you three times deny that you know me.'

Thus when Christ said, 'Strengthen your brethren,' he did not base this command on the particular qualities of Peter. Humanly speaking, Peter was not specially endowed to 'strengthen' the others, in spite of all his enthusiasm and good will. After the Resurrection, when Christ asks him three times, 'Do you love me more than these?', he does not hesitate to reply, in spite of the tragic night in the courtyard of the high priest, 'Lord, you know that I love you.' I think that he had in himself the guarantee needed to say so.

Note that he does not say, 'I love you more than these,' but simply 'I love you.' And he was not relying on his own conviction, but on what Christ knew of him: 'Lord, *you know* that I love you.'

On that last night, on the road to the Mount of Olives, the Lord had said to him: 'I have prayed for you that your faith may not fail.'

Well, it didn't fail. No, it didn't fail, in spite of the triple denial.

1. Luke 22:32

It didn't fail at Jerusalem, or Antioch, or Rome, or ever until his death on the Vatican hill, in the time of Nero.

Peter knew that if his faith 'did not fail', if he could 'strengthen his brethren', it was because the Master prayed for him, in an intercession that still continues. Moreover, in the hour of danger, when he was imprisoned by Herod and already condemned to death, the whole Church prayed for him, as we are told in the Acts of the Apostles. She prayed as if she guessed Christ's intentions.

Why am I telling you all this? Because I cannot reply in any other way to your question, which bothers me a little . . .

It is good that the Gospels tell the inner story of Simon Peter, the story of his human weakness in which the power of Christ is revealed.

And how much evidence there is of this same truth in the apostle Paul, evidence written, so to speak, in the living blood of his heart!"

# III

If the Pope did not travel, he would be accused of indifference to the world and human affairs; he would be reproached with living like a monarch in his palace and paying no attention to the age in which he lived. Since he does travel, he is reproached for travelling, for leaving Rome too often, for thereby neglecting the government of the Church in order to cultivate in the five continents a popularity which can only be a cheap popularity. For the very ones who speak only of 'the people' and 'masses' despise crowds when it is not hatred that assembles them. The same people who call on the Church to go out into the world blame her when she does so. The same people who are so concerned to make themselves heard by 'the men of this day and age' are irritated when 'the men of this day and age' meet to listen to the Pope. One could say a good deal about the mentality of these new pharisees who are only interested in the people in the abstract form which it assumes in ideological discussions, and who cannot find enough gibes with which to mock the 'ignorance' and 'naivety' of the simple hearts who rush to see John

Paul II pass by. I suspect them of being less concerned to fill the churches than to empty them of their last believers, whom they regard as ignoramuses, so that they remain in the hands of the connoisseurs of the pure doctrine, with which only these people are familiar.

However, it is not my purpose to analyse the élitist, gnostic state of mind of these curious evangelizers who speak Greek to the modern world, on the pretext that Latin is no longer understood, and who have only to utter the word 'festival' for everyone to understand that they are going to be bored to death. I preferred to learn from the Pope himself why he was in such a hurry to travel the world, as if little time were left to gather the flock of people of good will before the storm broke, as if some 'state of emergency' had been declared. People ascribe to him the saying, 'One must travel to live, and live to travel.' I asked him if he had really said it.

"I don't remember having done so, and I find it difficult to believe, but I may have done.

As for my journeys – made in the context of my apostolic ministry – this is the position.

First of all, it was not I who started this practice. It was started by two great predecessors, the Popes of Vatican II, especially by Paul VI. But John XXIII had already let it be understood that the Pope must not only be visited by the Church but that he himself must visit the Church. In spite of his eighty years he had taken the first step in this direction with the pilgrimage to the shrine of Our Lady of Loreto before the opening of the Council. As for Paul VI, travelling was part of the programme of his whole pontificate. I can still remember with what enthusiasm the Council fathers learned of his plan to make a pilgrimage to the Holy Land, at the end of the second session of the assembly. He could not have made a better start.

So I found this chapter in the history of the pontifical ministry already started. I was soon convinced that it was necessary to carry on with it. How could a relatively young Pope who in general[1] enjoyed good health not have taken over this duty and followed the

1. This 'in general' may be regarded to-day as an allusion tinged with humour to the Pope's stay in the Gemelli hospital. We shall see in the last chapter of this book how his vigorous constitution enabled John Paul II to recover three times in ten days from two operations and a virus infection.

example of an octogenarian Pope and a Paul VI of advanced years and delicate health?

The first time I had to make up my mind very quickly, because of the congress of Latin American bishops at Puebla, where they were counting on the presence of the Pope. As early as January 1979 I went to Mexico. Then I visited my own country on the occasion of the ninth centenary of the death of St. Stanislaus, for which I had long made preparations as Archbishop of Cracow. There followed other visits which I will not mention, since they are well enough known. If God permits, I shall accept most of the invitations I have received.

I have said all that to a certain extent to justify myself. Here now are the underlying reasons for these journeys.

I have to go back to my twenty years' experience as a bishop. During that period I used to attach special importance to parish visits. These visits, which in my view were essentially pastoral, were intended to help the communities enjoy a deeper experience of Christian unity and to feel at home, thanks to the presence of the bishop, in the Church as a whole – not just the local Church, but the universal Church. I emphasized this many times in the homilies which I had occasion to preach. For the pastors, these visits were also the occasion and the means of gathering their parishes more closely together, which is one of the basic functions of every shepherd of souls – to gather his community together. In the Mass, the third Eucharistic prayer proclaims this in very beautiful terms: that God may gather together his people from East and West, through Christ, in the power of the Holy Spirit. Thus as shepherd of souls, the priest must gather together the people of God in the name of Christ. This is even truer of the bishop. Here our first models are the apostles, especially St. Paul.

When, in 1976, I had occasion to preach the Easter retreat at the Vatican at the invitation of Paul VI, I spoke of parish visits as 'a particular form of pilgrimage to the sanctuary of the people of God'. I found this idea fully corroborated in the constitution *Lumen gentium*.

During the course of the retreat in the chapel of St. Matilda in the Vatican, I pictured the bishop on a pastoral visit to a parish. The parish is not only an administrative cell of his diocese; it is a community of the people of God participating in the triple function of Christ, of which we have already spoken, and bearing in itself, with all the human weaknesses, all the sins, all the failures, the attributes of the 'kingship' which Christ has conferred on it. One has to *feel* this kingship, this dignity, apparent in young people receiving the sacrament of confirmation, in married couples renewing in the bishop's presence the sacramental commitment of the marriage blessing, in the sick and old receiving their pastor in their homes or in hospital and recollecting themselves with him in prayer. This dignity, this royal aspect comes from Christ, who has conferred 'royalty and priesthood'[1] on the whole people of God. This is perceptible in these meetings in which the solemn atmosphere is nevertheless full of human warmth.

The more difficult the life of men, of families, of communities and of the world becomes, the more necessary it is for them to become aware of the presence of the Good Shepherd 'who lays down his life for the sheep'. The bishop visiting the parish communities is an authentic pilgrim who, on each of his visits, betakes himself to another sanctuary of the Good Shepherd.

The people of God is this sanctuary, the people that shares in the royal priesthood of Christ. And every man is this sanctuary, whose mystery is only illuminated and revealed in all its fullness 'in the mystery of the Word incarnate'.

There you have a first reply to your question."

The world is his parish. The people of God, or any fragment of the people of God, is a sanctuary of Christ. And every human being, too, *is a sanctuary*. That is why John Paul II calls his travels *pilgrimages*; that is why he kisses the soil of the countries in which he has just arrived; that is why, were there only left in the world one shepherd lost in the Andes, he would still go in search of him, for in his eyes this man would be the Church, this man would have received the investiture of Christ, this man would be sacred. This vision of humanity is not that of the prevailing ideologies, to which man is very far from being a tabernacle. But when a Pope goes out into the world with these ideas, dare anyone maintain that he is 'stealing the limelight'?

"Finding after Paul VI this policy of travelling well established, I continued to follow it because it fitted in with the ideas which I had formed during the preceding stage of my life. The notions of episcopal service put into effect at Cracow were just as valid in

1. Apocalypse 1:6

(198)

Rome for the pontifical ministry. The development of the means of communication created conditions particularly favourable to their application, and the need to which they correspond had become more and more explicit. It even seems to me that the life of the post-conciliar Church has changed this need into an imperative that is both a command and a moral obligation.

I feel very deeply the multiplicity of Churches in the one Church, a multiplicity that is not only quantitative but also qualitative, and results from a number of factors and circumstances. Is it not the task of Peter's successor to see that this Church, in her multiplicity, gathers round Christ in her visible unity? I thank Providence for opening to me so many paths towards the sanctuaries of the people of God; conscious of my unworthiness and weakness, I beg Providence to give me the strength to perform this service as it should be performed.

I shall add these words of the apostle Paul in his epistle to the Romans: 'For God is my witness, whom I serve with the spirit in the gospel of his Son, that without ceasing I mention you always in my prayers, asking that somehow by God's will I may now at last succeed in coming to you. For I long to see you, that I may impart to you some spiritual gift to strengthen you, that is, that we may be mutually encouraged by each other's faith, both yours and mine.'[1]

If I had to pick out any words in this letter, I should choose, 'I long to see you . . . that we may be mutually encouraged by each other's faith, both yours and mine.' I think these words really explain everything and answer your question.

You may point out that I have said nothing of the state of emergency of which you spoke. In my view, it would be better to speak of an 'urgent situation'. This would be closer to St. Paul and the Gospel."

Undertaken in this spirit, all the Pope's journeys are obviously important. However, some have attracted more attention than others – those, for example, to Brazil, Poland, France, Africa and Great Britain. The journey to Brazil, because, as we have already said, all the problems of the Church of to-morrow are already visible to-day in this huge country which, in thirty or forty years, may alone form half of Christendom. The journey to Poland, because many people think that Christianity will return to us one

1. Romans 1:9–12

day from the East, and everyone was curious to see the enthusiasm of a country where joys are few and which had felt tremendous pride in the election of John Paul II. The journey to Africa, where the Christian faith is discovering a new youth; the journey to Great Britain for reasons which I will explain later on; and finally the journey to France, for France can be read like an open book, since the French are in the habit of expressing themselves in plain language and of carefully legislating about everything, including the absurd, to such an extent that it is perhaps easier in France than elsewhere to form an idea of the state of people's minds. I asked the Holy Father if he shared this point of view. He was to answer me in general terms.

"I have just read an article in which the author tried retrospectively to sum up the results of the Council. One of his expressions struck me. For him, through Vatican II, the Church became, much more than before, 'a Church of the whole world'. I think this formula applies less to the pastoral constitution on the Church in the modern world than to the dogmatic constitution *Lumen gentium*, especially to the chapter dealing with the people of God.

All men are called to belong to the new People of God. This People therefore, whilst remaining one and only one, is to be spread throughout the whole world and to all ages in order that the design of God's will may be fulfilled: he made human nature one in the beginning and has decreed that all his children who were scattered should be finally gathered together as one. It was for this purpose that God sent his Son, whom he appointed heir of all things, that he might be teacher, king and priest of all, the head of the new and universal People of God's sons. This, too, is why God sent the Spirit of his Son, the Lord and Giver of Life. The Spirit is, for the Church and for each and every believer, the principle of their union and unity in the teaching of the apostles and fellowship, in the breaking of bread and prayer. The one People of God is accordingly present in all the nations of the earth, since its citizens, who are taken from all nations, are of a Kingdom whose nature is not earthly but heavenly.[1]

I have just quoted *Lumen gentium*. Developing its thought on the universal character of the Church, the Council then speaks not only

1. *Lumen gentium*, 13

of the Catholic community but of all those 'who have the honour to bear the fair name of Christians' and even of those who, although they have not yet received the Gospel, are nevertheless in various ways 'related to the People of God'. Paul VI's first encyclical takes the same line. In it the Church appears as a community of faith and salvation, seeking in the name of his faith the dialogue of salvation with all men.

In the last analysis, you did not so much ask a question as express an opinion about my travels, with a few observations which seem to me to be accurate enough.

Once again, these pilgrimages to the sanctuaries of the People of God which I carry out one after the other all have their own importance, for the precise reasons mentioned in *Lumen gentium* and in Paul VI's first encyclical; each of them serves in a certain way and to a certain extent to bring the Council to life; each of them expresses faith in the Church, which thanks to Vatican II has become particularly open and ready for dialogue. She has become aware of being the Church of the whole world. This expression certainly has nothing triumphalist about it; it only emphasizes the rôle of servant which is that of the Church, for everywhere and always she serves the Father, the Son and the Holy Spirit in their will to save. Everywhere – so obviously even where the Pope cannot travel."

John Paul II has already travelled to every part of the world. In Poland the happiness of a whole people could be read on their faces. This was perfectly reflected by the press and somewhat less perfectly by television, whose cameras remained for most of the time unfortunately trained (during his first visit) on an empty corner of the platform or an empty horizon.

If the welcome which the Pope received in Poland did not surprise anyone, the same cannot be said of the welcome which he received in Great Britain. The circumstances seemed unfavourable owing to the Falklands War, which might give the Pope's visit a significance which it did not possess. Well before the outbreak of the Anglo-Argentine conflict, some people predicted that the visit would be a failure, the somewhat stiff reserve ascribed to the British character not lending itself very well to collective demonstrations except in football grounds, and certain sectarians having made known their intention of spoiling the stay of the man whom they depicted as a sort of Antichrist from the impure Babylon on the banks of the Tiber. In addition, certain points of disagreement between Catholic and Anglican theologians (to set beside results which as a whole were remarkable), had just been made public, and this did not make things any easier. Everyone advised against the visit, and John Paul certainly seemed to hesitate right up to the last minute. It was only an apparent hesitation. In reality he does not hesitate; he lets his judgement ripen like a fruit, which he never picks too soon. When he felt the moment had come, he made known his decision to make the visit and at the same time his intention to go subsequently to the Argentine, which destroyed the argument based on the state of war. He did not want this first invitation from England to Rome, after a rupture of several centuries, to come to nothing; and if he had avoided or postponed it, people would have been quick to accuse him of practising only a superficial ecumenism. So he went, in order not to let slip a historical chance for a rapprochement between the Churches, and to plead in favour of a settlement of the Falkland conflict which would not aggravate the break between the Western democracies and Latin America (he was to speak in the same terms a little later on to President Reagan). In the event, all the pessimistic forecasts turned out to be wrong. The denouncers of the Antichrist gave vent only to a feeble buzz of disapproval, British reserve melted in the twinkling of an eye and soon the only typically British phlegm and sobriety on the route of the official procession were those of the Pope himself, who, so as not to upset the religious prerogatives of his hosts, made his blessings very restrained. His famous charisma (in the sense of that 'gift of communication' which is as difficult to define as to exercise) had come into play again.

On his return he told me that he was not expecting to find such Neapolitan warmth beside the Thames. He had found much to admire, in particular the skill of the organizers, who in Cardiff and Edinburgh had succeeded in containing the exuberance of his young audiences without in any way suppressing their spontaneity. After this trip one may observe the paradox that although the Catholic Church may have fewer doctrinal differences with the Orthodox Church than with the Anglicans, it is with the Anglicans that an understanding seems closest.

Whether in Britain or elsewhere, John Paul II's journeys have strange effects. In France, for example, his visit revealed the existence of a vast layer of underground Christianity, in the state, so to speak, of fossil energy, like oil in shale. Each of his speeches caused Christianity to spurt up like a gusher of crude oil, where it was generally thought that there was nothing. Yet all pastoral thinking has been based for over forty years on the idea that France, not to mention the world, is deeply de-Christianized and that the only thing to be done is to re-inject Christianity in small doses, with a big politico-social sweetener. The Pope's visit proved on the contrary that the French remain Christians, even if they no longer know much about their religion, and that, even when they belong to Marxist parties, it is still Christianity that most of them are looking for in these parties.

I asked the Pope if all this did not call for a change of strategy on the part of the Church.

"We are talking about the world, and for each of us there is a fragment of this human world which is properly his own. For you, of course, it is France; and so I listen to you, since I have less to say about it than you!

However, although France is not that part of the world which is mine, as it is yours, geography and especially bonds of history and culture have always made it close to me. It was already like that when the centre of 'my' universe was at Cracow, and it is the same now that it is in Rome.

When the time came for my pilgrimage to France, I set out for your country that I knew already with the wish to speak to it intimately, person to person.

My longest stay in France took place in the university holidays of 1947, in July and August. It was then that I read with great interest Godin's book, *France, pays de mission?*, and that I visited Father Michonneau's suburban parish. I also read Father Boulard's studies and had occasional contacts with the Mission de France. At Marseilles I had a short meeting with the community of Father Loew.[1] I took part in a *Semaine sociale*.[2]

---

1. Father Jacques Loew, a convert from Protestantism and a Dominican, was the first French 'worker-priest'. A doctor in Marseilles, he is the founder of the *Mission ouvrière Pierre-et-Paul* and of the *Ecoles de la foi*. He has written numerous books which are as luminous, strong and gentle as he is himself.

2. The *Semaines sociales* ('Social weeks') are an important aspect of Catholic action. They were launched in Lyons and take place every year.

Naturally I went to Lourdes, and I visited your cathedrals, whose Gothic splendour is one of the high points of art.

During this short but crowded stay, I was impressed by the evidence of the French priests, who were convinced of the de-Christianization of vast social strata in France, not only in working-class circles but even in the countryside. These visits and meetings filled me with esteem for the pastoral enterprises which I was permitted to study and with a certain admiration for these priests who go with total determination in search of a de-Christianized world, sometimes working in a factory to be closer to the working class which the Church has allowed to slip away from her.

In Paris, I realized that something remained of the meetings of days gone by. Of course, thirty years had passed and I had had new experiences. As the days went by, I was able to observe the sequels to what I had noted in 1947. In my memory there persists a sort of association of ideas with the shepherd in the Gospel who abandons ninety-nine sheep to go in search of the hundredth, which is lost . . .

If you are right, we must push to its extreme the parable of the Good Shepherd, who went off in search of the lost sheep. The parable tells us that, having found it, the shepherd put it on his shoulders and took it back to the ninety-nine sheep which, with it, formed the whole flock. Thus what counts is not simply to find the lost sheep, but to keep the whole fold intact.

It is perhaps in this direction that we shall find an indication of the 'strategy' of which you spoke."

Under the inspiration of the Gospel, the Holy Father was beginning to speak in parables. Carried away by his example, I felt a strong desire to say that to-day's shepherds often seemed to me less inclined to bring back the lost sheep on their shoulders than to set their flock loose and follow it to perdition. However, I did not say so.

We live in an age in which abstraction plays a considerable rôle, as both painting and ideology show in their own ways. Now it is clear that ideologies have largely proved their inability, not only to respond to the deep aspirations of man, but even to solve his material problems. Liberalism, based on the creative instinct, the individual initiative, the need to possess (or dominate), favours the production of wealth, but usually lacks justice; on the other hand, collectivism, in its urge to correct the inequalities which it calls injustices, before re-establishing them and sometimes aggravating them in a different social order, suppresses liberty. Will humans be eternally compelled to choose or suffer one or other of these two iniquities, one of which offends their moral sense while the other reduces them to silence? One day at Castel Gandolfo John Paul II gave me a real philosophical course on 'alienation' according to the successors of Marx, an extremely aggressive theory which has already made quite a few converts among Christians themselves, and on the cases of conscience which arise to-day for Western societies.

I remember asking him if it was possible to find or trace a new path between the errors with which the world is swarming and from which it is dying. But he was called away to an audience, and I was left alone with my question. Now I repeated it again: is there a *third way*?

"In the first part of your question you spoke to me of ideologies, in the second of the political systems based on these ideologies.[1] Your view of both is critical. The problem raised would need a book to deal with it fully. Obviously, there is an answer in the teaching of the Church, particularly in her social ethics; for the Church, it has long been a subject of concern.

When they propose their programmes, the ideologies base themselves on a certain conception of the world, which guides their social, economical and practical solutions. Amid them, the Church never ceases to proclaim man's vocation, both temporal and eternal, and she strives to treat economics and politics as functions of this vocation. Her voice may seem weak compared with the means of expression controlled by governments and by the ideologies which they represent.

Nevertheless, everyone is aware that the Gospel makes serious demands on man, both on the social and on the personal plane. In recalling these demands, the Church acts in the midst of men subject to the pressure of ideologies, in the midst of men subjected to specific régimes. These systems create in the life of the men of this age tensions and antagonisms through which one can discern the huge threat that weighs to-day on the whole of humanity, since

1. The term is used here in its current meaning of a conscious structure of ideas, not in the sense sometimes given to it of a collection of received values, admitted or accepted without examination by this or that civilization or social class.

they rely on military programmes and means of reciprocal destruction that could end in the self-extermination of man on this earth. It is not along this path that the truth is to be found. The gulf between the rich countries, at the pinnacle of technical and economic development, and the countries where people are dying of hunger, continually grows wider.

When one reads and meditates on the Gospel, one is certainly obliged to observe that the path of truth is there. It is there that is to be found the answer to the deep aspirations which you mentioned. In the Gospel we find all the principles of morality which, if put into practice, should free the lives of individuals and societies from the various forms of injustice, those arising out of economic exploitation and those that violate the just freedom of the individual.

Does this mean that the Gospel and Christianity constitute the third way? I do not think so. The third way should be of the same sort as the two others, and this is not the case. The Gospel is not an ideology. No political, social or economic system limited by its nature to the temporal corresponds to it. The Gospel is a different way. Based on the truth of man as such, the Gospel is in permanent conflict with the ideologies which wish at any price to be stronger and more decisive than it. With the help of their abundant means, they succeed to a large extent. The Gospel is the word of Christ, passed on by poor means, which do not prevent it from being a 'road', even where its voice does not seem able to make itself heard. The Gospel is a path to which none of the human paths is alien.

When the wide paths traced by the ideologies turn out to be dead ends and offer no way out, the path of the Gospel remains open; intended for men, it awaits men. All those who are converted from the bottom of their heart find it.

As for the Church, the guardian of the Gospel, she wishes to be man's servant. That is why she asks herself what can be retained, for man's good, from these paths into which ideologies, systems and régimes have led him. The Church never ceases to ask the supreme Wisdom and Providence what can be saved from all this for the real good of man. For the Church writes her truth on the curving, muddled lines of history, those tangled lines on which man gradually rediscovers this truth, not without the hardest and most painful tensions and experiences."

At this point, an incidental question. Among the régimes in force in the world of to-day, some seem to have arisen out of the natural development of the forces exerted for some centuries by human genius, forces more or less controlled by reason and disciplined by law; the others are the product of a certain *a priori* conception of the world and of history. It has become a matter of course to label the former 'capitalist régimes' and the latter 'socialist régimes'. Now can one in fact define Western societies as 'capitalist' without giving economics the value of an absolutely primary principle and without thereby becoming involved in Marxist logic, from which no one is ever known to have successfully escaped, contrary to the notions of good souls who imagine they can reconcile it with their personal beliefs?

The Holy Father seized in particular on that part of my question which alluded to the actual priority accorded to economics by the materialism common to contemporary societies, whatever their basic ideology. This led him to reflect once again on the person, his rights and his relations with the material universe.

"In your question I see rather a diagnosis of the state of our civilization, especially of our Western civilization. It seems sometimes as if we need to go back over two centuries and to start to rebuild this civilization, in order to be able to implement the real content of the individual's code of rights and to incorporate in it the rights of human communities: on one level, the rights of the family, and on another, the rights of the nation. I'm simplifying! And in any case history does not allow this kind of revision or 'second thoughts'. History does not develop backwards. As one of your writers has remarked: 'History does not offer second helpings.'

Yet, if I express myself in this way, it is because the reversal of the right relationship between man and matter, and between the person and the thing, goes back at least as far as that! In this phase of history, man has made a tremendous effort to dominate the world, but at the same time he has made himself into an 'epiphenomenon' of material relations and economic laws, into an object of historical materialism. Far from subordinating the world of things to himself, he lets himself be subjected to it; he even does it in a programmed and 'scientific' way.

The real liberation of man demands profound changes in the modes of thinking, evaluating and acting that the civilizations based on materialism impose on humanity. Meanwhile, the interpretation and realization of the rights of man come up against the fundamental, pre-existing obstacles of a liberal and individualistic type, or on the contrary of an anti-individualistic and, strictly speaking, totalitarian type. It must also be understood that systems assign different meanings to the words."

Chateaubriand said in his day: 'In every age, the mission of the Popes has been to maintain or vindicate the rights of man.' In a very short time John Paul II has become in popular opinion 'the Pope of human rights', and it is true that he has never ceased to recall them, not only from Rome but in all the countries which have opened their gates to him, and even before governments who are not above reproach on this subject. People accordingly expect him to proclaim right and justice on every occasion – for they have never so badly needed to be defined. But I wanted to know where these rights came from that are proclaimed, ratified, invoked and violated, and what their counterpart was.

"Everyone knows that the International Declaration of the Rights of Man was devised after the Second World War. You would think that man has to pass through the most painful experiences finally to discover these apparently obvious principles and truths which form the code of a healthy conscience, or of natural law, to use the sort of language that people do not like to listen to these days. The most tragic experience of our century, with the cruelties of 'total' war, the extermination of tens of millions of people, the frightful experiments in the death camps, the programmes of genocide, the explosion of the first atomic bomb – this terrible experience must to some extent have cleared the path to the codification of the rights of man. People must have understood after this tragedy that at the centre of the dangers which threaten us there stands first of all man himself. People must have also understood that the renewal of the nations and of the whole human family must be based on man in all his truth and dignity. The effort to repair the evil, to re-establish peace between nations, continents and systems must be based on the objective rights to which man is entitled – for the sole reason that he is man.

It cannot be denied that, in the tangled web of contemporary history, the proclamation of the Declaration was an important event, a sort of indication that the right path had been found again.

The Declaration has certainly not solved all problems; it has not crushed all the various forms of evil exhibited by individuals, communities, nations and continents, but it cannot be denied that it has become the source of a certain amount of light, a point of reference and of recourse, some kind of witness to the just priority of man and morality in a materialist world.

As the guardian of the Gospel, the Church wishes to serve man; she has often proved it. Accordingly, she welcomed the proclamation of the charter and the foundation of the United Nations Organization, which adopted this charter as its basic document and foundation stone. It would be difficult not to note the explicit points of similarity between this great initiative and the teaching of Vatican II, especially *Gaudium et Spes* and other texts like *Pacem in terris* and *Populorum progressio*.

That said, neither the adoption of the Declaration nor the efforts of the UN and its dependent organizations such as the FAO and Unesco have been able to prevent the world filling with dangers, tensions from increasing and the rights of man from being flouted in different ways in different areas.

Finally, it should be added – since you spoke of 'counterparts' – that the Gospel, which is certainly an important source of the rights of man, equally implies the demands that man must impose on himself and of which he must continually be reminded, so that the moral balance of his existence does not waver. It is enough to recall verses like 'Whatever you wish that men would do to you, do so to them,' or again, 'As you did it not to one of the least of these, you did it not to me.'[1] How many similar verses there are! Thus at the base of all the rights of man there is an objective ethical order, including, for every man, the right and the duty to demand from himself his just measure of humanity."

An attractive formula, but the fact remains that in many cases men seem inclined rather to a generous measure of inhumanity, and that goes for the lands where the Biblical religions were born and where people seem to have no suspicion that the secret of all true peace is concealed in these words of the Gospel: 'But I say to you, Love your enemies.'

"We have already emphasized, I think, the extreme importance of these words of Christ, though I forget at exactly what point in these conversations.

In any case, for the world which is ours and which we call 'our world', for this world in which we live and in which future

---

1. Matthew 7:12 and 25:45

generations will live, it is of capital importance to eliminate the idea of the struggle against man as a necessity and principle, at whatever ideological level it may be, as a way of settling problems between individual persons and nations. I am speaking of the struggle conducted against man with the intention of annihilating him or of subjecting him to establish some new power.

I repeated this several times, in particular at Saint-Denis, during my visit to Paris. I'll look for the speech. Of course, there is no question of conceding to quietism.[1] To fight is often a moral necessity, a duty. It shows strength of character and it can develop authentic heroism. 'The life of man on this earth is a struggle,' says the Book of Job – man has to confront evil every day and to struggle for the good. True moral good is not easy; it has continually to be acquired by conquest, in oneself, in others, and in social and international life. 'Fight the good fight,' writes St. Paul to Timothy.

There is a wide area of events and actions where combat merges with justice, and truth with love.

However, there is a tremendous danger of this area of struggle becoming permeated, under different forms, by hatred, hostility, alienation, contempt for man, the desire for destruction, everything that tramples under foot the dignity of man on the pretext that he is on the wrong side of the barricades.

When Christ says, 'Love your enemies,' he seems to be demanding at least this: do not allow hatred, whatever mask it may wear and however strong it may be, to become a motive force and to be made into the principle and main imperative of policies.

This is of absolutely central importance for the world to-day – as it was yesterday and will be tomorrow."

Before the visit to France – to which the reference to the talk at Saint-Denis brought us back – people said in the East that the Pope would doubtless be warmly welcomed in France 'except by the workers, the young and Unesco'.

Well, at Saint-Denis communication with the working-class public was immediate, which showed that if, as is often said, 'the Church has lost the working class', the loss has not been irrepar-

1. The doctrine of the Spanish theologian Molinos, fairly widespread in the seventeenth century, particularly in France, thanks to Mme Guyon. It advocated a rather resigned sort of contemplative passivity.

able, even supposing that it has in fact occurred. At Unesco John Paul's speech made a vivid impression on the audience, which did not consist solely of practising Catholics; and finally, in the Parc des Princes, the enthusiasm of the young people completely broke up the programme for the evening. To these audiences, which seem to have few points in common, John Paul spoke in exactly the same terms directly inspired by the Book from which all his thinking springs – with the necessary adaptations, but without the smallest demagogic variation, without the slightest concession. If the Christian message, which receives such a poor reception when it is daubed with sociology or repainted in the abstract style, does so well when unadulterated, is this not a sign that what the world desperately awaits is nothing other than the Gospel?

"Since you speak of Saint-Denis, I have found the homily to which I referred yesterday. Here is the passage that I wanted to quote:

'The World of human work must be built on moral strength; it must be a world of love, not of hatred. A world of creation, not of destruction. Human work is deeply inscribed with the rights of man, of the family, of the nation, of humanity. The future of the world depends on respect for these rights.

'Does this mean that the fundamental problem of the world of work is not justice and the struggle for social justice? On the contrary, it means that the reality of human work cannot be separated from this justice and this noble fight . . . However, this hunger for justice, this ardour to fight for truth and moral order in the world are not, cannot be hatred, nor a source of hatred in the world. They cannot be changed into a programme of struggle against man, simply because he happens to be, so to speak, "on the other side". This struggle cannot be transformed into a programme of destruction of the adversary; it cannot create social and political mechanisms centred on collective egoisms that grow more and more violent, powerful, murderous, ready to destroy without scruple whole nations, social groups that are economically or culturally weaker, by depriving them of their independence and national sovereignty and by exploiting their resources . . .'"

Before answering my question the Holy Father was going to recall me to moderation. He has no taste for compliments; he hands few out and does not like to receive them. He had already accused me several times of presenting him in too favourable a light, of making him 'the hero of a romance'. I should prefer to say a romantic hero, but that would not please him any better.

"There are more observations than questions in your remarks. That's natural when the subject is France, which is your domain, your 'share of the world'; you are at home, so to speak, and I listen to what you say about me and try to distinguish what seems right from what I find excessive and cannot accept or approve. If through all those meetings at Saint-Denis, Unesco and the Parc des Princes, a certain amount of good was accomplished, then I quite simply give thanks for it to God, the dispenser of all gifts, and to the Holy Spirit, who acts not only on the heart of him who speaks but also, and to the same degree, on the hearts of those who listen. This does not of course mean that one needs to make no effort to communicate!

In any case, it is clear that these three meetings took place in three distinct *milieux*, each of which represented a different and specific dimension of the world of to-day. And each time, I was somewhat surprised by the reactions of the audience and by what radio engineers would call the quality of the reception. At Unesco, for example, I was amazed by the way in which the gathering responded to certain key thoughts or observations which my experience has led me to regard as essential. I felt that there exists in the world a tremendous agreement, if not always a conscious one, a wide consensus not only on certain values but also about certain threats. The people in the audience came from countries all over the world, from every continent. I had the feeling that it was the representatives of the young nations and the new states who reacted most warmly to my words on the meaning of culture and the conditions for its flowering. That gave me a good deal to think about. The same is true of the basic fact itself, namely the atmosphere of this meeting about the problems of culture. This, too, seems to me to be symptomatic: culture always implies a certain protest by man against his reduction to the state of an object. It signifies the march towards a world where man can achieve his humanity in the transcendence proper to him, which calls him to truth, good, beauty.

So far as the Parc des Princes is concerned, we have already spoken of it twice. To your question whether 'what the world desperately awaits is the Gospel', I reply emphatically 'yes'. And the stronger the denial, the stronger and more deliberate the opposition, the greater the expectation."

The principles according to which human beings – if they were more human – ought to behave have been explained and repeated by John Paul II throughout this book. The rest is events, and events have the grave defect of being forgotten even more quickly than books. Newspapers swallow a topical event like a boa-constrictor swallowing a rabbit: at first it fills their mouths and nearly dislocates their jaws, then it gradually disappears without trace. However, there is a certain kind of topicality which never completely disappears, or reappears from time to time in the same generally hideous form, and that is the sin against humanity. A good example is anti-semitism and its twin, racism. After so much suffering, is it really over? What can the Church tell us to-day about this recurring nightmare?

"At Auschwitz, on 7 June 1979, during the Mass concelebrated on the site of the camp, I invited the congregation to stop with me in front of the inscription commemorating a people whose sons and daughters had been doomed to total extermination. The sons and daughters of a people descended from Abraham, the 'father of our faith', according to Paul of Tarsus.

A people which had received from Yahweh the commandment, 'Thou shalt not kill,' was killed.

Need one quote St. Paul again? 'As regards election [the children of Israel] are beloved for the sake of their forefathers. For the gifts and the call of God are irrevocable.'[1] 'They are Israelites, and to them belong the sonship, the glory, the covenants, the giving of the law, the worship, and the promises; to them belong the patriarchs, and of their race, according to the flesh, is the Christ, who is God over all, blessed for ever.'[2] St. Paul's recognition of the election of the Jews does not prevent him from speaking in these terms to Christians: 'For as many of you as were baptized in Christ have put on Christ. There is neither Jew nor Greek, there is neither slave nor free, there is neither male nor female; for you are all one in Christ Jesus. And if you are Christ's, then you are Abraham's offspring: heirs according to promise.'[3]

1. Romans 11:28–29
2. Romans 9:4–5
3. Galatians 3:27

The declaration *Nostra aetate* energetically condemns anti-semitism and the acts of hatred which proceed from it: 'The Church reproves every form of persecution against whomsoever it may be directed. Remembering, then, her common heritage with the Jews and moved not by any political consideration, but solely by the religious motivation of Christian charity, she deplores all hatreds, persecutions, displays of anti-semitism levelled at any time or from any source against the Jews.'[1]

So much for anti-semitism.

As for racism, this is what we read further on in the same Council document: 'Therefore the Church reproves, as foreign to the mind of Christ, any discrimination against people or any harassment of them on the basis of their race, colour, condition in life or religion. Accordingly, following the footsteps of the holy apostles Peter and Paul, the sacred Council earnestly begs the Christian faithful to "conduct themselves well among the gentiles" and if possible, as far as depends on them, to be at peace with all men and in that way to be true sons of the Father who is in heaven.'[2]

That is the voice of the Council. Is the 'sin' of which you speak in process of disappearing or of starting again? We have to return to one of my earlier answers about loving one's enemies. There is no other way of radically eliminating the attitudes, which rightly worry you. There is no other way but the commandment to love our neighbour."

# IV

This last conversation about 'the world' took place at Castel Gandolfo, in the library of the private apartments, towards the end of a summer afternoon. The room, built jutting out above Lake Albano, has windows on three sides. To my right, the setting sun, itself invisible, shone through the pine trees, and in the depths of a big bluish void tiny boats criss-crossed the lake. The Holy Father

1. *Nostra aetate*, 4
2. *Nostra aetate*, 5

looked at them for a few moments with a touch of nostalgia. The only remaining physical exercise he is allowed is to dive into the swimming-pool in the park, where everyone, be it said, bathes before or after him, from the Swiss guards to the palace chamberlain. The evening came noiselessly, darkening the hills, and the whole conversation was to be a long lesson in serenity, temperance and love of one's neighbour. I know that what I have just said will not please the Holy Father. There is one subject on which we differ, and that is himself. He finds me too 'papalist'. He seems to have absolutely no suspicion of what he represents for Christians who trembled for a Church threatened in her doctrinal unity and deserted by a silent stampede of faithful who no longer knew what they should or should not believe. So disorientated that they could no longer reply to the major question of their faith, to Christ's fundamental question, 'And you, who do you say that I am?', they had sought safety in flight. Then this man came, solidly rooted in unshakable faith, who spoke to Christians in a language inspired by a sort of solar vision of the Church which has warmed many hearts. He began to revive the tissue of Christianity cell by cell. He has woven round the world a network of good will which makes him, unarmed though he may be, a power equal to the greatest powers on earth – powers that history will have shrouded in darkness when the Church is still shining beyond the shores of time.

Does he know this? In any case, he does not like people to talk to him about it, and when I told him that the subject did not figure on the day's agenda he sighed, 'Thank goodness for that.' However, he cannot be unaware that he came just at the right moment to utter that resounding 'Be not afraid!' which touched people to the quick in a century which, as the year 2000 approaches, sees terrors comparable to those of the year 1000 – minus the religious fear, plus the apprehension of a deliberate or accidental apocalypse. That exhortation of John Paul II at the dawn of his pontificate was taken by many as an encouragement to moral resistance and to bear witness, and by some – not many, it is true – as a paternal way of reassuring anxious minds. The Pope himself had followed it up with its correct interpretation: 'Be not afraid to open your frontiers, to open the doors of your life to Christ.' Whatever their interpretation, no words could have suited our time better, for this century is afraid, and its innumerable fears drive it to every kind of excess. It is afraid of war, a fear justified in a dialectical universe that knows no other law but that of the confrontation of opposites, but a fear that produces, in the West at any rate, those 'pacifist' movements which aggravate the risk of conflict by giving the various hatreds at work good reasons for persevering in their enterprises. On this point John Paul II was to remind me that the reasoning of the Church on the subject of peace is by no means that of the pacifist, since the Church does not separate peace from respect for the rights of man and for the rights of peoples. There is another sort of fear, more widespread than one would think: fear of reality, which drives many young people to drugs, so much so that it will soon be possible to invert Karl Marx's famous dictum and say that opium has become the religion of the people. The same fear leads adults to take refuge from reality in front of the cinema or television screen, which reflects the outside world as fiction, dream or nightmare, switched on or off at the touch of a button. Fear of the modern world unleashes fanaticism, as if the fanatic were trying to take refuge in his past, like the child who, according to psychoanalysis, seeks to return to its mother's womb. States are afraid of each other, not without reason, but they are also afraid of their own citizens or subjects, whom they keep imprisoned or drugged, for fear that the individual wakes up and says 'no' to the system. For in the depths of his dungeon the individual has not completely forgotten the promises of eternity which he received in days gone by and which in principle should make him for ever unreceptive to counterfeits of the absolute.

The great fears of the century are well known – fear of the future, imaginary pictures of which are no longer popular, fear of the present with all its violence; even fear of the past in so far as people fear nothing so much as to appear out-of-date; and a quite new fear of science, which in spite of all its benefits is beginning to worry people more than it comforts them. But alongside these big fears there are little ones that do no less harm. I cited to the Holy Father the fear of looking ridiculous to contemporary rationalists, a fear which pushes certain Christians, some of them in Holy Orders, to deny more or less skilfully their traditional beliefs, like young upstarts ashamed of their old mother in front of their new smart friends. I also mentioned the fear of commitment – I mean lasting commitment – whether in the priesthood, in which innovators advocate ordination for a period renewable by mutual agreement, or in marriage, whose hazards have given obliging ecclesiastics the idea of the 'trial marriage', in which the boy is not obliged to keep his promise and the girl promises nothing. Then there is the fear of not seeming to be sufficiently to the left, of which Péguy said that it would never be known 'how many acts of cowardice it had caused Christians to commit'. But the Holy Father, as we know, rejects these divisions between Left and Right, between conservatism and radicalism, which in his view should be avoided at any price. For him, the faith is to be lived with simplicity, and 'following the Gospel does not consist in choosing between what is ahead of the times and what is behind them, but in serving the truth.' Of all the minor fears which I had just enumerated, the fear of commitment is the one that most engaged his attention.

"This, too, comes, like several of the disorders which you have mentioned, from a loss of the sense of life. People no longer see life as a whole, which implies a choice and a direction. They see it in successive stages, without seeing further than the end of one period and the start of the next – if even these are noticed! But one has to commit oneself totally. The religious life and married life are two varieties of an absolute commitment of this sort. Unfortunately to-day people lack a clear vision of the finality of human existence. It is a real disease, a weakness, perhaps even a sin against the spirit. One does not live in the same way before God, and before the void."

The Pope lives in the presence of God, without the shadow of a doubt, and I see nothing that could distract him from his vigil. He answered all the fears that I lined up before him with the response of faith: God wishes all these men who simultaneously build and destroy the world to be saved and to attain the knowledge of the truth. Whether they know it or not, they are all writing the history of salvation, which is the soul of their common destiny. 'Be not afraid!' he says. But what about himself? Is he never afraid? Is there nothing that he fears?

"From the beginning of this conversation it has been easy to see from my answers what my fears are. We live between fear and hope. The Gospel is a hope for this world, where the Kingdom of God is already being realized. We must fear and hope. And be not afraid to hope."

As it has been possible to observe more than once, in John Paul II confidence in God engenders a confidence in man to which the virtue of hope brings, where necessary, if I dare say so, the assistance of religion. The vigour of his mind, instead of revealing to him in this world only reasons for bitterness and consternation, leads him on the contrary to seek any good that may still exist in the bad, and the less bad elements in the worst.

This rare disposition of mind does not make him in any way subject to illusions. It does not hide from him any aspect of the hardest realities – with which in any case he soon became acquainted in his short family life. But all his thoughts find their conclusions and are resolved in Christ, whose light illumines his own intelligence.

However, while he spoke as a man of peace about a world which is not peaceful, I thought of the wars that will not end, of the violence which struck the Pope himself, of the ubiquitous lies which threaten like noxious weeds to stifle the truth, and finally of pathetic, hateful, suffering humanity which, in the view of the believer, has been entrusted to him. I thought also of Christ calling on Peter to 'feed his sheep', currently assailed by wolves in various parts of the world. And since prayer is the only weapon employed by this Pope, I asked him one last question which summed up many others, and which was to receive the shortest answer in this dialogue. I asked him what his prayer for the world was, and he replied:

"I call on Mercy. Yes, I call on Mercy."

# THE
# ASSASSINATION
# ATTEMPT

# I

She is Polish, lives for most of the year in Rome and examines people and things with a sharp and candid eye that reveals to her what many others do not see. Unless she is prevented by her official duties – and they have to be really pressing – she never misses an audience.

I was near her, in the 'Polish corner', on the day, four months after the attempted assassination of 13 May 1981, when John Paul II appeared again for the first time in St. Peter's Square, standing in the same little white vehicle to travel through the crowd by exactly the same route that had been interrupted a few months earlier. In the same way, an airman who has had a crash starts to fly again as soon as possible to shake off the hold of an unpleasant memory.

In our 'Polish corner' I think we were both trembling. It was not fear, but a sort of retrospective horror at the thought of the crime perpetrated there in the midst of a happy, sunny family gathering – a crime which had made me write almost despairingly the following day about a world through which Cain still stalks, bearing on his forehead the mark that makes him invulnerable.

So she was there on 13 May at five o'clock in the afternoon, and, like a general describing a battle to his guests by moving the cups and teaspoons about on the tablecloth, she arranged on her work table the books and anything else that came to hand to simulate the scene, the basilica, the colonnade, and the railings that divide the square into enclosures like paddocks separated by paths.

'This is the armchair, the Holy Father's throne, opposite the central avenue. To the left of the façade, under the big clock, *l'arco delle campane*, The Arch of Bells: that's where the Pope emerges from the Vatican.

'That day, exceptionally, the crowd was not very numerous, nor were the Poles, and I took advantage of this to approach the railing along the road.

'When the Pope arrived in his white jeep, you know, the one that we saw just now and that people here call the *papamobile*, his face was completely relaxed, pink and smiling. His eyes were as clear as a child's, and I thought, "How young he looks! How handsome he is!" He wasn't looking in my direction, but into the distance, towards the back of the square. He passed, he went round the obelisk by this avenue, once, then a second time. As I couldn't see him any longer I sat down. Next to me a lady from Cracow whom I didn't know kept talking to me all the time. I wasn't listening to her; I was following the Holy Father's progress by the crowd's applause, and every now and then I could see him at the end of an avenue.

'Well, this is what happened. This is the colonnade, with a Red Cross ambulance always there for people overcome by the heat or for any other reason; and these are the columns in front of the Bronze Door.'

This is the central door of the Vatican; at the top of the steps stands a Swiss guard with a halberd who is probably the most photographed man in the world after the Pope.

'The lady from Cracow was still talking. Everything was quiet. To judge by the noise of the applause, the white jeep must have been between the Bronze Door and the ambulance.'

The assassin, after asking which was the best place to see the Pope, had reached the railing.

'Suddenly I heard the detonations. The shots. In the convent where I live, bells are always ringing to call one or other of the guests or nuns to the telephone or the parlour; everyone has her own code – mine's "three, two, one" – so I have acquired the habit of counting subconsciously, and I counted the shots like bell-rings: one, two, three, four. Five! I heard five shots; I don't know why, there weren't five. At that moment all the pigeons in the square flew up. I had already realized that it was an assassination attempt, for I was always afraid that something would happen, and yet I thought, although I knew what it was, "Who dares to shoot at pigeons in the presence of the Pope?" For I didn't want to admit the reality; I didn't want to hear my own thoughts. Then I asked the lady from Cracow, as if with the hope that she would give me a different explanation from the one I wanted to evade.

'"What was it?" She replied: "What?" She was talking so much that she hadn't noticed anything. And suddenly the crowd which a moment before had been applauding and showing its joy lapsed into a sort of stupor.

'I don't know how many people there were. Twenty thousand

perhaps. And after the pigeons had flown up nothing more was to be heard but a huge sigh, a sort of groan from the crowd.

'Then it was uproar. Guards ran up, the people massed on the other side of the square. I tried to see what was happening and I noticed the white jeep retracing its route. Since then I have hated that car. It was coming back very quickly and I saw the Pope supported by Don Stanislaus, as you may have seen him in the photographs. His face was completely white and I thought he was dead. He was in that inert attitude of pictures of Christ being taken down from the cross, in which the whole body is slumped in the arms carrying it. He was peaceful, with something like a smile, but I said to myself that the dead often smiled like that.

'Then I had to sit down, and although I weep easily I wasn't weeping. I had the feeling that the whole of St. Peter's Square was slowly sinking with us, that everything was falling into the void – the open space, the crowd, all the statues on the colonnade, whose baroque gestures seemed to indicate fright and disapproval. Since that day I have loved them. The pain I get in my side when I become excited started up and hurt me a great deal. Everyone around me had gone pale, and in the avenue the faces of the shocked guards were bloodless. One of them near me had a face the colour of chalk under his black hair and I wondered if he was going to faint. No. He was weeping.'

There were shouts and sobs. By this crime a whole people felt wounded in its noblest sentiments, which make it particularly welcoming and attentive to those who entrust themselves to its hospitality.

'Now, imagine the square. The armchair, the throne of the Holy Father was there. No, here. My compatriots, some two or three hundred of them perhaps, had brought from Poland a picture of Our Lady of Czestochowa, who in Poland is always there when something happens. So they had brought this copy with them, not a very good one, as a matter of fact, and they put it on the ground against the armchair. A gust of wind blew it over, and everyone could see what was written on the back: "May Our Lady protect the Holy Father from Evil." Then the Poles wedged the picture on the armchair in place of the Holy Father, and immediately people came up and began to pray.

'No one knew anything. I couldn't say how much time passed before a priest eventually came to announce that the Holy Father was only wounded, that no vital organ had been hit, and it was true; but he didn't say that the wounded man was at death's door through losing over six pints of blood, which is fatal. Then the Poles, who had stood up to listen, knelt down again with the bishops and the whole crowd – it was magnificent – and no one left the square until night fell and the news was better.'

# II

If it is difficult to get into St. Peter's Square on audience days, it is quite as difficult to get out of it, and the assassin was caught. It was soon learnt that he was a known Turkish agitator, that he had already killed some one in his own country, and that he had only given up the idea of killing the Queen of England because he had remembered in time the Koran's directions about the treatment of women. He simply had to assassinate some one for reasons known to himself alone, and his deliberately or involuntarily confused explanations to the court enlightened no one. If the police knew anything about his real motives they kept it to themselves. Their communiqués were laconic, the enquiry was extremely swift and the trial very brief. The defendant seemed to expect the intervention of some mysterious and all-powerful *deus ex machina*, who did not show up. After reconstructing the curiously complicated itinerary which had brought him to Rome, and after hearing his demands (he wanted his case to be heard in the Vatican, where this sort of affair is not dealt with) and the statements of a few witnesses, who could shed little light on anything, his judges sent him to prison and he disappeared there with his secret, if he had one, which I doubt. I think he was one of these terrorists organized in little groups drunk on macabre dialectic who have been floating about in Europe since the nineteenth century, in the void left first by the disappearance of old structures, then by the slow collapse of morality in the democracies. But of course there are other hypotheses.

Neither the victim nor his entourage having been called upon to give evidence, since the court saw no point in issuing useless subpoenas, much that is correct and much that is incorrect has been said and written about the actual circumstances of the crime. For example, it is not true that the Holy Father asked, 'Why?' or 'Why me?' during his journey to the hospital. It is an idle question. Good attracts evil, and when Abel's pure fidelity attains a certain degree of splendour, his brother takes up arms in the shadows.

But it was necessary to satisfy history, which is sometimes interested in the facts, and no one knows these better than the Pope's private secretary. He was in the jeep. He did not leave his master – I use the word in the scriptural sense – day or night, until the latter was completely cured and it became necessary to send the secretary himself on convalescence, since he was losing his strength as quickly as his patient was regaining his.

Don Stanislaus, or *Monsignore Stanislao*, as he is called in Rome, is a taciturn man. Confidence, which he does not waste, gives him a sprightliness which he gladly allows to go as far as humour, but no further. The intervention of the Pope was needed to induce him to break the vow of silence which he seems to have added to his natural discretion. Here is his story, to the best of my recollection. The emotion is to be found between the lines; it is there all right.

'On 13 May the Holy Father had lunched with Professor Lejeune, his wife and another guest. The audience began punctually at five o'clock, in a perfectly orderly fashion. Nothing foreshadowed what was going to happen. Then, when the Pope was going round the square for the second time and approaching the Bronze Door, the Turk Mehemet Ali fired at him, wounding him in the stomach, the right elbow and the index finger of the left hand. In my view, two bullets were fired, but there are different opinions on this point. One grazed the index finger before going through the abdomen. I was sitting as usual behind the Holy Father, and the bullet, in spite of its force, fell between us in the car, at my feet. The other one injured the right elbow, seared the skin and went on to wound other people.

'What did I think? No one thought that such a thing was possible and I did not understand immediately what had happened. Was it an explosion underneath the car? The noise had been deafening. The nun who is the Pope's housekeeper was looking down at the square from the height of the palace, and she heard it. All the pigeons flew up. Naturally I soon realized that some one had fired.

But who? And I saw that the Holy Father was hit. He was tottering, but there was no sign of blood or a wound on him.

'Then I asked him, "Where?"'

'He replied, "In the stomach."'

'I asked him again, "Does it hurt?"'

'He answered, "Yes."'

'Standing behind the Holy Father, I supported him so that he did not fall. He was half sitting, leaning on me in the car, and that is how we reached the ambulance, in front of the first-aid post.

'At the time of . . . the accident there was a doctor in the ambulance. The decision to leave was taken immediately, to avoid confusion and possibly a fresh attempt. I had only one thought – hospital, and it had to be the Gemelli hospital. For two reasons: it was ready for such an eventuality, and in a conversation after his election the Holy Father had said that if he ever needed medical attention he was to be sent to hospital like anyone else and that the hospital could be the Gemelli.'

Thus the hospital was ready to receive the Pope at any moment, and the decision to go there was taken immediately. No one knew how far the Pope's life was in danger or even what his wounds were.

He was moved twice, first into an ambulance which was not equipped with oxygen, then into another with the necessary apparatus, and this one took him to hospital.

'The Holy Father was not looking at us. His eyes were closed, he was in great pain and he kept repeating short exclamatory prayers. If I remember correctly, it was mainly: "Mary, my mother! Mary, my mother!"'

'Dr. Buzzonetti and a male nurse, Brother Camillo, were with me in the ambulance. It went very fast, without any police escort. Even the siren stopped working after a few hundred yards. The journey, which normally takes half an hour, took eight minutes, and that in Roman traffic!

'I didn't know if the Holy Father was still fully conscious. He was in intense pain and from time to time repeated a prayer. It is not true that he said, "Why me?" or that he formulated any reproach. Nothing like that. He uttered no word of despair or resentment; simply words of profound prayer springing from great suffering.

'Later, the Holy Father told me that he had remained conscious until we reached the hospital, that it was only there that he had lost consciousness and that the whole time he had been convinced that his wounds were not fatal.'

At the hospital there was confusion. It is one thing to get ready to receive a pope and another to see him arrive drained of blood and unconscious. The services had had time to get organized, but nevertheless there was a moment of panic. The doctors were ready, everyone rushed up, but excitement had caused a general loss of nerve for a moment. The Holy Father was taken up to the tenth floor, where his room was, according to plan, then he was taken down to the operating theatre a few minutes later. Don Stanislaus went in with him. The operation was to last five hours and twenty minutes. During the preparations Dr. Buzzonetti had said that the patient's condition was very serious. His blood pressure had fallen terribly and his pulse was almost imperceptible. Everyone feared the worst.

'So extreme unction had to be given. I administered the sacrament in the operating theatre, just before the operation. But the Holy Father was no longer conscious.

'Hope gradually returned during the operation. At first it was agonizing. Then it gradually became clear that no vital organ had been hit, and that he just might survive.'

In the most difficult conditions, since it had not been possible to prepare the patient as is normally done, it was necessary to cleanse the abdomen, cut away twenty-two inches of intestine, sew up the colon in several places and make good the haemorrhage: the Holy Father had lost three-quarters of his blood. His blood group was known and a transfusion always ready. Then a drainage system had to be inserted, which saves the patient but leaves him with a very painful memory.

'The operation was carried out by Professor Crucitti, assisted by Professor Corrado Manni, the anaesthetist; the heart specialist Manzoni; the house surgeon Breda; and a Vatican doctor. Professor Castiglione, the head of the clinic, arrived from Milan at the end of the operation.'

The news had gone round the world in a few minutes. Immediately visitors arrived – cardinals, archbishops Martinez and Silvestrini from the Secretariat of State, politicians like President Pertini, Prime Minister Forlani, Signor Craxi, Signor Berlinguer, men of all shades of opinion, or almost.

After the operation the Holy Father was taken to the intensive care unit, and until 18 May he remained under the continuous supervision of the doctors, especially Professor Manni, and the surgeons.

Everyone hoped for the best but said nothing. Anything could still happen.

It is amazing that the bullet did not destroy any vital organ. A nine millimetre bullet is an unspeakably brutal projectile. It had to follow an unlikely trajectory not to cause irreparable devastation in this very complex part of the body.

'It passed a few millimetres away from the central aorta. If it had hit it, death would have been instantaneous. It did not touch the spine or any vital point. Between you and me, it was really miraculous. The rest is due to the immediate move to the hospital and to the presence of doctors who operated marvellously; I repeat, marvellously. The operation was perfect; there were no complications after it. Many antibiotics were administered every day for fear of an infection. During the first two days the patient was in very great pain, mainly because of the drainage tubes. But his reactions improved from hour to hour.

'During the night following the operation Signor Pertini, the President of the Republic, came. The Holy Father, who was awake, thanked him for his visit, but the next day he did not remember it. President Pertini came three times. On 17 May he offered to carry the Holy Father's good wishes to Switzerland, which he was to visit.

'A family atmosphere reigned in the whole hospital. The doctors and nurses gave the Holy Father every attention, tried to talk to him or to be present at his Mass. He welcomed them with his customary simplicity and expressed his gratitude to them.

'I was always there. Like Father Magee, I only left the hospital very occasionally. Together with the Polish sisters and our assistant Angelo, we did not leave the Holy Father for three months.

'The Holy Father received communion on the very first day, and from the very next day onwards he concelebrated Mass with us from his bed.

'We were always afraid of complications, mainly because of a persistently high fever, which was not caused by the operation. Almost immediately we thought of an international medical consultation, not to check but to give support to the Gemelli doctors, who had done everything with devotion, skill and filial piety. In our view, such a consultation should also establish future treatment.

'After Wednesday's operation the Holy Father was already capable on the Sunday of speaking at the Angelus (he never missed one).'

People will remember this first brief allocution, uttered in a weak voice which was unrecognizable to all those who still had his normally deep voice ringing in their ears. The words were words of pardon and of trust in Providence. The victim called the would-be assassin his 'brother'. Still stunned by fright, I wrote at the time what I thought, that, all round, I should have preferred this brother to find another means of entering the family.

'There was a crowd at the clinic waiting for news of the Holy Father. Letters poured in. We received 15,000 telegrams.

'On Monday 18 May at half-past one in the afternoon the Pope was taken up to the tenth floor, which was staffed by the sisters of Maria Bambina. The departure from the intensive care unit was quite emotional, and I can still see the tears in Professor Manni's eyes.

'The same day saw the arrival, at the invitation of the Secretary of State, of the first specialists from the United States, Münster, Cracow, Barcelona and France. In their presence he took his first steps.'

At this point an amazing detail was disclosed.

'The Holy Father never failed to say his office.

'I remember that the day after the attempted assassination, when the Pope had scarcely recovered consciousness, his first question was: "Have we said compline?"

'But it was already midday and consequently too late. During his first and second illnesses, when his weak state did not allow him to say the office himself, it was recited aloud in his presence so that he could follow it in thought. As soon as he could he said it alternately with one of us.

'Every day he was visited by Cardinal Confalonieri, the dean of the sacred college, by the Cardinal Vicar General Poletti and by the latter's deputy, Martinez Somalo. Cardinal Casaroli came twice a day, and Archbishop Silvestrini came often. They followed the course of the illness with great attention and kept in close contact with the doctors.

'May 17 was a day of added suffering: Italy voted on abortion, the opponents of which were defeated. This legalization of murder, against which the Pope had fought so hard, was another blow on top of his wounds.

'On 20 May the fever abated. The Holy Father, fed until then by drip, ate his first meal, soup with an egg. In the evening we recited the *Te Deum* together.

'The Holy Father saw all this as a sign from heaven, and we – doctors included – regarded it as a miracle. Everything seemed to be guided by an invisible hand. No one spoke of a miracle, but everyone thought of one. For example, the injured finger recovered of its own accord. During the operation no one had bothered about it. They thought of amputating it. An ordinary splint and the medicines intended for the patient's general state were sufficient to cure it. Yet the second joint had been broken. Now it's perfectly all right again.

'We used to say Mass every evening, and afterwards the litanies of the Holy Virgin. The Holy Father sang with the sisters. The greatest desire of the staff was to be present.

'On 23 May the doctors signed a communiqué announcing that the patient's life was no longer in danger.'

But the fever had returned. And another sorrow was added to the others: Cardinal Wyszynski was dying. At 12.25 on 25 May there was a last telephone conversation with the Primate of Poland, who asked the Holy Father for his blessing. The Pope replied by blessing 'his mouth and his hands', as though to approve and ratify all that the cardinal had said and done during his life.

'The patient's general condition was better, but not yet satisfactory. Fever and high blood pressure.

'On 27 May, after recording a talk to pilgrims from Silesia, the Holy Father felt very tired. His condition remained precarious. There was "something" amiss. Difficulties with breathing, shortage of breath and pains in the heart indicated fresh trouble. In fact, we know now that it was the start of that virus infection that was about to break out violently.

'Cardinal Wyszynski died on 28 May. We put off telling the Holy Father until the evening Mass. The Mass was said for the primate.'

On the Sunday he joined in the funeral of Cardinal Wyszynski by following the service on the radio and then by saying his own Mass at the same time as the one in Poland.

During his stay in hospital he had never stopped attending to

Church affairs, discussing them with his assistants, taking decisions and giving his signature.

'Then an improvement occurred, and on 3 June the doctors agreed to let the Holy Father go back to the Vatican for what people thought would be a period of convalescence.'

He was all right, but was obviously still in pain from his wounds, from his finger, from his elbow – and from the tooth broken during the anaesthetic, to the great chagrin of the anaesthetist.

He had hastened his return to the Vatican for two main reasons: to preside over the solemnities of 7 June connected with the anniversary of the Council of Ephesus and of the first Council of Constantinople, a big ceremony to be attended by delegations from all the bishops' conferences in the world; and to consecrate the world to the Virgin Mary. This had in fact been done at Santa Maria Maggiore during his absence. He had to confine himself to reading a message from the balcony of St. Peter's.

He was very pale, his strength would not come back and the fever started up again on 10 June in its capricious way, suddenly going up to 39.5 centigrade and then quickly falling again without anyone's being able to discover the cause. All the tests were negative and this curious fever caused everyone fresh distress, almost worse than the first, while the patient gradually became exhausted. It was a nightmare, Don Stanislaus said. The Pope's face was grey and emaciated, his nose pinched, and in their almost black rings his eyes, now an unusual green in colour, did not focus on anyone and looked simply vacant. Once again fear reigned round him.

None of the most modern apparatus brought in to sound the organism furnished any clue to the origin of the fever, which did not yield to antibiotics. A drip was used again.

On 12 June the Pope's staff requested a wider consultation, with the participation in particular of a virus expert. The idea was to make sure that this obstinate fever was not due to any detail neglected during the operation.

On 20 June it became necessary to return to the hospital for fresh analyses, which at first were no more informative than the previous ones. It was enough to make one tear one's hair. How could one treat a disease that had no name?

It was at this point that Professor Sanna discovered and isolated the cytomegalovirus, the cause of all the trouble. He said it would take six weeks to eradicate, during which time the patient's condition would remain precarious and liable to sudden onsets of fever. It was on that very day that a slight improvement became perceptible; but subsequently a touch of pleurisy brought further complications.

During this stay in hospital, as during the earlier one, the Holy Father never omitted to say his office or any of his usual prayers – the rosary and the Way of the Cross on Fridays, the meditations on which were read to him at the foot of his bed.

At seven o'clock in the morning, when the day staff took over from the night staff, the day began with an Our Father said together, sometimes a hymn and a blessing. At last, between 15 and 16 July, the storm subsided: the fever left the patient and, to all appearances, the virus too.

Then people began to think of the second operation, which was to free the patient from the drainage system of which I have spoken. The doctors wanted to put it off as long as possible, but the Holy Father, who was extremely inconvenienced from every point of view, wished it to take place as soon as possible, and in any case had no desire to go back to the Vatican only to have to return a third time to the clinic. Finally he himself fixed the operation for 5 August, the feast of Our Lady of the Snows. He was in a hurry to resume his normal activities, which he almost reproached himself for having had to slow down.

The operation, though less hazardous than the first, nevertheless presented the risks involved in any surgical operation. It lasted an hour and was very successful. On 14 August the Holy Father returned to the Vatican and on the next day was able to celebrate the feast of the Assumption with the fifty thousand pilgrims gathered in St. Peter's Square, which had never witnessed so many people on 15 August, a date usually kept as such a thorough holiday that there is not a Roman left in Rome. At 5.30 in the afternoon the Holy Father went by helicopter to Castel Gandolfo.

'The rest was the return to health.' With these words Don Stanislaus's account came to an end.

# III

I went over the route from St. Peter's to the Gemelli hospital through the new districts of a Rome which will leave no ruins. The avenues are wide but full of traffic, and they are crossed by others no less busy; all the ingenuity of Roman drivers is required to prevent these crossroads, at which traffic lights indicate the problem without pretending to solve it, from turning into cemeteries for cars. After skirting a market which overflows into the street and crossing the moving flood of the Via Aurelia, like a canoeist forcing his way through rapids, one finally glimpses on a spur of Monte Mario the glass walls of the polyclinic and the Catholic faculty of medicine, which occupy as much space on their hill as the Vatican on its own. I do not know how the ambulance driver, deprived of his siren, managed to reach this haven in eight minutes.

In the lobby there is a big portrait of a thoughtful friar in a homespun habit with a white girdle – Brother Agostino Gemelli, the founder of this medical Babylon, which is not, as I had thought, the work of some fabulously rich donor but that of a poor man by vocation who, like his creator, made a great deal out of nothing, while so many rich men make nothing out of a great deal. In olden days an inspired pope had gone, to everyone's amazement, to kneel before a young man in rags near Assisi, who preached to the birds and carried the Gospel in his heart. Centuries later, a dying pope was to be welcomed by the likeness of a disciple of this same empty-handed young man and restored to life under his discreet patronage. Nowhere in the world would John Paul II have been cared for better.

With its five operating theatres and eighteen hundred beds, the Gemelli complex employs four thousand people, including five hundred doctors.

On the tenth floor a section of the central building shut off by smoked glass doors, previously reserved for doctors on duty, has since been allotted to important people who cannot fall ill without affecting the health of a whole state and who are accompanied everywhere by the staff which links them to the outside world. John Paul II inaugurated this *reparto speciale* which comprises, to the right of a wide hall ending in a waiting room, a room furnished with a few armchairs, a chest of drawers, a low table and shelves containing a few books to which the Holy Father had added some of his own. An inner door leads into the bedroom, small, of exemplary sobriety and like all the others, except for the bullet-proof glass in the bay window. I hasten to say that John Paul II does not like this kind of protection any more than the other sorts, and that he particularly detests the *papamobile* topped with a glass cage which separates him from the crowd whence he draws part of his strength and which he thinks has a right to his confident and unarmed presence. He only agrees to climb into this strange vehicle to calm the apprehensions of his hosts. After the bedroom comes a bathroom on the scale of the Baths of Caracalla. On the other side of the hall is Don Stanislaus's bedroom and also a big room in which the college of doctors used to meet. The Pope was to call it the Sanhedrin.

With the Holy Father's consent, I wanted to know how things had happened from the point of view of the doctors.

On 13 May, at 5.25 p.m., Professor Tresalti, director of the medical services, received a telephone call from the Vatican and the wounded man at almost the same time. The Pope, according to the telephone message, was *colpito*, that is, 'hit', 'struck' or 'affected'; the word covered a heart attack, a cerebral thrombosis or a physical accident; hence the ascent to the tenth floor before the hurried descent to the operating theatre.

The 'emergency' team was ready and so was the blood, though not in sufficient quantities for the huge transfusion necessary. The operation began just before 6 p.m., on the arrival of Professor Crucitti, who was to take charge of it. At 8 p.m. Professor Tresalti was able to read a first, fairly reassuring communiqué to the journalists who were besieging the hospital in hundreds, microphones held out towards the slightest murmur. At a quarter to one in the morning a second communiqué announced that the operation had ended very successfully at 25 minutes past eleven. The patient's condition was satisfactory. The communiqués continued to become more and more encouraging until 3 June, the day on which the Holy Father left hospital. They remind me of the famous bulletins of Napoleon's 'Grande Armée', which reported victory after victory up to the burning of Moscow and the retreat from Russia. On 19 June it was announced that a flare-up of fever, due to an unidentified infection, necessitated a return to hospital. That day Professor Tresalti welcomed the Holy Father at the entrance to the Gemelli with a wheel-chair which the patient at first did not want to use. However, he was so weak that after a few steps he had to make use of it after all. The professor, a shrewd and cultivated man, subsequently told me with a twinkle in his eye how his patient, who normally never complained, did complain once to the 'Sanhedrin' in the name of 'a sick man's rights'. I shall recount his remarks later on. For the moment I simply wish to note that on the first occasion the Holy Father arrived at the hospital exhausted by an internal haemorrhage which could easily become fatal. Everything was ready for the operation, but the patient had still to be prepared for it, however briefly. For a few minutes the Pope's life hung in the balance. While the dying man was being taken down from the tenth floor to the operating theatre on the ninth, a call went out in all directions for Professor Crucitti, a world-class surgeon whose colleagues would just as soon have him with them. Naturally they had decided to operate without waiting for him, but without any doubt they would have preferred him to be there.

In fact he was over two miles away, in a clinic in the Via Aurelia, where he was visiting a patient. A nun who was listening on the radio to the live broadcast of the weekly audience heard that the Pope had been the victim of an attempted assassination and that an ambulance was taking him to the Gemelli hospital. She ran to tell Professor Crucitti, who found the news so incredible that he telephoned the hospital. The number rang but no one replied. Those few seconds during which the telephone rang unanswered seemed to him interminable, but revealing. He changed from his white coat into his jacket and jumped into his car. It was the rush hour and traffic was heavy.

'I did the first part of the journey in the left-hand lane to overtake the traffic, but at the junction where the Via Aurelia crosses the avenue leading to the Pineta Sacchetti I had to get back into my proper lane to turn at the traffic lights. It was then that the wailing of police sirens removed my last doubts; the news was clearly correct. In trying to creep into the line of police cars I got in the way of one of them and found myself at odds with a policeman who was threatening me with his sub-machine gun. I gave him to understand in sign language that I was in just as much of a hurry as he was.

'I started to press continuously on my horn, and although the police cars, which were driving very fast, left me behind I was able to stay in their wake for a minute or two. I was not very far from the hospital when I saw in my mirror a police motorcyclist chasing me. I thought he was going to delay me. On the contrary, he was an intelligent lad, for I only had to shout to him, when he drew level, "I must get to the Gemelli at once," and he replied without the slightest hesitation, "Step on the gas, I'll help you." He led me at full speed to the hospital. At the porter's lodge I shouted, "It's true then?" They replied: "Yes, yes, the Pope's in the operating theatre."

'On the fourth floor, where the normal entrance to the hospital is situated ( it is built on a slope), some unknown genius had thought to call all the lifts. I was able to go straight up to the ninth floor, where a nun shouted to me, "Quick, quick!" Assistants and nuns literally threw themselves at me to tear off my jacket and trousers and put on my theatre gown, scattering all round me everything in my pockets – keys, small change, wallet. I ran to scrub my hands while some one fastened my gown and some one else put my feet into my boots. During this time a doctor called to me from the theatre: "Blood pressure is 80, 70, still falling." When I went in, anaesthesia had begun, the Pope was unconscious and I had my scalpel in my hand. The emergency team had already made the necessary preparations and I had only one thought: to open up without losing a second.

'So I made the incision.

'And I saw blood everywhere. There were some six pints in the abdomen. We sucked it out, staunched it, sponged it up by every possible means until we could see the sources of the haemorrhage. I was then able to proceed to stopping the flow of blood. Once the patient had stopped losing blood and the transfusion had been set up, his blood pressure rose again. At that stage we could continue more calmly.

'So I explored the abdomen and saw the series of wounds. There were multiple lesions of the small intestine and the colon. Some were due to direct wounds – cuts or perforations on the trajectory of the bullet – others to blast. The mesentery, the membrane which is the starting point for the blood vessels which irrigate the small intestine, was cut in several places. I did the necessary resections and anastomases, washed out the peritoneum and sutured the

(236)

sigmoid. There, in the last part of the colon, I found a terrible laceration caused by the direct passage of the projectile.

'After stopping the flow of blood and checking the cardio-vascular functions, and having noted the gravity of the wounds, I reckoned that what the situation required above all from me was a cool head. Although I was perfectly aware of the difficulty of my task, I was already convinced that the result would be successful.

'No vital organ, such as the aorta or the iliac artery, had been touched, nor had the ureter. The bullet had gone through the sacrum after entering by the front wall of the abdomen. The sacral vein system, which was bleeding copiously, posed a difficult problem: we had to use sterile wax to stop the haemorrhage. But the essential organs, damage to which would have caused death, had only been grazed and the nerve centres next to them had not apparently suffered. Frankly, it was surprising. However, since the patient was anaesthetized, we could not tell if he had escaped damage to the nerves. We were not sure of this until he started to move again.

'The operation itself lasted less than five hours, but as soon as the haemorrhage had been stopped we gave the organism a little time to regain strength. Similarly, after the sutures we took some X-rays to make sure there were no other bullets or fragments. We attended to the wound in the arm and X-rayed the finger, which the ortho-paedic expert looked after.

'After the operation the Pope stayed in the operating theatre for a little while. We did not transfer him to the neighbouring room, known as the recovery room, as we do when patients are awaiting their turn; that day he was the only one to be operated on.

'The intensive care unit, where he was subsequently taken, is on the third floor. He stayed there five days. His cardio-vascular and pulmonary condition was good, and any other patient would not have remained so long in intensive care; but with him we preferred to take more precautions than were strictly necessary. The in-tensive care cubicles are sterile and always ready, with all the equipment necessary to check the vital functions, whereas this equipment was not present in the Pope's room; we installed it later.

'After the operation I was dehydrated. Yes, we can drink during an operation: the nurses put a glass or a straw to our lips, since we cannot touch anything. But I preferred to wait. I drank some water and smoked a cigarette.

'No, I didn't panic. Everyone has asked me that. Of course, I had a moment's anxiety before opening the abdomen. Afterwards, once the haemorrhage was under control, I simply had before me a patient to be operated on, a seriously ill patient to be operated on as quickly as possible. I had to carry out a rational act and that was all. In a situation like that a surgeon cannot indulge in emotions or philosophical considerations; he thinks only of doing his duty. The problems raised by the personality of the patient on whom he has operated come later, when he leaves the theatre and notices that hundreds of people, television, photographers and a horde of journalists are waiting to hear what he is going to say, and the world with them.

'Some of the team accompanied the Pope to the intensive care unit. The crowd had been moved out of the corridors. We were on our guard against photographers, but presumably not enough, since one of them succeeded, I don't know how, in taking a picture of the move, in spite of the Vatican guards and all the checks.

'Once the Pope had been settled in, the doctors all met for the first time to decide on treatment. President Pertini was there and said to me, "You smoke too much." I pointed out to him that he seldom let go of his pipe. He replied: "That's because politicians cause me a lot of worry, too."

'During the night the Pope was still unconscious as a result of the anaesthetic, but all was going well, as the second medical bulletin indicated. I kept my eye on the patient for a few more hours; then I went to bed. But I wasn't able to sleep. Very early in the morning I had a coffee and went back to the intensive care unit. The news was good, and our little group met, as it was to do twice a day.

'My first contacts with the Pope were purely professional: "Are you in pain? How do you feel?" and so on. It was like that the whole time he was in intensive care – our relations were those between doctor and patient. Subsequently they became those between an ordinary man and the Pope, between a Catholic and the shepherd of the Church.

'A journalist claimed that we had broken professional secrecy, and some one even wrote that "we spoke of the Pope as if he were a man"! Certainly. The Pope is not a pure symbol; he is a real figure who has a direct and fraternal contact with the world. And this man-to-man relationship was established between us.

'We talked about everything – about the assassination attempt, about what could lie behind it, about my country and his country, of the world situation, about my family and his family, about his friends and my friends, about my colleagues and his; the field was enormous.

'Our conversation about the crime left me with the impression that he had pondered in vain about the significance of this incomprehensible act. And indeed, why him, a person who is not mixed up in politics, why this attempt to murder a man of hope and peace? And again, did the Turk act on his own account, or was he only a tool? That is one question which he asked himself. If he found the answer, he did not impart it to me.'

On this point, people have never got any further than constructing hypotheses. I doubt whether one could find any power, great or small, ready to take the risk (even via 'secret' services, which in any case are never all that secret) of being unmasked in an enquiry or trial. But that said, it is certain that the Turk was not alone and that he had organized his escape. A *monsignore* of the Curia, who on the day of the incident had left his car alongside the colonnade, was invited to clear off by two individuals in dark glasses who showed no card or badge to back their demand. Accomplices? The *monsignore* is sure of it. It is very unlikely that the would-be assassin went alone to St. Peter's Square with the intention of leaving again under his own steam protected by a weapon that could betray him, and which in fact jammed after the fourth shot (one of the miracles of that day).

But the professor returned to his patient. He had to perform a colostomy.

'The Holy Father wanted a detailed explanation of the intestine, of its anatomy, of its normal functioning and of the way in which we had had to compensate for its provisional failure, not that he was already thinking of the second operation which was to free him from this problem, but simply to get an accurate idea of the situation. And from then on he accepted all the medical treatment without argument.

'During the second stay in hospital we increased the number of examinations, including the "computerized axial tomography", which we call CAT for short, and on the day when the analyses proved that he was clinically cured we decided to carry out the operation which would restore him to normal life. But when? Should we operate straightaway, in spite of the recent cytomegalovirus infection from which he had only just recovered? Knowing that a patient in this state is not on his best form and that there was a considerable risk of the reinfection, I said to him, thinking, I must admit, to gain time, "Your Holiness can go back to the Vatican right away." For it was clear that the danger would decrease all the time. But he did not see it like that at all. He did not wish to leave hospital until he was completely whole again. He did not want to leave us before the second operation. And so on the day when we met to fix the date he intervened unexpectedly to say in substance: "Don't forget that although you may be the doctors I am the patient, and that I am entitled to explain to you my problems as a sick man, especially this one: I should not like to return to the Vatican until I am completely cured. I don't know what you think, but personally I feel very well, even supposing that the analyses indicate the contrary. I feel quite strong enough to undergo a fresh operation." In the last analysis he was trying to convince us that in the relationship between the patient and the doctor, the latter must not act as a sort of oracle sending down his decisions from on high. These decisions must be taken by mutual agreement, for if on one side there is the skill and knowledge of medicine, on the other there is the individual's knowledge of himself. We know this, but sometimes we forget it. The reminder was useful.

'The Pope has been cured since 14 August 1981. There have been no complications.

'One could say that he was "surgically" cured a week after the assassination attempt. Then came the virus infection, which he overcame very successfully. After which the second operation cured him of the handicap that we imposed on him – the colostomy. On the seventh day after the second operation we took out the stitches and said to him: "Your Holiness is cured and can leave to-morrow." He left hospital on 14 August.

'I kept on eye on him in August and September after a short week's rest. I went to visit him at Castel Gandolfo, where he continued his convalescence until October. We advised him to take up his activities again slowly and progressively. Without success. Feeling better, he did not spare himself.

'It is true that he had lost weight. This wasn't a consequence of the operation, of the infection or of the work that he immediately imposed on himself. No. It was we who suggested that he watch his weight. Before the assassination attempt he was overweight! A man of over sixty should weigh too little rather than too much. He followed a diet and feels the better for it.

'The finger? It mended of its own accord, under the supervision of Professor Fineschi.

'As for the final result, the whole world can judge for itself.

'Another thing: the Pope works too hard. I told him so again recently. I wasn't talking as a doctor, for he no longer needs one, but – if I may be allowed to use the word – as a friend. Past a certain age, every man should work at a reasonable pace, especially when he has just suffered a severe shock. Overwork can harm even the young!'

Professor Crucitti told me all this between two operations, two coffees and two cigarettes. He left me with this remark: 'Physicians deal with patients. But that is not always the case with us surgeons. For example, some one with a hernia is not really ill. It is we, with the anaesthetic and the operation, who inflict the surgical illness on him. One more reason for establishing a trusting personal relationship with him and not just knowing him as a medical card with a number on it.'

Another great surgeon had already said to me one day, 'I operate on people, not on X-ray plates.'

# IV

The sister blushed at the idea of appearing by name in this book. So let us spare her modesty. The sister, then, is one of those contagiously healthy nurses who succeed in squaring the circle by looking simultaneously round and four-square. Happy, full of vitality, she reminds me of those gardeners who are said to have 'green fingers' because they are so good at bringing back to life plants on the point of dying. Her patient benefited from this gift. She must have looked after him with energetic devotion.

She is a sister of Maria Bambina. She went to fetch a transparent plastic box containing, like a great florist's orchid, a pretty baby in swaddling clothes with a halo intersected by the pillow.

'You don't know this devotion to the infant Virgin? That's a

pity. Our order bears another name, but they call us the sisters of
Maria Bambina because of a miraculous statuette. There's the Holy
Father's sitting-room. No, he didn't change anything and he didn't
bring much, except for files, a lot of files. Clothes? No, not even
clothes. He wore hospital clothes, the white collarless shirt with a
little belt and the blue dressing-gown, like the other patients.
That's how he strolled up and down his corridor. Or up and down
ours, to go to the chapel. We have a little chapel in the section of the
tenth floor reserved for us. When he wanted to work, we took into
the sitting-room the table from his bedroom, the one from the foot
of his bed which was also used for saying Mass. He was so
undemanding! He never asked for anything. In his view, people
took too much trouble over him. Naturally on the first day I
approached him with some apprehension. The Pope! The next day
it was all over; I was in command of myself again. I even said to
him, one day when he didn't want to leave his bed, "Most Holy
Father, you *must* get up to regain strength." He laughed and said,
"Well, well, sister has got over her shyness!" He can put you at ease
with a word or a smile. It's true that his bed was not very big. No,
it's not because we are sisters of Maria Bambina that we put
children's cots in the rooms. They are the same all over the
hospital, light, on castors; it's convenient for moving a patient
without having to transfer him to a trolley with all the apparatus.

'Yes, he found the bed a bit short, but he got used to it. He put
up with everything. He was a very easy patient. And so simple!
Who would have thought it was the Pope, if there hadn't been so
many people around him! Yes, that's quite true, he was the first
patient to be accommodated in this part of the building, which had
previously been used as rest rooms for the doctors on duty. He left
us this picture, this Virgin Mary, with sick people round her and
himself arriving in the background. And this big picture of Czestochowa on the wall facing his bed. No, he didn't go off to the other
floors. He often went through the door down there at the end of the
corridor, to pray in our chapel. He always acted in the same way:
first he knelt down on the floor and then, after a moment, on the
first bench he came to, his head in his hands. Morning and evening.
One Sunday he opened the door when other patients were already
there. What excitement! Like all foreigners, he did not talk much.
He liked to joke from time to time. One day he left his room and
when he could see no one in the corridor we heard him saying:

"There you are, they've gone, they've all abandoned me." We were all there, in one room or another, busy doing this or that, not to mention the guards on the landing, at the back entrance and on the floors above and below. The window panes are bullet-proof and, as you can see, they can be covered with opaque panels. But he used to go to the window to bless the patients in the wing opposite. As for those in his own building, who could not see him, he had them brought on the last evening, yes, if need be in their beds or wheelchairs. No, the other people wounded in the assassination attempt were not treated at the Gemelli. The young American woman wounded in the arm came here. He received the other one at the Vatican. He used to pray. He said to me once: "The whole world has a right to expect much from the Pope, so the Pope can never pray enough." No, I didn't imagine him differently, perhaps because I saw him here when he came to visit his friend Mgr. Deskur before going into the conclave. I had already found him very straightforward and "approachable".'

As approachable as the *Maria Bambina* in its little shrine of imitation glass, which she carried off carefully before returning to her patients, whom she would look after as if they were popes.

Professor Manni is extremely sensitive, and during the course of the story which he was going to tell me I was to see him interrupt himself more than once to murmur an excuse, shaking his head from side to side like a suffocating diver trying to get his breath back. It was not so much a question of 'collecting his memories' as of loosening their grip on him.

'I had already taken part in an operation on a pope – Paul VI – in 1967, with my teacher, Professor Valdoni. It was I who gave the anaesthetic. But it wasn't the same thing at all. Everything was ready, including the patient. Paul VI was operated on in the Vatican, in a room in the private apartments which Pius XII had turned into a cinema. We moved everything to set up our operating equipment – table, lamp, anaesthetic apparatus and so on. No one would have dreamed of sending the Pope to hospital. We were worried less by the operation itself, for which careful preparations had been made, than by the fear of having forgotten – you know – that famous drug that's never used but could turn out to be indispensable.

'On 13 May the situation wasn't really the same at all. After learning the news of the attempted assassination on the radio, I rushed to the hospital, where the Holy Father had already arrived. He had been carried in almost unconscious, drained by a haemorrhage which could quickly become fatal, and his blood pressure was falling all the time. When I saw him on the operating table, covered in blood, a blood transfusion attached to one arm and a drip feed to the other, he looked the very image of Christ on the cross. Yes, I felt I was looking at the crucified Christ.

'I bent over him to take off his ring, something which no one had yet thought of in the general confusion, and directed the administration of the anaesthetic. The operation, as you know, lasted several hours. The reconstruction of the intestinal tract, which had been terribly damaged, was a very long business, complicated by a perforation of the sigmoid which had caused pollution of the abdomen, with all the dangers that this can involve during an operation.

'Fortunately, everything went off very well. Towards midnight we moved him to the intensive-care unit. A little while afterwards the effects of the anaesthetic began to wear off. I leaned over him and said: "Most Holy Father, it's up to you to help us. The doctors have done a great deal for you; now they expect your total co-operation to get through this difficult moment." He moved his head to indicate his acquiescence.

'He scarcely gave vent to a complaint, and as soon as he was able to speak his first words were words of thanks, almost of apology for all the inconvenience he was causing the hospital, the doctors, the nurses and all the staff present. Then he went to sleep again.

'I was dead tired, a crowd of people was jostling in the corridors and I had to draft the medical bulletin. President Pertini took advantage of the confusion to ask for a gown and to go into the intensive-care unit; he was quite proud of having been the only person to succeed in getting in there.

'The Pope stayed there five days, the most decisive days, for obviously it is during this period that complications can arise. Fortunately the operation was a total success. On the last day the red danger light went off and we moved the Pope to the tenth floor. He asked to see me and gave me a picture by Signor Fanfani, the president of the Senate, who is a talented painter, of the Virgin of Czestochowa. "Professor," he said, "please accept this picture in thanks for what you have done."

'And I wept, as I am weeping now.

'He thanked us all again. Excuse me. I cannot think of that moment without emotion.

'I said to him: "I will not leave you. My assistants and I will come up to see you with our medical colleagues. You must be glad that the danger is over. What a great joy for us!"

'When I went back, he reminded me of this episode, and seeing that I was still in an emotional state he said: "Professor, your great emotion risks arousing mine."

'Well, there I was with the Pope, and he spoke to me of my emotion, as he was to speak of it a few months later to my wife and my sons (one is a doctor, the other a lawyer). I still have tears in my eyes.

'Did you know that on 12 May, the day before the assassination attempt, the Pope had visited the medical centre in Vatican City? A few months before, at the suggestion of Mgr. Fiorenzo Angelini, Catholic doctors had offered to buy an ambulance with resuscitation equipment to help people taken ill in St. Peter's Square. There was already a little tent for first aid, but it wasn't sufficient from the medical point of view. The new ambulance had been presented to the Holy Father on the occasion of his visit to the centre; it was this ambulance that was to take him to the Gemelli the next day.

'I call the Pope's stay here "my ninety days of clausura". From 13 May to 14 August we had to withstand a positive siege, and the things we had to listen to! Everyone wanted to treat the Pope, and everyone constructed the most unlikely hypotheses or invented his own treatment, and even when it had been established, on irrefutable evidence, that the Holy Father's fever was caused by the cytomegalovirus, there were still people trying to demonstrate that it was something else. It is true that the Pope belongs to the whole world and it is normal that the whole world should worry about him in such circumstances. But it was painful to see the tiniest incident distorted and exaggerated in the most fantastic way, if indeed it was not purely imaginary.

'That said, we were glad that eminent foreign colleagues came to examine the Holy Father. It was thus made evident that the operation had been faultless and that the treatment was suitable.

'At the time of the second stay in hospital, I was among those who suggested putting off the fresh operation until later. The weather was hot. We would not have operated on any other patient in those conditions. We said to him: "You have undergone a serious operation and you have withstood it; you have had an infection and you have overcome it. That's fine, but you now need a month or two's rest. We'll operate in October."

'But the Pope has a will of iron. He did not wish to leave hospital before he could live normally again. I said to him jokingly: "Naturally, if Your Holiness wants to stay here, you will not be thrown out."

'He replied: "Either the Pope is ill and cannot leave, or else he is well and must depart completely cured, without any handicap." His colostomy prevented him from feeling like a normal person.

'He was tenacious. He used to say jokingly: "What did the Sanhedrin say to-day? What did the Sanhedrin decide on my behalf?"

'That's how he came to attend the meeting at which we were to fix the date of the second operation.

'He asked to be allowed to speak, and he went on speaking for half an hour or more. He dealt thoroughly with the subject of the relations between doctors and patients. There must be a continuous dialogue between them, he said. The lesson was a good one. It convinced us. If some one had told me in advance that I would give way, I should not have believed him. But one cannot resist him. When he has taken a decision he sticks to it; for example, all the objections in the world did not stop him going to England and Argentina.

'I saw him again recently at the opening of the new cardio-surgical wing of the Bambino Gesù paediatric hospital on the Janiculum. He said to me, "You are in very good form," to which I replied that I was just going to make the same remark to him. He is an exceptionally robust man, and he owes his strong reaction after the assassination attempt partly to his mountaineer's physique.

'He is obliged to make an enormous physical and intellectual effort every day. His life frightens me. It's a continual commitment. And to think that a man of peace like him was nearly murdered by a terrorist! To plead for peace and to be paid in pistol shots! Psychologically, that must be very hard for a man who is so human, so kind, so good at building bridges. One day when he was walking in the corridor he surprised me picking chocolates from a box that a nun had just offered me. "Well, well, are you fond of sweets, then? Like grandfathers and young children?" I replied that I was no longer a child and not yet a grandfather – my children are not yet married – but that nevertheless I liked chocolates. He laughed. It's only a little thing, but it shows how he can seize on a detail and turn it into a gesture of friendship.

'He is an incomparable person. I shall never forget the days I spent near him.

'What an extraordinary adventure! I said to my sons, "Children, your father was very lucky!"'

From what the father had just let me glimpse of himself, so were they.

From 3 to 24 June there was no medical bulletin. The bulletin of 3 June, no. 18, announced that since the post-operative condition was progressing satisfactorily and the 'clinico-functional parameters remained within the normal limits', there was no longer any point in keeping the Holy Father in hospital and he had just left. The communiqué ended with a tribute by the doctors to their patient for the example of patience and serenity which he had never ceased to give them.

At that moment the Holy Father's friends, of whom there are two or three thousand million on this earth, felt a weight lifted off them.

However, it was only a respite. On 24 June bulletin no. 19 announced that after a period of general improvement a high fever had appeared in the patient, bound up with 'an inflammatory pleuro-pulmonary process' which suitable treatment had quickly reduced. However, the recurrence of the fever had made it seem indispensable that the patient should return to hospital. Additional examinations and 'computerized axial tomography' had ruled out post-operative complications. On the other hand, virological analyses had disclosed the existence of a cytomegalovirus infection.

I wanted to know how this kind of auxiliary terrorist had managed to infiltrate into the Holy Father's organism and to cause it to decline so rapidly. Professor Sanna, dean of the Catholic faculty of medicine and a renowned microbiologist, started by describing the symptoms of the illness: fever, changes in the composition of the blood, pulmonary and liver disturbances.

'It's fortunate,' he said to me, 'that none of this was a consequence of the surgical operation, for, in view of the patient's condition, it would have been difficult for him to withstand another operation. On the other hand, the presence of the cytomegalovirus was revealed very quickly, from 20 June.

'You should know that this virus can be transmitted by a blood transfusion. During the operation on the Holy Father a large quantity of blood had been needed. As his blood belongs to a special group, several donors were necessary. Naturally we have an organization for this, but that day the donors came from all parts of Italy. I remember seeing the head of the Rome Fire Brigade arrive with a number of flasks. By sheer bad luck, one of the donors must have been a carrier of the virus. Such accidents are not rare. Three viruses can be transmitted by a blood transfusion – hepatitis B, infectious mononucleosis and the cytomegalovirus.

'We thought of this straightaway, and on the first day that the Pope was in hospital again we conducted examinations for hepatitis, mononucleosis and the cytomegalovirus. The first two were negative. The third was positive and showed the presence of IGM antibodies, which form and disappear very quickly and indicate a recent infection. Subsequently these antibodies went on increasing and reached very high percentages.

'The laboratory analyses were done in record time – three days.

'To grow a cytomegalovirus artificially we use human cells, for it is a virus of a specific kind that lives only in these. These cells are fibroblasts, swollen cells. The virus enlarges them; that is why we speak of cytomegalia. It produces a focus that we call cytopathic. We can demonstrate that the cytomegalovirus is indeed at work by 'cementing' the virus to specific antibodies. That is how we were able to identify it in the Holy Father.

'No, there is no appropriate antibiotic. The only therapy is a general one, a supporting therapy: one has to help the organism to eliminate the virus itself. Antibiotics, which are so useful for surgical complications, are of no use in a case like this. We therefore stopped administering them and in fact the patient did not take long to react effectively. It was his organism alone that overcame the virus.

'As a matter of fact, he wanted to see the virus, so I showed him the slides.'

I wondered if one could be sure of having defeated this haunter of cells, or if it could suddenly rear its head again when it was thought to have been eliminated.

'Yes, the cytomegalovirus can persist a long time in an organism and be reactivated. But we followed the Holy Father's progress closely and we have not observed any worrying signs in this respect. Far from it! Considering that he has been to Fatima, Britain, Argentina and Switzerland, where apparently he made twelve speeches in ten hours, I'm tempted to say that he is almost too well; he lays burdens on himself that no one else in the world could bear, and it worries us. But it was the same thing in hospital. As soon as the fever gave him a respite, he started work again. We would see him go past with files under his arm and we learned later that he revised and corrected the encyclical *Laborem exercens* while he was in hospital.'

Professor Sanna then told me about the famous session of the 'Sanhedrin' at which the Pope ended by convincing the doctors, who wanted to delay the second operation as long as possible (if only to avoid the dangers of another blood transfusion), to fix it for 5 August, the feast of Our Lady of the Snows, so that, if all went well, he could be at St. Peter's on 15 August, the feast of the Assumption. The liturgical calendar overcame the medical one. Professor Sanna, like all his colleagues, was struck by the Holy Father's address, which Professor Tresalti summarized rather nicely in these words: 'All my life I have defended the rights of man. To-day I myself am "man".'

After seeing the doctors – all admirably competent and devoted men – I asked John Paul II if he remembered the speech of complaint which he had made to them. He replied that at that time he already felt very strong, although several doctors thought that he was still too weak, and that he had given them this information in order to try to help them. Then he had explained to them how the patient, in danger of losing his subjectivity, had to fight constantly to regain it and once more become 'the subject of his illness' instead of simply remaining 'the object of treatment'. He pointed out that the doctors are certainly not responsible for this state of affairs, since it is purely a matter of inner feelings, but that they ought to be aware of the danger and of the efforts which the person concerned is obliged to make to regain control of himself. This problem of the transformation of the individual into a thing occurs everywhere in the realm of social relations. According to John Paul II it is one of the biggest problems of philosophy – and one of the most serious problems in the modern world.

# V

When I went to Castel Gandolfo after the second operation the hill
above Lake Albano looked even prettier than usual, and the sun
softer. The square with the parasols in front of the imposing
mansion was almost empty and had the deserted charm of a little
beach at the foot of a cliff. The carabinieri posts at the entrance to
the town and in the corner of the square had been doubled, but
there were still only two Swiss guards in the porch and their
halberds were no sharper than usual. In the lift that serves the
private apartments I went up with the vegetables from the garden,
and found the Pope in sports clothes, that is, in a white soutane
without a hard collar or mantle. He had just been for a walk in the
park that lies on the other slope of Castel Gandolfo, on the side
facing the sea, which is about twelve miles away. At every step on
these long flowering terraces you come across the remains of
Domitian's huge summer villa, the tiny theatre in which the actors
played their parts almost in the emperor's lap, the cryptoportico
the size of a cathedral to walk in on rainy days, and here and there
lumps of masonry made to defy Time and which Time has stamped
into the ground. The persecutor little knew that one day the
ruins of his luxury would assist the peaceful meditations of the
persecuted.

At table, the Holy Father was given a big glass of what looked
like a pulpy mixture of fruit juices. At the end of the meal some one
gently pushed towards him a glass of that exquisite wine from the
vineyards of Loreto which seems to have been filtered through
roses. The antibiotics had made him take a dislike to this drink and
this was his first attempt at reconciliation. He drank his wine as he
had drunk his vitamins; he showed neither pleasure nor distaste.

He was very much thinner, his gaze had not yet recovered all its
sharpness, and I had the impression that pain was still fighting a
rearguard action in him. The reader will remember his words: in
his youth, suffering *frightened* him and he almost reproached
himself for being exempt from it when it affected so many other
people.

This stranger springing from the depths of hatred came up to him one feast day and did not leave him again for a long time. He experienced suffering's refined jealousy, which isolates you from your friends and puts a tiny but unbridgeable gap between you and the compassion that reaches out to you. He went through two successive agonies of suffering without a complaint, without any but physical weaknesses, undergoing with faith untouched, like a baptism once secretly desired, these two suffocating immersions in the infinite.

However, he never feared death.

'Not from courage, but because at the very moment when I fell in St. Peter's Square I had this vivid presentiment that I should be saved. This certainty never left me, even at the worst moments, after the first operation and during the virus infection.'

Yet the latter was the hardest test. For a week he was not afraid of dying, but rather, I think, of living diminished, a burden to everyone and to the Church. That is my impression; but this fear did not destroy his confidence. For although his staff, at the clinic, may have hesitated to speak openly of a miracle, he dares to do so himself, quite calmly: 'One hand fired,' he said to me that day, 'and another one guided the bullet.' For him, there is no doubt about the protection which saved him from death, and the miracle is authenticated by its date – the anniversary of the first apparition at Fatima.

He was going to give thanks for this the following year when a turbulent priest tried to stab him and very nearly succeeded. He already had the bayonet clenched in his hand and was squatting like an infantryman ready to jump from his foxhole when he was arrested by the chief Vatican guard. The state of mind of the all-or-nothing Catholic who conceives it his duty to kill a pope, that is, to prise away the stone on which his whole doctrinal edifice is built, is quite simply incomprehensible. In any case, from the prison where the man was taken came no echo of a regret, either from him or from his relations. It is thus not true that the family asked for an audience, which John Paul II had declared himself ready to grant. With him, assassins have an easy time: no sooner are they caught than they are pardoned. His justice is not that of the Middle Ages. A Pole confided to me one day that, although we might not know, he himself knew very well, 'who had put the weapon in the Turk's hand'. I hastily replied, 'Don't tell the Holy Father. He would make us pray for them!' For there is not the slightest room in him for resentment. The whole space is occupied by the Gospel, and has always been. So it is a waste of time to ask if the harsh experience of May 1981 has changed him.

'I am becoming what I am,' Democritus used to reply to those who asked for news of him. Suffering has strengthened John Paul II in his faith, by making him for a time the companion of the sick to whom, as he sometimes murmurs, he entrusts the Church, and who are in fact perhaps the only ones who can help him. Through the test of suffering he has become what he was. I shall not say here what that is, in case he pencils in the margin one of those question-marks which are his discreet way of indicating his complete disagreement.

However, all the question-marks in the world will not prevent me from saying that this man of peace is a man who believes sufficiently in men – including those who raise their hand against him – to make them feel like believing in them too, and who believes sufficiently in God to give them the inclination, perhaps, to believe with him.

Such is the Pope. The *acta apostolica*, the crowds and the newspapers call him John Paul II. But the name that Christ gives him is Peter.